THE BBC: AFTER THE LICENCE FEE?

Edited by John Mair, Andew Beck, and Janine Chandler

Cover by Dean Stockton

Bite-Sized Books Limited
16 High Holborn, London, WC1V 6BX England
Registered in the UK. Company Registration
No: 9395379

ISBN: 978-1-0682808-4-9

CONTENTS

FOREWORD

Lord Tony Hall

I fear it's happening all over again. The debate about the BBC is the wrong way round. When I was Director-General, the Government first announced the financial settlement for the Corporation. This was all done behind closed doors over a matter of days with the Treasury taking the lead. Then the Government moved to talking about the Charter and what the BBC could do. Pretty much the same thing happened under my predecessor but one. The result is a licence fee that has decreased by nearly 40 per cent in real terms since 2010. And that's all happened without an intelligent and full debate about whether that was what people, the licence fee payers, wanted.

There is still time to get it right this time round. The BBC has launched a survey to gather the public's views on what they want from the BBC. The Government has announced plans to engage the public too. All this promises well. But the public should also be informed about what the BBC does and could do to help them come to a judgement. The trouble is that at present most of what they hear and read about the BBC centres on whatever crisis is dominating the moment.

Local reporting in news deserts

So what should they be thinking about? For a start we should be considering the role of BBC News in our democracy, to help us all keep properly informed. We all need information you can trust in a rogue world. How can the BBC enhance its role as the place you go to for news and information you can trust? But beyond that, up and down the country, the provision of local news is patchy to say the least. Who is it who represents our communities to themselves, tells the stories that matter to them, and celebrates their achievements? The House of Lords Communications and Digital Committee I was a member of pointed to the growth of news deserts, places where they used to be local journalism but now there is none. Some years ago we built the local democracy reporter scheme which provides reporting on local councils which would otherwise not happen. Could the BBC build on this? Could they become a supplier, the guarantor of local news and information which anyone could use to build their own new local services. Then there are those services that the BBC supplies or supports in Welsh or Gallic. How should they develop and thrive?

Global reporting in a disinformation age

We should be discussing the soft power of the BBC with its global services. They're already reaching over 400 million people a week providing information to countries that otherwise have no free news media. The importance of this to the UK is immeasurable when countries such as China and Russia are pouring huge sums into new services promoting their values. The late Shirley Williams called the BBC Britain's greatest export after Shakespeare. Should we be doing more to promote the values we believe in?

The BBC also fulfils a vital role at the heart of the creative industries. However good they are, and they are, the streamers will never supply us with programmes about who we are, what we care about, what defines us, to the degree that the BBC and the other Public Service Broadcasters do. I'm thinking about dramas like *This City Is Ours*, or programmes like *Country File*. And all that is before you've considered the BBC's role in audio, or the Proms, or Wimbledon fortnight, or the Women's Euros 2025 — all free-to-view. By moving its work to places like Cardiff or Salford the BBC has demonstrated how it can act as a catalyst for others to move in and grow. What should the BBC do in future to reflect ourselves to ourselves and to help our economy grow?

Further, we need to consider how the BBC is governed. Its demonstrable independence is crucial. But so too must be its accountability. I'm much taken with the current Chair, Samir Shah's, idea of a forever charter. He's right to argue that the constant shadow of Charter Review hanging over the corporation is a threat to its independence. So too is the inability of the Chair to do what any other Chair does — to choose their own board.

How do we pay for it?

At that point, let's debate how we want to fund these services. In 2022 the Lords Select Committee I served on produced a first-rate guide to comparative ways of funding the BBC. In the end, if you believe in universality — good programmes and services available equally for everybody — then you have to choose either a licence fee or a household tax.

What could enhance the debate is taking up an idea put forward by the Voice of the Listener and Viewer (VLV) in October 2024. And that's setting up a body to examine the case for every increase in the licence fee and suggest to the Government what that rate should be. The Government could then accept it, amend it, or reject it. Germany has a not dissimilar system. It could help us all consider openly what we thought the BBC was worth to us.

For the point that often gets overlooked about the BBC is its role in the social infrastructure of the nation. At its best it can bring us together and allow us to reflect and enjoy the diversity of these isles. Of course the BBC is a media business. But it's also a cultural organisation, one of the great creative organisations in the world.

This contribution draws on Lord Hall's contribution to the 24 June 2025 Royal Television Society event about BBC funding.

About the contributor

From 2013 to 2020 Lord (Tony) Hall, Baron Hall of Birkenhead, was the sixteenth Director-General of the BBC. Before that he was Chief Executive of the Royal Opera House (2001-2013), and BBC Head of News and Current Affairs (1993-2011).

Acknowledgements

This is my seventh edited book about the BBC. I could enter *Mastermind* on the subject. This book could not be more timely. The BBC is facing a perfect storm, an existential crisis in the making, with Charter renewal and licence fee setting to be settled by the end of 2027. Almost every week storm clouds gather over the Corporation. In the summer of 2025 the noise was about *MasterChef* presenter Gregg Wallace, live coverage of Bob Vylan's Glastonbury set, and two Gaza documentaries, one shown, one not. If and when they die down more storms will brew or be created. Media organisations, press barons, politicians, keyboard warriors, all with their reasons to see BBC funding and influence wither, can be relied on to criticise the Corporation for crimes real and concocted.

These books are carefully curated from blank sheet to publication at great speed. Team efforts. I am especially grateful to my chief engineer — Andrew Beck — for relentless and dogged copy-editing, fact checking, and contributor liaison. This time Janine Chandler has added a totally fresh insider dimension to the project. She took the cast beyond the usual suspects to fresh intellectual pastures. Roger Packer brought his forensic copy-checking skills to the manuscript. As ever, Dean Stockton added his design brilliance to the cover. Julian Costley, our ever-patient publisher, contributed his wisdom and skills. Most of all I thank the contributors. All are approached out of the blue and then chivvied to produce very readable copy. I leave you, dear reader, to decide whether we all have created a vital and necessary debate or produced a mouse.

John Mair, Oxford, August 2025

The cover explained

The building blocks or bricks represent all the BBC entities which are stacked precariously on top of the single TV licence brick. That is their foundation. A Government official (note the emblem or logo on the cufflinks) is about to remove the TV licence brick and it could all come tumbling down.

Dean Stockton

The editors

John Mair was born in the then-British Guiana (to an 'Old Guianese' mother — heritage not age) in 1950. He went to Sacred Heart RC School in Georgetown. John won the top scholarship in the Common Entrance examination in Guiana in 1961. Then his parents emigrated to the UK. He returns regularly to Guyana. He writes there under the nom de guerre Bill Cotton/Reform. John is the proud owner of a Guyana UK High Commission Award. He attended the LSE, Sussex, and Leeds universities. John has taught journalism at the universities of Brunel, Coventry, Edinburg Napier, Guyana, Kent, Northampton, and at the Communication University of China. He has edited sixty-four hackademic collections over the last twelve years on subjects ranging from the health of investigative journalism, reporting the Arab Spring, three volumes on the Leveson inquiry, and six collections about the BBC. His most recent books have been about the UK 2024 General Election, Inspector Morse in Oxford, ten Oxford author walks, reporting the war in Ukraine, Boris Johnson's clownish time as UK Prime Minister, climate change coverage, and the Guyana oil boom. He created the Coventry Conversations which attracted 350 media movers and shakers to Coventry University. Most recently he began the My Jericho (Myjericho.co.uk) series of talks in Oxford – 350 not out so far. In a previous life, he was an award-winning producer/director for the BBC, ITV, and Channel 4, making programmes in Belfast, Glasgow, and London, and a secondary school teacher. He often defends the BBC when interviewed by GBNews and TalkTV.

Andrew Beck taught in UK secondary, further, and higher education for forty-two years. For twenty of those years he held department or faculty head positions, and for fourteen years he had faculty-wide management responsibility for international development. He is the author of best-selling and oft-cited works such as *Cultural Work* and *Communication Studies: The Essential Introduction*, as well as having served as chief examiner for UK public and professional examinations. Retired from full-time work, he continues to teach at and advise international universities, as well as researching and publishing on a range of media issues. Recent publications include contributions to and co-editing books on Covid-19, the Ukraine war, Boris Johnson's premiership, the British monarchy, as well as occasional features for *China Eye*.

Janine Chandler is a seasoned strategist with over 35 years' experience helping organisations navigate change, define their purpose, and build organisations that matter. She began her career in the commercial sector, working in brands and innovation with some of the UK's best-known companies, before moving into the public and social spheres. She was BBC Interim Head of Brand Strategy in 2006/07, working for Tim Davie, now Director-General, helping shape the corporation's brand architecture as BBC iPlayer was launched. Today she leads Jump in Puddles, a certified B Corp consultancy based in Oxford. She works with purpose-led charities, social enterprises, and public bodies to drive innovation, unlock fresh thinking, and deliver meaningful impact. Her work combines behavioural science, strategy, and play to help teams tackle complex challenges and create breakthrough change. A passionate believer in public service broadcasting, Janine has long been both a supporter and a challenger of the BBC. She believes the institution is one of the UK's greatest assets — but to stay relevant in an age of fragmentation and AI, it must radically reimagine how it connects with audiences and earns public trust.

The contributors

Richard Addy is a co-founder of the international audience strategy consultancy, AKAS (www.akas.london). He is an award-winning global expert in strategy, media, comms and media. In 2024 he was named a top 100 media expert. He has over thirty years' experience working as a strategist and government economist, advising C-suite executives, third-sector leaders, and government ministers. Previously he was the Chief Adviser on strategic and audience issues to the BBC's Deputy Director General who headed up BBC journalism, locally, nationally, and internationally. He currently sits on the boards of theguardian.org and Africa No Filter.

Robin Aitken is a former BBC news correspondent on *Today*, *The World Tonight*, and *Breakfast News*. He now writes columns for *The Daily Telegraph* mainly on media matters.

Prof Paul Anand is professor of Economics, Decision Sciences, and Philosophy Emeritus at the Open University, and participates in a health economics group in Primary Care at Oxford University. Among his other publications are *Foundations of Rational Choice Under Risk* (OUP), and a recent report for the UN on AI and Human Development.

Prof Patrick Barwise is emeritus professor of management and marketing at London Business School, chairman of the Archive of Market and Social Research, and co-author with Peter York of *The War Against The BBC* (Penguin 2020). After an early career at IBM he joined LBS in 1976 and has published widely on management, marketing, and media.

Andrew Beck has never worked for the BBC although he has appeared on local and national programmes since the winter of 1963. He has been listening to and watching the BBC for more than seventy years with equal degrees of delight and distress.

Roger Bolton was a BBC general trainee, who edited *Tonight*, *Panorama*, and *Nationwide* at the BBC. He then moved to *This Week* at ITV. He presented *Right to Reply* on Channel 4 between 1994 and 2000, Radio 4's *Sunday* from 1998 to 2010, and *Feedback*, also Radio 4, from 1999 to 2022. He now curates his own podcast *Roger Bolton's Beeb Watch.*

Maggie Brown was the media editor of *The Independent*, a *Guardian Media* writer, and *Observer* contributor. She is the Channel 4 historian.

Janine Chandler is a seasoned strategist with over 35 years' experience helping organisations navigate change, define their purpose, and build organisations that matter. She was BBC Interim Head of Brand Strategy in 2006/07, working for Tim Davie, now Director-General, helping shape the corporation's brand architecture as BBC iPlayer was launched. Today she leads Jump in Puddles, a certified B Corp consultancy based in Oxford.

Prof Barnie Choudhury is an award-winning journalist who worked for the BBC for 24 years, and is now an editor-at-large for *Eastern Eye*, Britain's number one south Asian national newspaper. The University of Buckingham appointed Barnie its first professor of professional practice in communications, and he now lectures in journalism at the University of East Anglia. He specialises in diversity and inclusivity, data journalism, and investigations.

Tara Conlan has written about media for the *Guardian* since 2005 and was previously the *Daily Mail*'s TV editor and columnist. She has also written for the *Observer*, *Evening Standard*, the *Sunday Times*, *The Independent*, *Radio Times*, *Variety*, *The British Journalism Review*, *The Journalist*, *Television*, *The Stage*, and *Broadcast*. As well as contributing to Radio 4's *The Media Show*, the Media Club podcast, Radio 4's *Today* programme, BBC *Ten O'Clock News*, ITV's *News at Ten*, BBC News Channel, and LBC, she is a Royal Television Society juror and an executive committee member of the Broadcasting Press Guild. She has also been a consultant for the newspaper industry's marketing body Newsworks and the TV industry body Screenskills.

Prof Sir John Curtice is Professor of Politics at the University of Strathclyde, and Senior Research Fellow, National Centre for Social Research, and 'The UK in a Changing Europe'.

Deborah Wilson David is Head of the Department of Journalism and Media at Nottingham Trent University. She has combined broadcasting and education for thirty years. Her research interests are broadcasting history, particularly the early days of the BBC, the BBC's reporting of World War II, and BBC local radio. She sits on the Board of the US-based Broadcast Education Association, representing the Association's International membership, and served for six years as the Vice President of the European Journalism Training Association.
Tim Davie is BBC Director-General.

David Elstein was a BBC general trainee, became a distinguished television programme maker, and was Director of Programmes at Thames Television from 1986 to 1992, Head of Programmes at BSkyB from 1993 to 1996, and the launch Chief Executive of Channel Five in 1997.

Daniel Freeman is the Managing Editor at the Institute of Economic Affairs.

Lord (Tony) Hall, Baron Hall of Birkenhead, was the sixteenth Director-General of the BBC from 2013 to 2020. Before that he was Chief Executive of the Royal Opera House (2001-2013), and BBC Head of News and Current Affairs (1993-2011).

Peter Heneghan is the founder of The Future Communicator, an AI and communications consultancy helping organisations navigate disruption and rethink strategy in the age of intelligent tools. He is the former Chief Digital Communicator for the UK government and has held roles at the BBC, Channel 4, and BuzzFeed. A guest lecturer at London Business School on Communications and AI, he advises global brands and institutions, including the United Nations and Diageo.

David Cay Johnston, a Pulitzer Prize-winning investigative reporter and four-time bestselling author, is a professor of practice at Rochester Institute of Technology.

Peter Kosminsky was a BBC general trainee and is now a writer and director of television drama, with approaching 45 years in the UK industry. He has worked for all the UK public service broadcasters, has served on both the Bafta and BFI boards, and is a Fellow of the Royal Television Society. In 2015 he made *Wolf Hall*, the BBC TV adaptation of Hilary Mantel's two Booker Prize winning novels. In 2024 he directed *The Mirror and the Light*, completing the adaptation of Mantel's trilogy.

John Mair is an award-winning producer/director for the BBC, ITV, and Channel 4, making programmes in Belfast, Glasgow, and London. He has edited sixty-four hackademic collections over the last twelve years including six collections about the BBC. He often defends the BBC when interviewed by GBNews and TalkTV.

Nick Manley teaches at Falmouth University where he is practice lead for their postgraduate programme in film and television. Since the mid-1980s he worked in factual and drama production worldwide both as a freelance cameraman and BBC staff series director. Credited as director of photography he currently has over 40 hours of drama work on BBC iPlayer, BritBox, Netflix, and Prime TV.

Dr Liam McCarthy is an Honorary Fellow in the Department of History, Politics, and International Relations at the University of Leicester. He worked for the BBC between 1978 and 2008, was Managing Editor of three BBC local radio stations, and Head of BBC Local Radio Training. His published works include *Finding a New British Asian Sound on BBC Radio* (2023).

Dr Daithí McMahon is a critically-acclaimed and multi-award-winning audio playwright, director, producer, and Associate Professor of Media and Culture at the University of Derby. He is a regular contributor to BBC Radio Derby, and BBC Radio Gloucestershire.

Dr Martin Moore is director of the Centre for the Study of Media, Communication and Power, and a Senior Lecturer in the Department of Political Economy at King's College London. He was previously the founding director of the Media Standards Trust (2006-2015). He is the author of *Democracy Hacked: How Technology is Destabilising Global Politics* (Oneworld

Publications 2018) and, with Thomas Colley, *Dictating Reality: the Global Battle to Control the News* (Columbia University Press, October 2025).

Chris Mundy has been Chief Executive of RSMB, a company specialising in audience measurement since 2020. Previously he was Head of Audiences for the BBC (1999 – 2008), and Managing Director of the TV advertising clearance body Clearcast (2009 – 2020).

Mark Oliver is Executive Chair of Oliver and Ohlbaum Associates which he co-founded in 1995. They advise media companies, sports organisations, investors, and regulators on strategy, commercial exploitation, regulation, and investment decisions. Between 1989 and 1995 he was the BBC's first-ever head of strategy.

Salil Pajwani worked in brand and marketing management at Procter & Gamble and Diageo then spent nearly twenty-seven years as global CEO of the innovation company ?What If! In 2019 he co-founded 2ndStage who undertake creative acquisitions for small businesses.

Adam Sherwin is the arts and media correspondent for *The i Paper*.

Raymond Snoddy OBE is the former media editor of *The Times* and the *Financial Times*. From 2004 to 2013 he was the sole presenter of BBC right-to-reply programme *Newswatch*. His publications include: *The Good, the Bad and the Unacceptable: the Hard News about the British Press* (1993), *Greenfinger: the rise of Michael Green and Carlton Communications* (1996), and *It Could Be You: the Untold Story of the National Lottery* (2001). He is now a freelance writer.

Dean Stockton worked for the BBC magazine *Radio Times*, before moving to the BBC Current Affairs and working on the *60 Minutes* programme. He has worked for the BBC, ITV, Channel 4, Sky, Disney, Chellomedia (AMC), Dorling and Kindersley, WRCTV, and Liberty Global. The recipient of awards from the Royal Television Society, New Media Awards, D&AD, International Promax Gold, as well as Emmy and Bafta nominations, he designed the book's cover.

Ben Tuff is a senior leader in brand strategy, with over 25 years' experience shaping and structuring brands internationally. He has worked across sectors including technology, hospitality, and consumer goods, guiding organisations in defining their identity and building frameworks that support growth. Ben's career includes leadership roles, both agency and client side, in Asia and the UK. His expertise in brand architecture focuses on helping businesses organise products and services clearly, enabling stronger connections with audiences and lasting value for organisations.

Lana Wrightman holds a doctorate from Goldsmiths, University of London. Her 2025 thesis, *From Great Society to Great Compromise: American Public Television's Struggle for Survival in a Neoliberal Era*, explores how American public broadcasting has been commercialised and its values eroded over its 50 year history. She has worked as a lecturer and journalist, and is a highly regarded public relations consultant.

Peter York is a capitalist tool by background, as a market researcher and management consultant. In parallel he is a social commentator, journalist, occasional television presenter, and author of twelve books, ranging from *The Official Sloane Ranger Handbook* to *Authenticity Is A Con*. His most recent publication is *A Dead Cat On Your Table* (Byline Books 2024).

SECTION ONE: THE BBC IN CONTEXT

Introduction

John Mair

The BBC (British Broadcasting Corporation) is 102 years old and revered throughout the world. 2028 is crucial to its continued existence. By then, its ten-yearly Royal Charter will have to have been renewed and the new level of the licence fee, currently £174.50, set. This is a crunch point, real not imagined. The enemies — the press, political parties, rival broadcasters — have been at the gate for decades. Now they are louder and more powerful than ever before. The cacophony rises to a crescendo at times of crisis for the Corporation. Those now come around far too frequently, not annually or bi-annually but almost weekly. As soon as one storm over the BBC abates, it is followed by another. The current BBC is almost in storm alley. The UK press, particularly the right-wing press, the *Daily Mail, the Telegraph* and *The Express*, smell blood and keep looking for more. Hyenas need red meat. This book is intended to offer some calm and informed reflection amidst all the noise about the BBC.

Much of the popular press opinion about the BBC is just that — opinion without facts. The first part of the first section of this book is deliberately designed to be factual; opinion then follows. First off is the eminent political scientist Professor Sir John Curtice, often seen on BBC screens especially at election time. That does not colour his view of popular opinion on the Corporation. His conclusion, while not bleak, is objectively cautious. Because the BBC has lost its 'role as a monopoly supplier of a rare resource, it will need to be grounded in an ability to a provide distinctive range of content that is widely regarded, not least by younger people, as providing a valued and valuable service in a heterogenous and fragmentated media landscape where reliability can be at a premium.'

Chris Mundy of RSMB, a company specialising in audience measurement, used to be head of audience research for the BBC. He looks at the rise of the streamers eating into BBC audiences on TV and radio. He offers his conclusion right from the start of his contribution: 'British media is at a pivotal moment. The streaming giants have embedded themselves in daily life. For many of Gen Z TikTok and YouTube content is more familiar than that of BBC One or Radio 1. In this fragmented and fast-shifting media landscape the BBC faces existential questions about how it serves the public — and whether it can remain truly universal'. Pretty clear then.

From 1989 to 1995 Mark Oliver was the BBC's first-ever head of strategy. Today he is a media industry consultant. Mark delivered a powerful scene-setter to a Royal Television Society event on BBC funding on 29 June 2025 where, in a tour d'horizon, he looked at the licence fee doubters and their doubts, and how the licence fee might be made more acceptable: 'Generally the licence fee is seen as the least of all evils. There is a real majority for subscription or advertising and value for money [...] People under 35 or under 45 are really moving away from linear TV and also moving away just from TV as we know it and towards social media and YouTube [...] There's also the basic conundrum, the BBC's, which is it needs high reach to justify its funding.'

Professor Paul Anand of the Open University puts a pure economic case for the BBC though that may need tweaking to a new reality: 'There is some current interest in developing a hybrid funding model, comprising a free core with subscriptions for additional services. So long as the core was substantial, its public interest ethos was not diluted, and users not confused by a mix of free and paid services there might be little reason to oppose such a move.'

Janine Chandler, herself a former BBC brand wonk and co-editor of this book, looks at the rise of the streamers in the UK. The numbers are big. The leaders are Netflix with 17.4 million UK households, 59.2 per cent penetration, and Amazon Prime Video with 13.4 million households, 45 to 47 per cent penetration. The UK is a mature streaming market with about 68 per cent of UK households now subscribing to at least one streaming platform. Those households that do have subscriptions tend to have multiple ones. In 2025 the BBC has 23.8 million licence fee payers, a reduction from the previous year's 24.1 million.

So far so factual. But what of the critics of the BBC and of the licence fee? Robin Aitken is a gamekeeper turned poacher. Since leaving the BBC the former radio and TV news correspondent has been scathing in his public views of the Corporation, usually in *The Telegraph*. In his contribution to this volume he sees the BBC losing political cover as the UK, in his opinion, drifts to the right: 'the Corporation will in the future find itself relying solely on the support of centre-left parties including Labour, the Lib Dems, and the Greens. Stripped of party political support from the Right, the future of the BBC will become another of those wedge issues that define our politics'. This could have profound consequences for the organisation's funding: 'For the BBC to continue more or less as it is, a new funding mechanism will have to be found because it will be politically unsustainable to go on charging people for the licence fee to pay for an organisation they dislike and mistrust and for which replacement services can easily be found.'

Has the BBC brand been diluted through too many services being created? (Look at the cover of this book for a visual representation of this proliferation.) Has expansion universality meant that not all audiences are sufficiently served?

Marketing and branding guru Ben Tuff finds a soft centre: 'The BBC doesn't need a rebrand. It needs a centre — one idea to unify its sprawl, earn attention, and make people feel that time with the BBC is time well spent [...] Brand BBC now exists in a world of near infinite choice [...] Brand BBC is no longer the box in the corner, but one of many always-on solutions, available in a multitude of locations [...] Brand BBC has legacy, but no longer dominates. It is now the challenger to global behemoths, no longer the first screen. But it doesn't appear to admit it. It is compensating, not challenging. A true challenger, comfortable in its own skin, behaves differently. They know what they stand for, make choices. They're brave enough to stand by it.'

Broadcasting is a series of mirrors. Producers and executives dominate yet the public, naturally, sees the person on screen as the most important. Retaining that talent has been a BBC blind spot in recent years. By accident, design, or self-inflicted injury they lose some big names. I conclude my analysis of the BBC talent drain: 'one of the major challenges for the national broadcaster is to grow onscreen and on-air talent, build them an audience, but also to keep them inside the tent. The BBC has not been good at that in the last decade.'

There are undoubted successes. Trust is still there, as is reach. The BBC World Service is one. It is almost universally respected but maybe increasingly irrelevant in the noise of modern state-funded propaganda stations. Richard Addy was at the epicentre of BBC News. Now a consultant, he finds life in the old dog yet. Adopting a hyperlinking analytical approach to the use of BBC news as a source for others he calls 'global peer hyperlinking', he reaches a positive conclusion about the BBC as a news source: 'In a world where international news providers make multiple and sometimes overblown claims about their influence and impact, the global peer hyperlinking analysis provides clarity based on actual behaviour. The analysis confirms that, according to the actions and preferences of journalists in the world's leading 5,000 news providers across the globe, the BBC can confidently call itself the world's most influential news provider'.

But yet, increasingly, questions are being raised about BBC journalism. From right, left, and centre. Objectivity, bias, and impartiality are the key indicators. A pioneer of UK media journalism Raymond Snoddy worries about how the Corporation deals with populism and purveyors of half-truths. He concludes: 'Simple impartiality of a traditional nature is unable to cope with those who either deliberately lie or who have only a casual acquaintance with the truth'. Might he be thinking of Donald Trump or Nigel Farage?

The Corporation does dip into commerce. It always has. The establishment of BBC Studios in 2018 was designed to top up the public service licence fee income. It sells programmes, formats, and more but yet much of its income is derived from *Bluey* a bought-in Australian children's animation series sold worldwide. The main Studios business is selling programmes to and from the

BBC. I've delved into their rather opaque accounts and found revenue of £1.8bn in 2023-24 with just £199m returned as earnings before interest, taxes, depreciation, and amortisation (EBITDA) to the BBC — £50m less than the year before! I conclude that BBC Studios is the piggy bank that does not keep giving.

The attacks on the Corporation come from diverse elements of modern Britain too. Barnie Choudhury worked as a BBC reporter, producer, and community affairs correspondent. Today he is a professor. He has, he says, 'a problem with the way the BBC portrays and reflects communities of colour, especially south Asians. It is all too superficial, all too stereotypical, and it is all too patronising. If we don't have to explain what Christmas is to south Asians, why does the BBC feel it needs to explain Diwali, Eid, or Vaisakhi to those living in London, Leicester, Birmingham, Bradford and Manchester, Glasgow, or Cardiff?'

To draw this first section of the book to a close we look first across the Atlantic, to the often vexed history of public broadcasting in the United States. Drawing on her research into why the US Public Broadcasting Service (PBS) never had the cultural or political impact the BBC enjoyed, Lana Wrightman identifies President Richard Nixon as 'the pantomime villain' of the piece. By placing PBS on a commercial footing he 'ensured it never fulfilled its promise to serve the entirety of the American public'. Her cautionary tale concludes the UK should not go down the US path: 'Abolishing the licence fee in favour of direct government funding renders the BBC politically vulnerable. Making it a subscription service that viewers can opt for in lieu of or in addition to their Netflix subscriptions ensures that it will be beholden to the tastes of viewer subscribers rather than the entirety of the British public in all its diversity.'

Finally, former innovation company CEO Salil Pajwani takes a delightfully sideways look at the BBC. Reflecting on the situation the BBC now finds itself in, as well as the journey it took to get there, he draws on his own and his family's experiences of the BBC. There can be no going back, he concludes, 'Now might be a good time to challenge the unthinkable'. He asks, 'Is impartiality the right mantra to take our great institution forward? Or do we need something with more edge and more energy, and more likely to survive modern media dynamics?'

All in all, the BBC is still there after more than a century, but in 2025 there is more debate about why it is there, what it is doing, and how we should pay for it. In my close to fifty years studying the BBC up close and from afar, I have never known more febrile nor more heated debate. Where the chips will settle, who knows?

Chapter 1

What do the public think of the BBC? How do they use it?

Prof Sir John Curtice reads the UK public's views on the Corporation and the licence fee

The original rationale for the BBC licence fee was straightforward. Radio, and subsequently television, sets were the only means by which broadcasting services could be accessed.

Moreover, listening to and watching such services were the only uses to which such equipment could be put. Meanwhile, the BBC was once the sole and, despite the subsequent advent of ITV and other commercial providers, long remained a major provider of broadcast programmes. In short, the licence fee funded a service upon which most users of radio and television sets were reliant.

All change

The advent of the internet – now used at home by as many as 94 per cent of UK adults (Ofcom, 2025a) – has fundamentally challenged this justification. No longer is the ability to publish audio and video content confined to a small set of companies that have been granted the right to broadcast material across a limited spectrum of radio waves. Now anyone can post material for others to read, hear, and see, not only in real time but also as and when the user chooses. Moreover, the one-to-one connection between equipment and access has been broken. Both radio and television services can be accessed by a variety of digital devices including laptops, tablets, and smart mobile phones.

Meanwhile televisions themselves are no longer simply a device used to access live TV broadcast via the radio spectrum but have also become a digital device that is widely used to watch material streamed via the internet. Of the four and a half hours that on average people spend a day watching video material, nowadays only just over one and a half hours are spent watching live television (Ofcom, 2025b: 18).

News on the news

Traditional broadcasting is even losing its grip in an area that it had once made its own – the provision of live news coverage. Unlike newspapers, broadcasters could cover news events and developments as they happened, backed by the resources of an army of journalists and producers. Indeed, this aspect of broadcasting has been regarded as so crucial that from the beginning the news coverage provided by broadcasters has been closely regulated, with a requirement on public service broadcasters, including the BBC, to display 'due impartiality' in its coverage of politics. The partisanship that characterises Britain's newspaper industry was never allowed to gain a foothold in the country's broadcasting structure.

However, people are now as least as likely to follow the news via an online service as they are via radio or television, both of which are in long-time decline. According to Ofcom's latest analysis of news consumption, more people (70 per cent) now use an online source to access the news than use live television (63 per cent), let alone live radio (37 per cent) (Ofcom, 2025c). Indeed, among online sources themselves, just over half of adults (51 per cent) use social media to access the news. People spend almost as much time accessing online sources (43 per cent of daily news consumption) as watching television or listening to the radio (49 per cent). Meanwhile, according to the 2024 British Social Attitudes survey when people were asked which single source they rely upon for their news, almost as many say social media (27 per cent) as television, however accessed (31 per cent) (Curtice et al., 2025).

Young people are losing the TV habit

Crucially, there is now a generational divide in people's viewing and listening habits. Ofcom's data show that live television accounts for 73 per cent of the time that those aged over 75 watch video content, whereas that proportion is just 9 per cent among those aged 16 to 24. Even if we include broadcasters' online offerings the latter figure is still only 19 per cent, less than half the time spent watching a streaming service (Ofcom, 2025b). More broadly, the younger someone is, the less likely they are to be watching television and the more likely they are to be viewing online. Meanwhile, although 69 per cent of all adults listen to live radio at least once a week, the figure for 15 to 34 year olds is a half (50 per cent) (Ofcom, 2024).

The same division is apparent in how people access news. Whereas according to Ofcom's data, 90 per cent of those aged 75 and over watch television to follow the news, well under half (43 per cent) of 16 to 24 year olds do the same (Ofcom, 2025c). In contrast, 81 per cent of the youngest age group use online sources compared with little more than a third (37 per cent) of those in the oldest age bracket. In the case of social media in particular, as many as three-quarters (75 per cent) of those aged 16 to 24 obtain their news that way, compared with just 8 per cent of those aged 75 and older. A similar age gap is evident in use of radio. Meanwhile, according to British Social Attitudes, no less than 58 per cent of those aged under 35 primarily rely on social media for their news feed, while just one in eight (12 per cent) say that television is their most important source (and only 3 per cent radio).

In short, those who have grown up as the internet has emerged have integrated the ubiquity and diversity of digital sources into their everyday lives. In contrast, those who can remember the days of just a few (black and white) television stations and crackly AM radio have not. Inevitably, however, this means that online sources are set to displace traditional broadcasting, much as in a previous age broadcasting displaced newspapers as the principal source of people's news.

Unpopularity of BBC licence fee

Meanwhile, the BBC licence fee is widely regarded unfavourably – and increasingly so. According to YouGov, only 25 per cent now believe it offers good value for money, down from 35 per cent in 2019. As many as two-thirds (66 per cent) take the opposite view. Even fewer, just 16 per cent (down seven points), believe that the fee is 'fair', while 63 per cent feel it is unfair. Only when people are asked to compare the licence fee with other possible ways of funding the BBC does the current system emerge in a somewhat more favourable light (Curtice, 2024). However, asking how the BBC should be funded presumes that people feel it is worth paying in some way or other for the BBC in the first place. If the BBC is still to be funded, the case for doing so needs to identify and focus on the things that the BBC does that people still value in today's very different media environment.

Is there a case for the BBC?

Here are three possible answers.

The first is that the BBC is not just a broadcaster. It is also a significant player in the online world. According to the Reuters Institute, as many as 41 per cent use BBC News online on at least a weekly basis, not far short of the 47 per cent who use BBC television or radio with the same degree of regularity (Newman et al, 2025). The BBC is as much the UK market leader in the provision of online news as it is of broadcast journalism. At the same time one in five (22 per cent) of those who watch TV news use the BBC's iPlayer service (Ofcom, 2025c). More generally, iPlayer use already accounts for more than a fifth (22 per cent) of the time people spend viewing BBC output (Ofcom, 2025b). The iPlayer, together with the market leading BBC Sounds facility that is used to stream radio programmes and podcasts, means the organisation is already well placed to make the seemingly inevitable transition from being primarily a linear broadcaster to being an organisation that provides a valued service in the nonlinear world of watching and listening.

Second, the BBC is widely regarded as doing a good job at providing the key attributes that people want from a public service broadcaster. In its 2023 Public Service Media Tracker Ofcom found that nearly half (49 per cent) regard the provision of 'trusted and accurate UK news' as one of the three most important attributes a public service broadcaster should have. This was closely followed by 'a wide range of different types of programme' (45 per cent), while the next most important was 'programmes that help me to understand what is going on in the world today' (29 per cent) (Ofcom, 2024). The most recent (2024) wave of the same tracker found that among the 85 per cent of people who use a BBC service at least once every six months (most of whom do so far more frequently than that), 61 per cent reckoned the BBC was doing well at providing trusted and accurate UK news, 65 per cent at supplying a wide range of programmes, and 62 per cent at helping people understand the world (Ofcom, 2025b). Although other public sector broadcasters also emerge well from this metric, none is thought to be doing quite as well as the BBC in satisfying these criteria. Even in the world of digital media, people may still value an organisation that provides the kind of service that has come to be associated with public sector broadcasting.

Third, much mired as it sometimes is in controversy, the BBC and its news are widely trusted. In repeated readings over the last four years YouGov have regularly found that just under a half trust the BBC to tell the truth 'a great deal' or a 'fair amount' to tell the truth, a rating that puts the institution well ahead of both journalists and politicians. According to the Reuters Institute, three in five (60 per cent) trust BBC News, while slightly less than one in four (24 per cent) do not, putting it at the head of the pack among mainstream media (Newman et al, 2024).

Trust and social media

The same cannot be said of social media. Ofcom report that just 19 per cent trust the information they see on social media (Ofcom, 2025a). Well under half think that social media are either an accurate (43 per cent) or reliable (44 per cent) source of news (Ofcom, 2025c). The latest British Social Attitudes survey indicates that just 32 per cent regard as 'very' or 'somewhat reliable' the news on political matters that can be found on social media, a figure that puts it in the same low league as newspapers. This figure is only around half that for television news (66 per cent) or for radio and podcasts (61 per cent). Moreover, some of this scepticism about social media as a news source is also shared by those who primarily rely on social media for their political news. Even among this group (of mostly younger people), only just over half (53 per cent) regard social media as a reliable source of political news. In contrast, 75 per cent of those who primarily rely on television for their news feel that it is reliable, while the equivalent figure among those who rely on radio is 83 per cent (Curtice et al., 2025). The kitemark of accuracy and impartiality is potentially even more valuable in the online world.

BBC - still relevant 102 years on?

A century on, the case for funding the BBC is inevitably very different from when radios first appeared in people's homes. Rather than based on its role as a monopoly supplier of a rare resource, it will need to be grounded in an ability to a provide distinctive range of content that is widely regarded, not least by younger people, as providing a valued and valuable service in a heterogenous and fragmentated media landscape where reliability can be at a premium. The shape of public opinion suggests the opportunity to make such a case exists, though it will need to be one that is well made.

References

John Curtice (2024) 'Public attitudes towards funding the BBC: A difficult decision?', in John Mair (ed.) *How Do We Fund The BBC After 2027*, Oxford: MGM Books.

John Curtice, Marta Mezzanzanica, and Katy Bailey (2025) 'Politics and social media: Scrolling politics – engagement, trust and polarisation in the digital age', in Elizabeth Clery, John Curtice, and Curtis Jessop (eds), *British Social Attitudes: the 42nd report*, London: National Centre for Social Research.

Nic Newman, Richard Fletcher, Rasmus Nielsen, Amy Ross Arguedas, and Craig T Robertson (2025) *Reuters Institute Digital News Report 2025*, Oxford: Reuters Institute for the Study of Journalism.

Ofcom (2024) *Media Nations UK Report*, London: Ofcom.

Ofcom (2025a) *Adults' media use and attitudes report*, London: Ofcom.

Ofcom (2025b) *Media Nations UK report*, London: Ofcom.

Ofcom (2025c), *News consumption in the UK: 2025*, London: Ofcom.

About the contributor

Prof Sir John Curtice is Professor of Politics at the University of Strathclyde, and Senior Research Fellow, National Centre for Social Research, and 'The UK in a Changing Europe'.

Chapter 2

The generation game

Chris Mundy tracks the BBC's battle to stay seen and heard

British media is undergoing rapid change, and the BBC is far from immune. Audiences are consuming less broadcast content, spending more time with global platforms, and finding content through algorithms not electronic programme guides (EPGs). Using data from Ofcom, Barb, RAJAR, and the BBC's own reporting, this chapter explores who the BBC still reaches, who it's losing, and what these shifts reveal about its changing relationship with the UK public.

British media at the crossroads

British media is at a pivotal moment. The streaming giants have embedded themselves in daily life. For many of Gen Z TikTok and YouTube content is more familiar than that of BBC One or Radio 1. In this fragmented and fast-shifting media landscape the BBC faces existential questions about how it serves the public — and whether it can remain truly universal. But to understand the BBC's future we first need to look backwards: at how its audiences have changed, who it reaches (and who it doesn't), and how its public role has evolved over two decades of seismic shifts in media behaviour.

Let's start with some of the biggest drivers of audience change over the past five to ten years:

- YouTube has become the primary 'channel' for 16–24s. It's now transitioned from mobile devices to the main TV screen and some of its creators command millions of viewers and should be considered as competing directly with traditional broadcasters.
- Global streamers such as Netflix, Amazon Prime, and Disney+ now produce both global and UK-originated content — with British shows like *Baby Reindeer* and *Adolescence* among the most talked-about series of 2024 and 2025.
- Mobile-first platforms like TikTok and Instagram serve up algorithmically-tailored, short-form content that not only soaks up time previously spent on TV but may also be contributing to declining trust in mainstream media.
- Broadcasters' own Video on Demand (VOD) platforms — iPlayer, ITVX, Channel 4, and others — have enabled new release strategies:

entire series dropped at once, on-demand-first launches, and access to deep archives. With these services increasingly accessed via connected TVs viewers are no longer bound by the tyranny of the schedule, and overnight ratings no longer hold quite the influence they once did.

All of this is underpinned by broader systemic shifts: widespread high-speed broadband, the ubiquity of connected TVs, content piracy, user-led content creation, and changing media economics, with ad spend increasingly flowing out of traditional media toward platforms such as Facebook and Google. Even the surge in non-English-language hits, from as far away as South Korea, has begun to reshape what audiences expect from mainstream content.

Who are the BBC's audiences?

The days of Auntie deciding what is good for us are long since gone. The BBC now has to earn its relationship with its audiences and, with so many competing ways to spend their time, audiences are consuming less TV and radio, and being more selective about what they watch and listen to. Funded by the licence fee, the BBC must provide value to as many households as possible to remain relevant. It must ensure that it at least maintains its current value-for-money score of 5 out of 10. One way that it does that is to keep a close eye on reach, the proportion of people tuning in on an average week. In its *Annual Report and Accounts* for 2014/15 the BBC reported that the percentage of UK adults who use BBC television, radio, or online each *week* was 97 per cent. By the 2023/4 *Annual Report*, and for the first time, it had changed emphasis to the proportion of *monthly* users of its services which was 95 per cent. The adult weekly reach figure for 2024/5 had fallen to 85 per cent for all adults.

This adult reach figure masks some notable differences by audience group, highlighting the challenges the BBC faces. For example:

Figure 1: Pan-BBC average weekly reach, selected audiences

	Adults	16-34s	55+	White 16+	BAME
Pan BBC average weekly reach	85 per cent	71 per cent	96 per cent	88 per cent	70 per cent

Source: *BBC Annual report and accounts 2023/2024*

Underlying these headline figures are notable differences, most notably between TV and radio, between linear and VOD, by different audience groups, and by genre.

Television

Both reach and hours to television have been falling for all audiences over time. The average weekly 15 minute reach for broadcast TV by all individuals is now just 74 per cent of the population, down from 90 per cent in 2018 (Barb/RSMB; Ofcom, 2024b). To make matters worse, those who are viewing are spending less time watching broadcast TV: average viewing time per viewer fell by around 20 per cent between 2020 and 2024 (Barb/RSMB).

Let's delve a little deeper and focus on the BBC. Figure 2 shows average weekly BBC reach since 2010 in five yearly intervals (Barb/RSMB). This time reach is based on people watching at least three minutes a week, long enough to catch the news headlines, and designed to catch the broadest number of people who may be defined as engaging with BBC content. The comparison is like-for-like across the period, that is, linear BBC viewing across time and including playback within seven days. We'll add back non-linear viewing and look at the difference that makes in a moment.

Figure 2: BBC average weekly TV reach across time

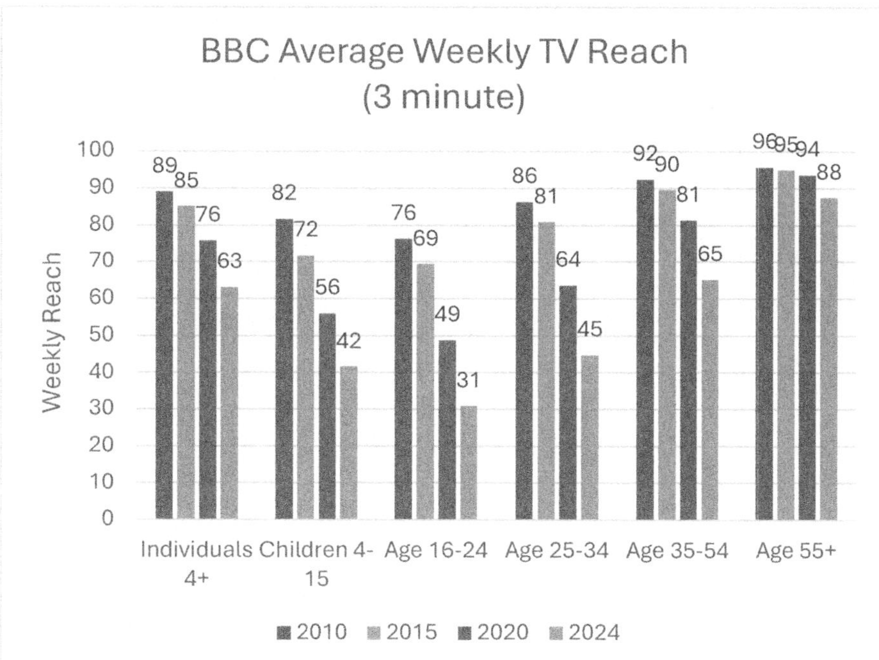

Source: Barb/RSMB

It's clear that younger viewers are much less likely to tune in to BBC TV channels than they once were. Only 31 per cent of 16-24 year olds tuned in each week in 2024, 42 per cent of children and 45 per cent of 25-34 year-olds. Viewing by over-55s has held up and, as they are heavier viewers, the total hours of BBC viewing and BBC share of viewing, whilst declining, has remained robust. This is a ticking time bomb for the BBC: as the population ages, and unless something changes, BBC viewing is likely to decline at an increasing rate as these 16-24-year-old viewers grow older.

Figure 3 shows average daily minutes viewed across the same period (Barb/RSMB). Although the number of people reached each week by the BBC has fallen 24 per cent across the period, average daily minutes fell by more, by 43 per cent, reflecting that even those who are watching each week are watching less. The decline in average daily minutes viewed is 'only' 29 per cent amongst over-55s, who are also the BBC's heaviest viewers and this has protected time viewed and viewing share to a degree. So the average age of a BBC viewer is creeping upwards. For example, the average age of a BBC One viewer in 2024 was nearly 63, up from 56 in 2011 (Barb/RSMB).

Figure 3: BBC average daily minutes viewed across time

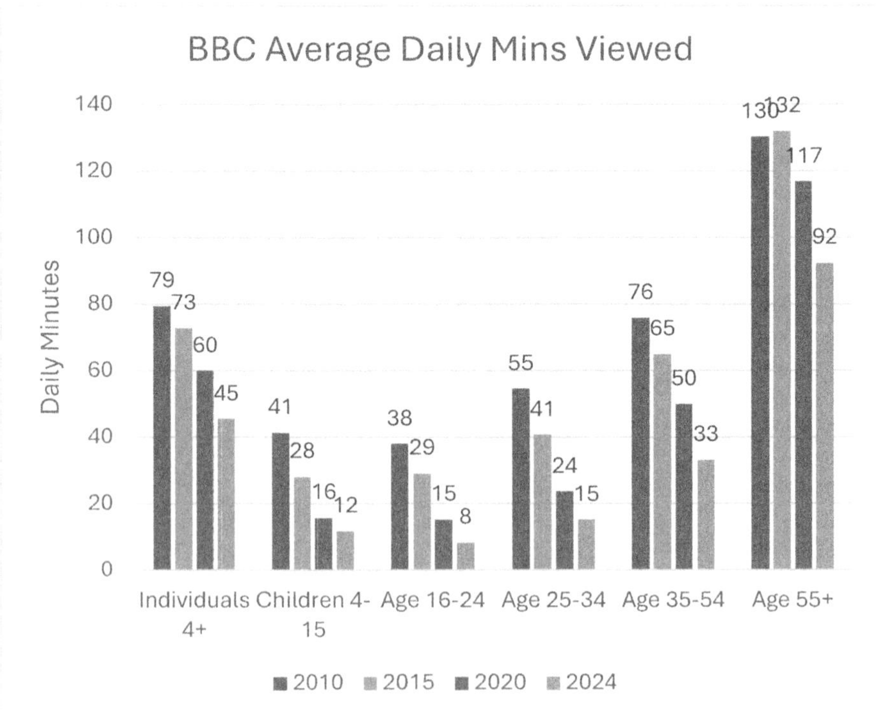

Source: Barb/RSMB

Figure 4: Relative genre performance 2024 vs 2010

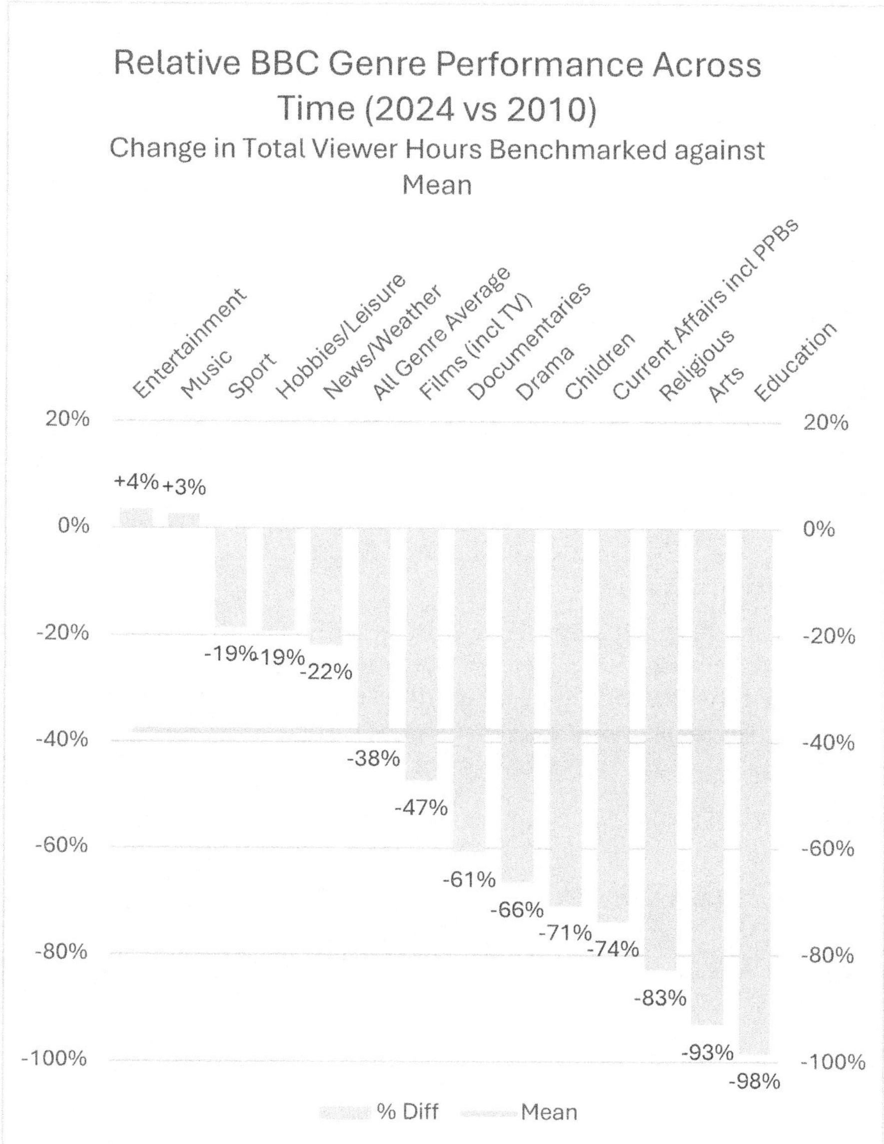

Source: Barb/RSMB

Analysing the data by genre shows further variation. We can see how the average decrease in BBC viewing hours breaks out across genre compared to the average across all genres and this is charted above in Figure 4. Obviously, as we are comparing with an average, some genres will do relatively better than others. It's also important to note that we're not necessarily comparing like-with-like here and scheduling changes, including any increase in repeats, will play a part. For example, Children's programming is no longer on BBC One; where *Blue Peter* on BBC One was averaging 380,000 viewers in 2010, its audience has now fallen to around 11,000 viewers on average across CBBC and CBeebies. Likewise, Education content is increasingly and more effectively served online rather than through broadcast. Changes will also reflect changing audience tastes and interests, for example, the role of religion in daily life.

First, the baseline. Total viewing hours to the BBC (excluding iPlayer) declined 38 per cent between 2010 and 2024. Total hours of BBC Entertainment viewing is up slightly on 2010 which may be surprising, but reflect a huge increase in broadcast hours: in 2010 Entertainment made up 5 per cent of the BBC's TV output but by 2024 this had risen to 15 per cent. Music is similarly up, and again hours of broadcast increased, however this genre makes up only 2 per cent of BBC TV output. All other genre shows decreased in hours viewed. Genres that declined less than the average include were Sport, Leisure, and News which were all down around 20 per cent. Genres performing less well than average include Documentaries, Drama, Children, Current Affairs, and Arts.

What impact does iPlayer have on BBC reach? Figure 5 shows that iPlayer does increase average weekly reach for younger audiences, most notably children and 16-24s. However, while iPlayer boosts reach and time spent among younger audiences, it doesn't close the gap.

Figure 5: Average weekly reach 2024 including and excluding iPlayer

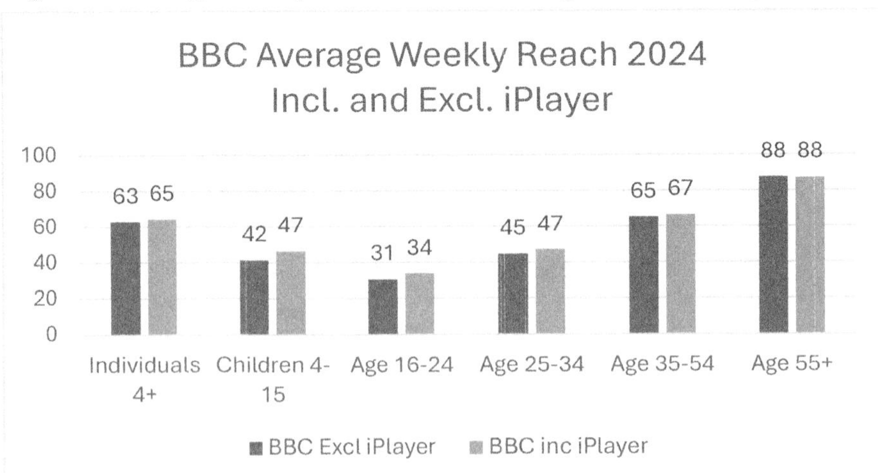

Source: Barb/RSMB. Data excluding iPlayer is 'as broadcast'; data including iPlayer is 'as viewed'

Radio

Moving to radio, changes in BBC listening over time have been shaped by several trends, most notably the increases in digital radio penetration, podcasts, and music streaming. In combination these have grown the size of the listening pie overall. Radio reach has held up surprisingly well although hours are down slightly (six per cent across this period). In the most recent quarter at the time of publication (RAJAR Q1 2025) 87 per cent of UK adults tuned in each week, and this is only slightly down on the twenty year record of 89 per cent in Q1 2024.

The big change over time is that now 76 per cent of the population tune in to digital radio each week, giving them access to a much wider range of stations than listeners on AM/FM radios. The number of commercial stations has risen far more than the BBC's, despite an ageing population that might otherwise favour the BBC. So, for example, in Q1 2015, the BBC's share of radio listening was 54 per cent with commercial radio at 43 per cent; the remainder is listening to other stations not recorded by RAJAR. In the latest quarter, Q1 2025, the position is reversed, with the BBC's share falling to 43 per cent while commercial radio has risen to 54 per cent.

A generation is growing up without the shared frame of reference that radio once provided. Among 15-44s the BBC's share is now 29 per cent of listening compared with 41 per cent in Q1 2015. The decline in overall share is not purely being driven by under-45s, though, it also fell from 63 per cent to 49 per cent for those over 45.

There is also a sociodemographic skew in BBC Radio that does not exist for TV: it reaches 62 per cent of ABC1s but only 49 per cent of C2DEs. This is unsurprising given BBC Radio 3 and Radio 4 attract more upmarket audiences.

There are notable differences within BBC networks as Figure 6 illustrates. Whilst BBC weekly reach (Q1 2025 vs Q1 2015) has fallen by 10 per cent over the period, with network radio as a whole broadly in line, weekly reach for BBC Local Radio has dropped by 28 per cent. There are notable differences between the BBC's national networks: Radio 1 reach has dropped 24 per cent across the period, with Radios 2 and 4 falling between 13 and 14 per cent. Meanwhile Radio 3 actually increased reach across the period. Radio 5 Live is down seven per cent, but this is less than the Network average, an indication of the audience loyalty that sports content provides.

We are likely to still be some way from reaching a stable equilibrium in audio listening. Half of adults now stream music at least weekly according to Ofcom/IPA Touchpoints data, rising to 74 per cent amongst 15-24s (Ofcom, 2024b). Whilst average hours of radio listening per head of the population has fallen only slightly, radio's share of all audio listening has fallen from 72 per cent in 2019 to 61 per cent in 2023/4. For 15-24s radio's share has dropped to just 34 per cent of audio listening (Ofcom, 2024b).

Figure 6: Change in BBC radio average weekly reach Q1 2025 vs Q1 2015

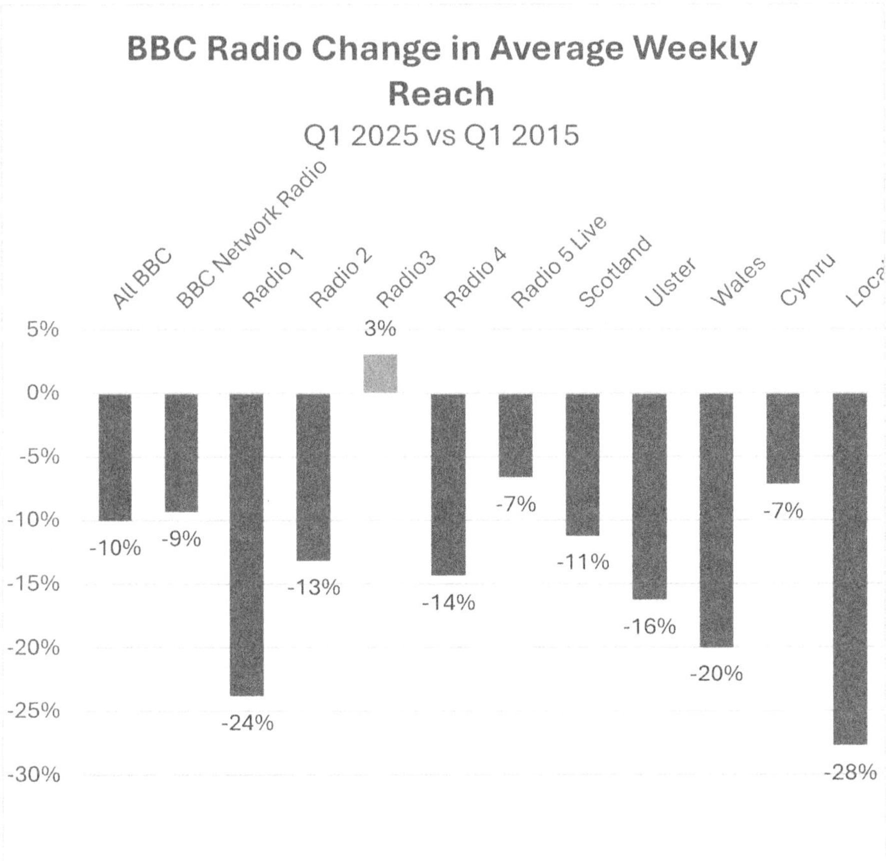

Source: RAJAR: Quarterly Summary Of Radio Listening Survey Period Ending 5 April 2015, RAJAR: Quarterly Summary Of Radio Listening Survey Period Ending 30 March 2025

Again, the BBC developed a strategy to try and meet the challenges of the evolving audio landscape, launching BBC Sounds in 2018. Ofcom research (Ofcom, 2024b) shows that BBC Sounds has established itself in the market, particularly for online radio where it dominates the competition with an adult weekly reach of 42 per cent. However this falls to 31 per cent amongst 16-34s, more of whom use other players for radio listening.

The BBC has also successfully made inroads into the podcast market with 32 per cent of adults and 20 per cent of 16-34 adults listening to these on BBC

Sounds at least weekly. A common theme for audio is that the BBC can't rely purely on BBC Sounds to distribute its audio content if it wants to maximise reach.

Online

Adult weekly reach for BBC Online is 61 per cent and skewed slightly male (65 per cent reach for men, 57 per cent for women). Unlike other BBC services, it also achieves a high 16-34 weekly reach of 59 per cent. With the BBC discussing a potential switch-off of traditional broadcast programmes, scheduled for the 2030s, this relatively high reach figure among younger adults offers a potential springboard for a successful reinvention of the BBC's video offer for this audience if it executes the transition successfully.

News

BBC data shows that BBC News was used by 75 per cent of UK adults on an average week in 2023/4 (BBC, 2024). BBC One alone has notable impact, with 42 per cent average weekly reach in 2024 according to Ofcom (Ofcom, 2024a). BBC News Online usage is also notable: 32 per cent of adults and 31 per cent of 16-24s use BBC News Online on average in a week (BBC, 2024).

Importantly, and although the scores may be declining, the BBC still leads the pack in trust, impartiality, and accuracy of news coverage.

Figure 7: Which provider news consumers say they turn to first

Which one source are you most likely to turn to	For news you trust the most	For impartial news coverage	For accurate news coverage
BBC	45 per cent	37 per cent	48 per cent

Source: Ipsos UK, 907 UK adults 18+ who follow the news, February 2024 (*BBC Annual report and accounts 2023/2024*)

However the BBC faces serious competition in news from new platforms. Ofcom data suggests that 40 per cent of adults get news from one of the Meta apps; Facebook alone is a news source for 30 per cent of adults (Ofcom 2024a). With social platforms growing in importance the BBC must ensure that its content is both seen on them and credited back to the BBC.

Again the demographic differences are stark when it comes to news consumption: 88 per cent of 16-24s say they get their news online, compared with just 49 per cent saying they get it from TV. However, 16-24s are actually less likely than adults as a whole to say that news on social media is accurate or trustworthy (Ofcom, 2024a).

The whole picture

The BBC continues to retain reach and relevance, particularly among older audiences and for major national moments. The BBC remains trusted but perceptions of impartiality and value for money have declined, especially among younger and diverse audiences.

Younger groups are spending less time with the BBC — and tuning in less frequently. Digital services like iPlayer and BBC Sounds are growing but still skew older. The BBC cannot simply rely on its own apps if it is to maximise reach and remain relevant. It can also no longer rely on being at the top of the EPG. Content discovery is increasingly shaped by third party algorithms and 39 per cent of people now turn to subscription streaming services first, rather than traditional channels, when browsing for something to watch (Ofcom, 2024b).

For the BBC to maximise its reach, and therefore the value it delivers in a world of near infinite choice, it's no longer enough for it to act solely as a 'broadcaster'; it must actively ensure that BBC content is surfaced by algorithms, shared, and actively sought out by users, often on platforms over which it has no control.

References

BBC (2015) *BBC Annual Report and Accounts 2014/15*, London: BBC Trust.

RAJAR (2015a) *Quarterly Summary Of Radio Listening Survey Period Ending 5th April 2015*, London: RAJAR.

RAJAR (2015b) *Quarterly Summary Of Radio Listening Survey Period Ending 30th March 2025*, London: RAJAR.

BBC (2024) *BBC Annual report and accounts 2023/24*, London: BBC.

Ofcom (2024a) *News consumption in the UK: 2024*, London: Ofcom.

Ofcom (2024b) *Media Nations UK 2024*, London: Ofcom.

About the contributor

Chris Mundy has been Chief Executive of RSMB, a company specialising in audience measurement since 2020. Previously he was Head of Audiences for the BBC (1999 – 2008), and Managing Director of the TV advertising clearance body Clearcast (2009 – 2020).

Chapter 3

Setting an agenda for the funding debate

Media economist **Mark Oliver** sets out the present BBC funding situation and some possible future scenarios

I started out as an antitrust and regulatory economist working on some of the large UK privatisations in the 1980s. At National Economic Research Associates I was told to look at the future of BBC funding in light of the Peacock Committee. Mrs Thatcher had insisted that committee, which reported in May 1986, be set up to bring advertising to the BBC.

To discuss funding in isolation of everything else you need to discuss about the BBC is always a bit artificial. That's why we start with funding because that's kind of what people get their heads around but it's part of a complex mixture of issues which will be part of the whole Charter discussions till the current one runs out on 31 December 2027.

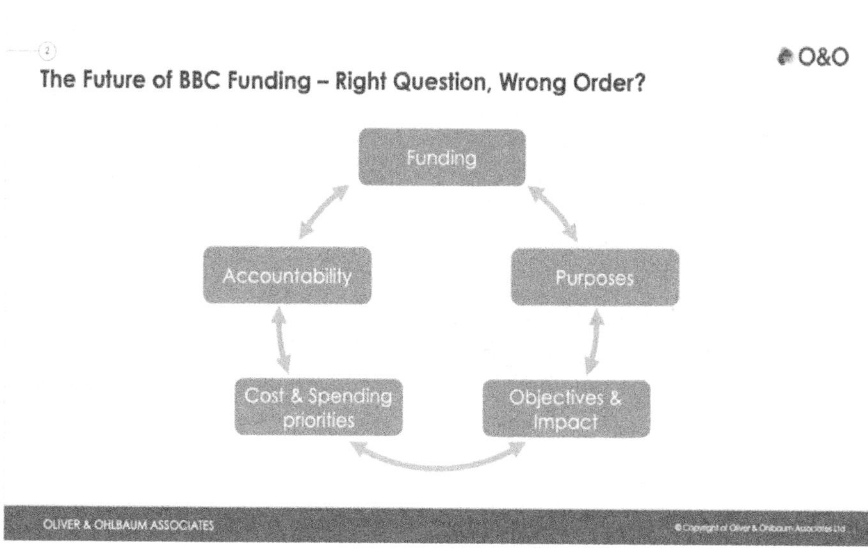

The first thing about the debate is it tends to divide people into two camps: either 'we're going to publicly fund it but how do we do that as the licence fee may not be fit for purpose?' or 'are there other ways of funding it publicly from taxation like a household charge or general taxation or even a lottery?'

The lottery was suggested by Peacock in 1986 but someone else got that money. On the other side there are streamers well-funded through subscription. Then you have the problem it's not universal any more, and it excludes people, and if only some people can afford it it's no longer a public service.

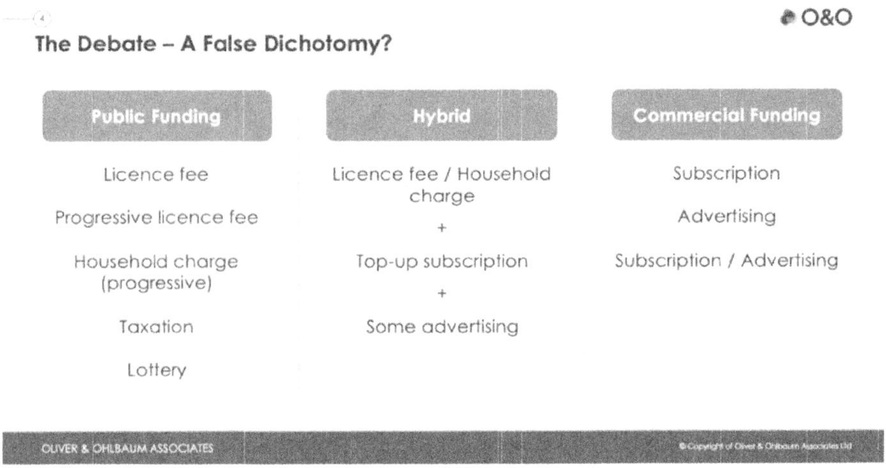

Advertising could be available to everybody but is there enough to go around and would it undermine the actual public service and subscription and advertising together? What tends not to get discussed as much is hybrid funding — some mixture of public or licence fee funding and commercial funding, which is what actually happens now.

To summarise things that have been said. Taxation is usually rejected because it's subject to short-term political pressures. The BBC doesn't want to be part of that because it means political pressure can be applied to the BBC in a way that's very direct and immediate. The lottery opportunity has gone and it's regressive, it tends to be poor people who bet more as a proportion of income. Commercial funding: subscription undermines universality and it won't be enough because there are lots of other pay TV players around. Nowadays it's a very crowded market. Advertising: there may not be enough and it would harm the commercial market and may undermine public purposes in the long run.

Hybrid tends to be rejected as just too complicated. It might create a two-tier public service and it would undermine long-term support for the public funding because if you start to grow your commercial income people always try and chip away at the public funding. In the end you always migrate to more and more commercial funding, less and less public funding, and so you move towards the commercial solution in the end.

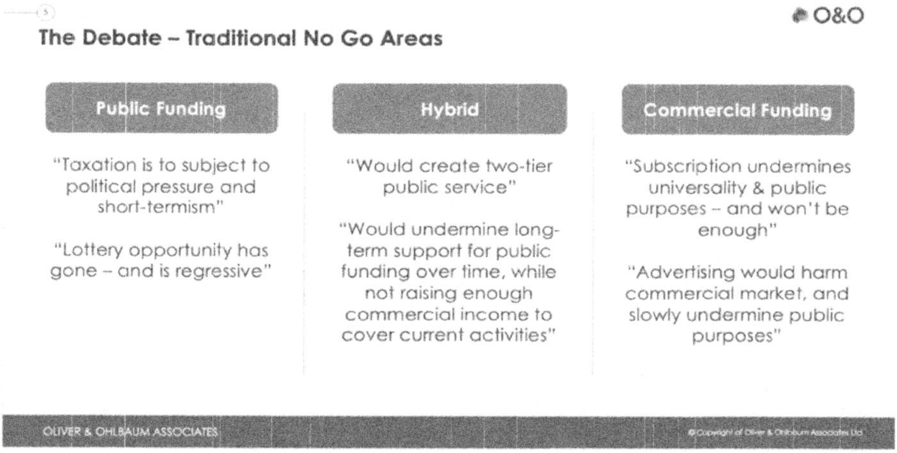

Another thing to note is that the people who object to the licence fee are not one homogeneous group. In fact it's a 'coalition of the unwilling'. There are at least six different groups, some of which overlap and some of which are very different.

You start with the very low-income people who just can't afford it or it's difficult to afford it. You then have non-consumers — 'I don't watch it; I don't use it' — and they have now got a way out. Then there are ones who are value-for-money, which is 'I do use it a bit but less than I think I should be paying for it and actually Netflix is better value for money'. Then there are the kind of very practical people — 'Can I afford it? Do I use it? How much do I use it? Does it balance why I pay?' Then the next three are more conceptual. There are people who just believe in free markets — they can't understand why you need to tax people to add to what the commercial market already provides. It's the in-principle objection to being taxed to provide a TV and radio product. There are people who are influenced by political bias. Then the sixth ones are fairness-focused; they are the people who say, 'it's regressive and I can afford it but many can't'.

O&O

The Debate – Licence Fee Objections – A Coalition of the Unwilling?

	Group	Issue	% of UK
1	Very low income	Can't afford it / difficult to afford	~10%
2	Non-consumers	Don't use BBC (TV) at all	~10%
3	Value for money focused	"Use it a bit, but less than I am paying" "Netflix better value for money"	~10%
4	Freedom / Free market focused	Imposition of a tax in a space where there is plenty of commercial provision	~5%
5	Political bias focused	"Group of lefties" or "Establishment stooges"	~5%
6	Fairness focused	"It's regressive – I can afford it, but many can't"	<5%

OLIVER & OHLBAUM ASSOCIATES

Another draws on the current societal trend at the moment to see everything you get from public services in terms of 'what does it give to me or my family?' or the other extreme 'what does it give to my group and my interest group? What can I get from it?'

What tends to get less airtime in debates is 'what's good for UK society as a whole?' You could argue the BBC was established because of that and so it's slightly subject to those two trends: on the one hand, there are the 'these are tougher times' attitude to life and, on the other hand, there are identity politics or group politics — what dominates my feelings?

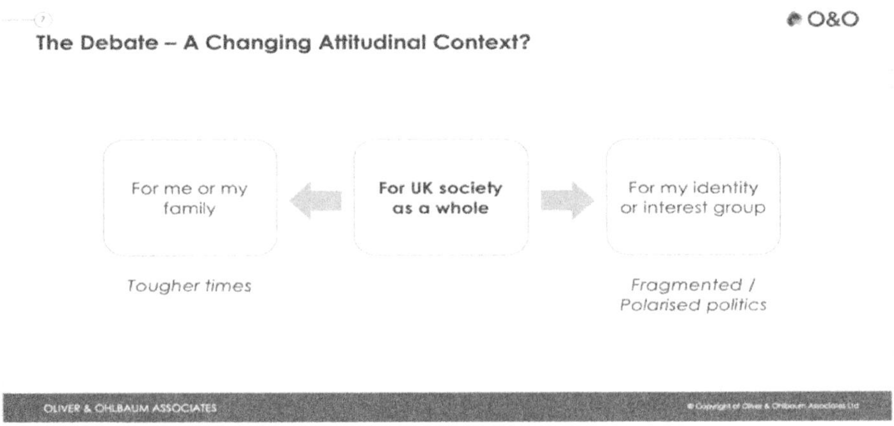

That sets a context to the debate when you're trying to argue for something that's supposed to be good for everybody and that may be difficult. There's been a lot of research done about various issues relating to the BBC cutting across those six groups.

One is about the trustworthiness and accuracy of its news. How well does it do and is it still well trusted by the majority of people? There are quite a few people who think it's too far right, some people think it's too far left, and some who don't know.

There's also preferred funding. Generally the licence fee is seen as the least of all evils. There is a real majority for subscription or advertising and value for money. It depends what survey you look at. The last Charter said that the majority of people either thought it was good value or were neutral about the issue. Surveys undertaken in 2023 (Reuters Institute, Ofcom) suggest that the number of people who think it's good value has shrunk but surveys are not consistent.

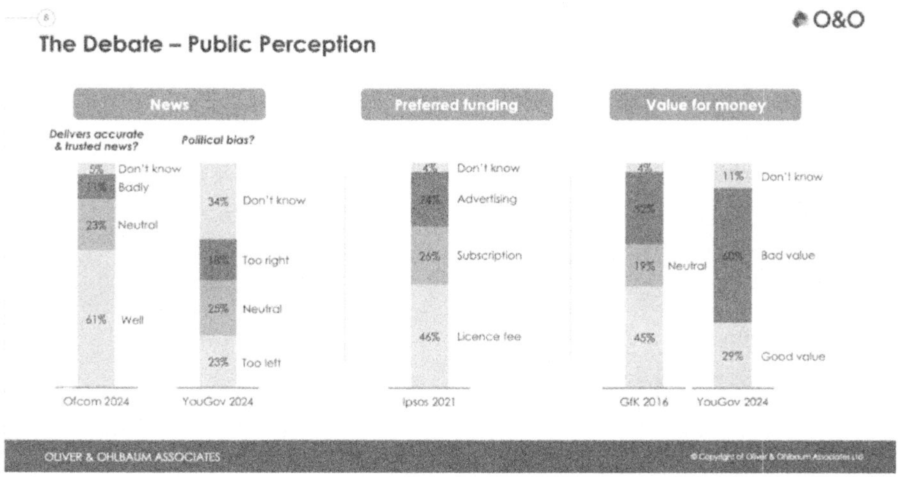

There is evidence about another way of assessing value for money which isn't just about asking a question. It's what's called a deprivation study, and the last one of these was done in 2021. This is where you take the BBC in its entirety away from a sample of people and say you can't use it. We technologically switch them off or just say you can't use it and monitor them. Then after nine days you offer them the money to buy back the BBC or to simply pocket the money. Once they've had it taken away their need to have the BBC goes up, so of those who said they would prefer to stop paying two-thirds said they'd pay in full now and 13 per cent said they'll pay something and of those who said they like to pay less 73 per cent said they'd pay a lot.

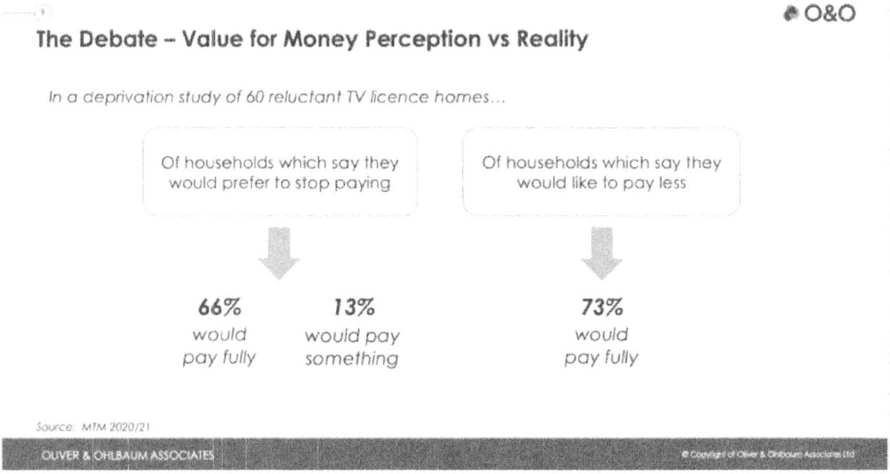

The first trend to notice is that the average number of people who've got TV licences is nowhere near the number of households, and the numbers are diverging. One should note that the number of people said to have TV licences actually includes the over 75s on pension credit because they've got a licence even though it's a free licence. There are people who evade the licence, there are people who have no TV, and there are people who have got through the IP access rule, which means you don't really have access to a TV signal just IP. If you don't use iPlayer you can claim that you really shouldn't pay the licence fee. That's a growing number and it's one of the main reasons for that divergence. It's really no longer a universal charge.

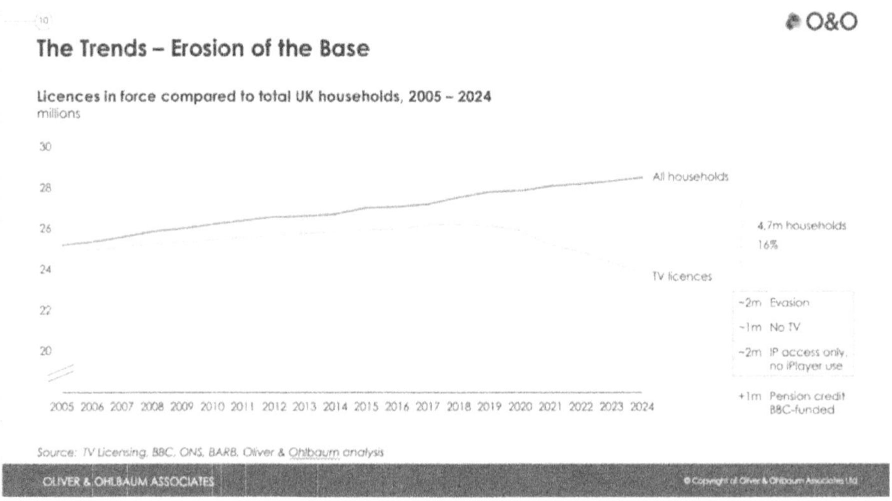

In terms of the inflation, why do people have a problem about the level of licence fee? Over twenty-odd years it's actually grown by much less than RPI or CPI. It hasn't inflated by as much as many other things, so in some senses it's quite odd that people should be so concerned about it, so it's probably more to do with enforcement and its flat fee nature.

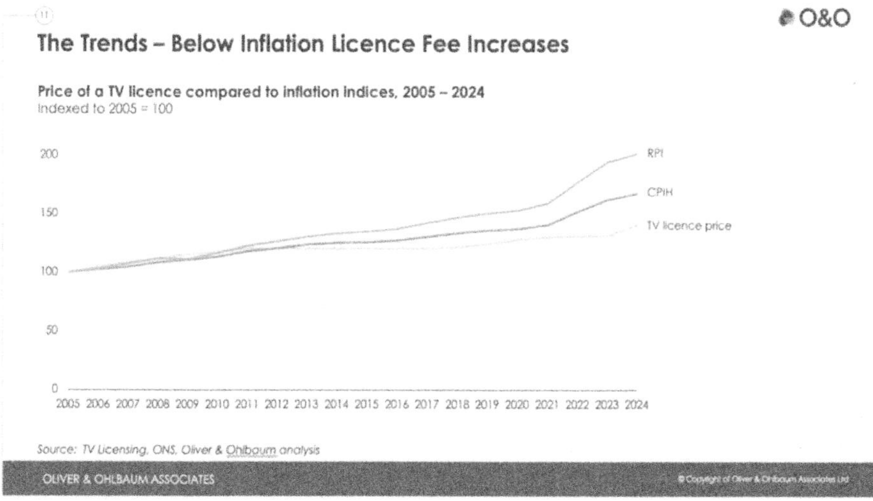

The other thing that comes into play is that the BBC's income may be flat but everybody's in the same boat. When you say everybody, that isn't the case for other public service broadcasters. The BBC is already richer than the other ones so it shouldn't really get much richer because it's got so many resources. Sometimes the commercial rivals say that the BBC shouldn't have more money because we're finding it hard to grow this number.

The lighter line at the top is the full contribution of commercial activities to the BBC. That's profits from commercial, its re-investment from commercial, and its contribution to overheads. To make a like-for-like comparison I've put on the ITV number that lighter bit which is actually the profits from ITV Studios so they are similar.

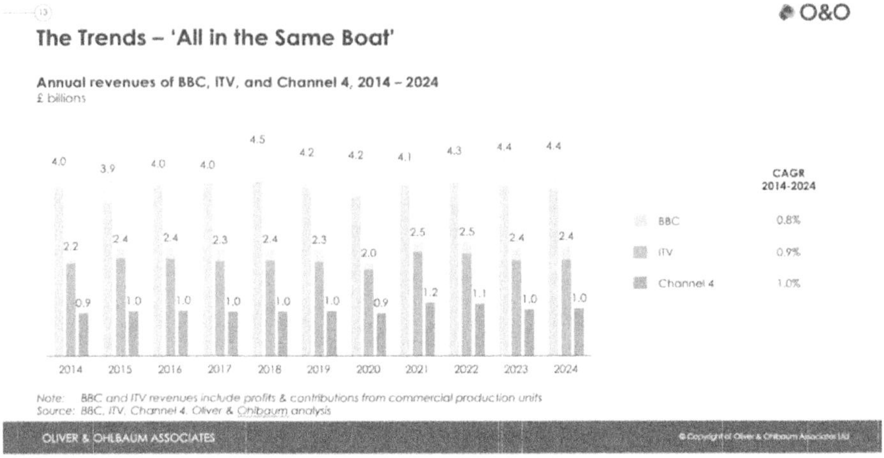

People under 35 or under 45 are really moving away from linear TV and also moving away just from TV as we know it and towards social media and YouTube. Obviously consumption in the end will affect people's view of the value but it's not actually just generational — each generation is moving away from linear TV.

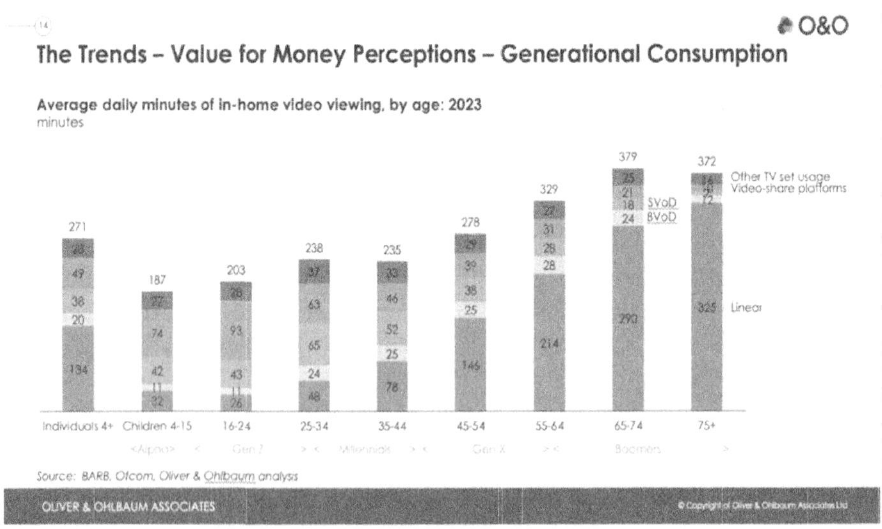

During Covid, older people adopted younger people's habits in terms of the BBC's performance. In terms of share, the BBC in TV has done very well and this is the share of the traditional TV audience in live and catch-up. It's what BARB has measured for many years and even its share of the 16 to 34 year old age groups is still at 30 per cent.

It's suffered more in radio because commercial radio has expanded its offering in terms of reach which in some ways is more important for the BBC: how many people have used it versus how many people pay? Again, standard measures of reach with traditional TV and radio consumption show quite a radical weekly decline, but if you then go to the reach of all BBC services, online news, online iPlayer, the reach there has started to decline as well.

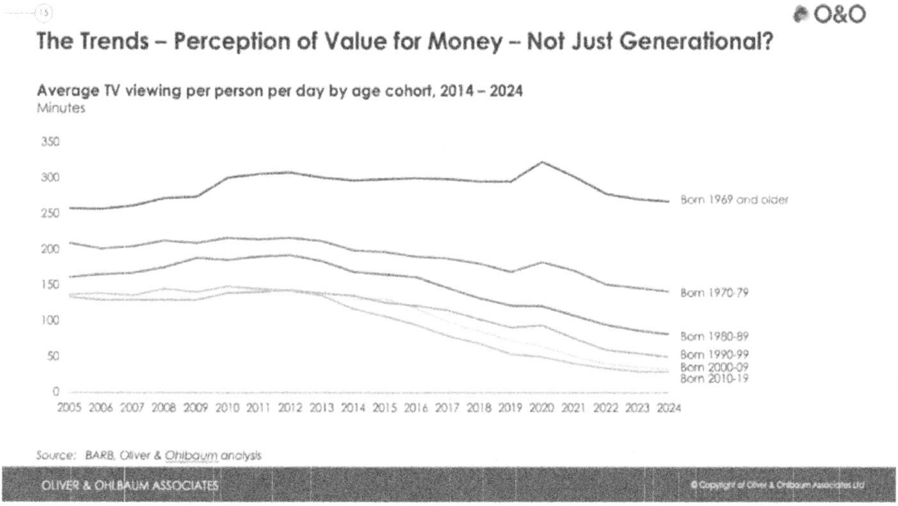

The weekly reach has gone down from 91 per cent in 2019 to 83 per cent in 2024. People using something on the BBC once a month is 95 per cent so 5 per cent don't indulge in the BBC at all.

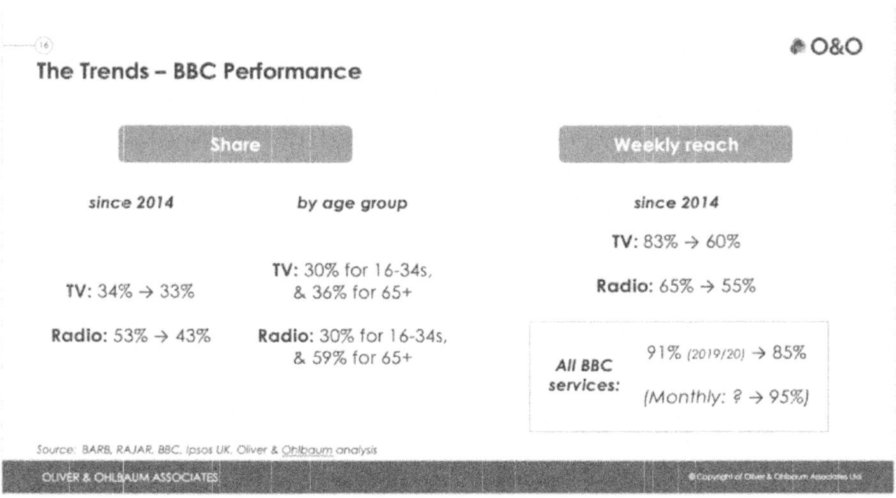

A few ideas about concessions. We already have a concession which is for the over-75s but now just those on pension credit. The over-75s used to be all households with an over-75 year old in them which is actually a bigger number, so if you actually add on more concessions you get back to all over-75 households.

With other measures such as households that qualify for free school meals, disability benefits, or incapacity benefits, there's overlap between them, and most of these are actually individuals rather than households. An estimate is that you might be able to give 5 million households a free licence fee if you extended concessions and the affordability issue was addressed.

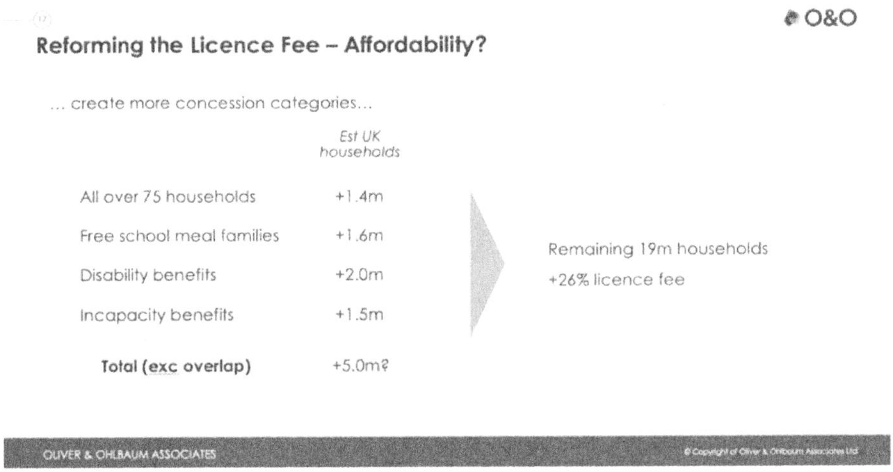

The issue here is if you wanted to maintain the system where everybody pays the same licence fee. That's the problem where the poll tax is always a poll tax. Council tax is always seen as a way because it's more progressive. It's got problems: there are many homes in band H. Widening areas of value. The south-east has lots in band H but if you got to the same kind of ratios of band A to band H then the top homes will be paying £350 a year for their TV licences.

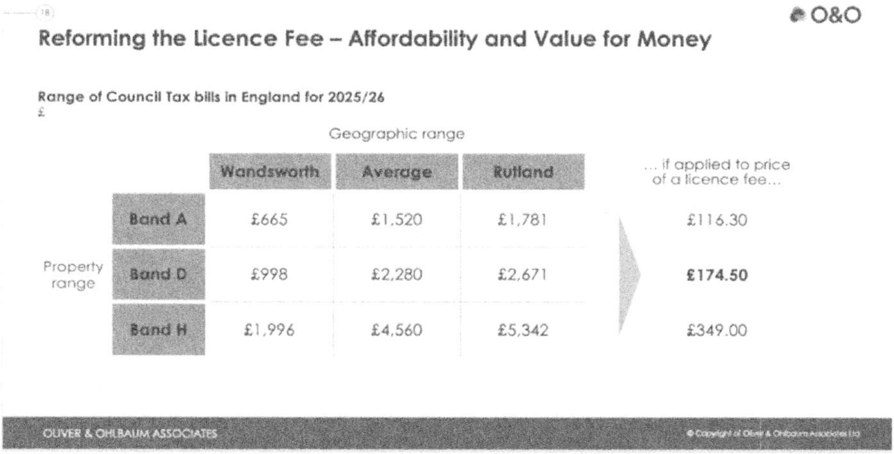

	Wandsworth	Average	Rutland	... if applied to price of a licence fee...
Band A	£665	£1,520	£1,781	£116.30
Band D	£998	£2,280	£2,671	**£174.50**
Band H	£1,996	£4,560	£5,342	£349.00

Public funding replacements are problematic. More concessions might be the way to go but of course that means pushing up the price for everybody; otherwise it's the same amount of funding and that will cause value for money issues and ads and subscriptions. A total replacement is unlikely — it's not really attracted the majority of consumers or commercial rivals but hybrid options hadn't really been looked at as fully.

There's also the basic conundrum, the BBC's, which is it needs high reach to justify its funding. Would a licence fee or a household charge give the BBC enough funding to generate the reach that then supports the fee? It's very easy to get into a downward spiral, a vicious circle, where we don't get enough funding to maintain the reach. More people start saying 'why am I paying it when you get less?' More people start saying 'why am I not paying it?' and that's exactly what's been happening over the last ten years so you've got to get out of that rut.

This chapter is an edited transcript of a presentation given by Mark Oliver at a Royal Television Society event on 29 June 2025.

About the contributor

Mark Oliver is Executive Chair of Oliver and Ohlbaum Associates which he co-founded in 1995. They advise media companies, sports organisations, investors, and regulators on strategy, commercial exploitation, regulation, and investment decisions. Between 1989 and 1995 he was the BBC's first-ever head of strategy.

Chapter 4

Some economic arguments for the BBC

Prof Paul Anand offers a cool examination of mainstream economic arguments supporting the BBC's current funding arrangements

To be transparent: I am broadly supportive of current arrangements that fund the BBC through a licence fee. On Radio 4 I listen to content which would be difficult to find anywhere else, even in this podcast age. I also listen to Radio 3 sometimes for Bach, jazz, and other music genres, and don't much care for advertising interruptions wherever they occur. Personal preference aside, there are several good public policy reasons why the current funding arrangements might remain and so I will focus on those from mainstream economics which appear to be particularly substantial. For while we live in activist times, substantive arguments remain important even if they need to hitch rides off good stories before they can fly. Here are some bare bones; further reading can be found in 'How Should the BBC Be Funded? in Gunter (2024).

Mainstream economic arguments

Public goods

There are some goods and services, like the police or public health, which benefit all and yet are difficult to charge for. The BBC offers objectivity and independent scrutiny of all aspects of society which for most people most of the time is beneficial. Excluding individuals who don't want to pay for such is nigh on impossible so in effect the service is a public good. If you can't charge beneficiaries you end up with undersupply so provision by the state, who can enforce charging, is necessary if we want to provide enough news.

Positive externalities

Another argument is that, even if you could somehow charge, there are benefits to society that would not be captured by the value of the economic transaction. Programing that embraces diverse cultures contributes to social cohesion yet the amount individuals are willing to pay to watch a programme or channel is unlikely to cover the broader benefits. You can't buy inequality in a shop.

There may also be environmental sustainability issues that public sector broadcasting can address. GDP figures do not include environmental externalities and the BBC can make arguments for change that might be harder to air in a broadcasting environment driven by advertising revenue.

Industry support and spillovers

There are positive spillovers into industry from the training and commissioning of professionals on the broader creative economy. One estimate suggests that for every £1 spent on the BBC benefits to the broader industry are over £2 (Sumner, 2021). Within the private sector, staff training programmes are often cut quickly when there is an economic downturn, yet the BBC has emerged as provider of some 250 apprenticeships and 150 graduate trainees a year across a range of professions from production to cybersecurity. While the private sector can do its own targeting training well it does not generally cover the full range of diverse training needs, at scale, and in a way that brings out public as opposed to corporate interests.

Skills development

BBC Bitesize, BBC Teach, and documentaries help create human capital at the population through improved literacy and numeracy, and greater civic competence while providing access to learning for socio-economic groups in society. Children's programming is delivered in a tone that is different to that offered by the US and is attractive to many countries around the world.

Universal access and equity

There are concerns about how universal and affordable access is as the previous point about skills development suggests. A flat licence fee, not related to income or wealth, is in theory regressive (proportionately to their income poorer households pay more) but there are various concessions, based on age, visual impairment, and residential care status that make allowance for at least some of the fairness concerns that are raised. Folding the fee into general taxation might help to make up for the failure of the fee to keep up with inflation as some have recently argued. However this is far from certain as a political party that was miffed with its coverage might find it easier to further cut or privatise the institution.

Support during shocks to the economy

During Covid the BBC broadcast daily government briefings and created a fact-checking team. It also upscaled its educational offering to children which would likely have cost taxpayers much more had it been done through private sector providers – if indeed they had the capacity.

Cultural political and administrative arguments

The following arguments feature in public debate overlap and relate to the economic arguments in some cases though the language and framing is generally more resonant with civil society or business.

The integrity of non-commercial content

Without dependence on advertising or subscriptions, there are no incentives for messages to be distorted by corporate interests. News education and cultural programming can be developed in ways that are shaped by considerations of individual and community wellbeing, and truth, rather than financial outcomes alone.

Cross-subsidisation of costly genres

Investigative journalism, science programming, and original children's shows are expensive to produce and yet may not generate the biggest audiences. Having an organisation that can cross-subsidise these activities follows industry-wide practice where cross-subsidisation is widespread if not *de rigeur* particularly in the digital world.

Predictable revenue without bureaucracy

It is claimed that a licence fee provides the BBC with a predictable source of revenue that is relatively easy to collect. Funding through general taxation would perhaps be even more efficient and perhaps just as or more progressive though political risk undermines predictability.

Soft power and cultural exports

One of the most common arguments made by politicians is that the BBC arises from the idea the cultural exports associated with BBC World Service and to a lesser extent programme sales contribute significantly to soft power. The World Service has an audience in the region of 400 million and as a result such power is viewed as a real, national asset which should, if anything, be funded from general taxation rather than the licence fee. That said, there is no simple consensus or evidence on how such power benefits the general population. One suspects the primary benefits are related to trust building and stability for business investment here and around the world, and for travellers, but I am not aware of any serious evidence on the topic.

Limits risks of monopoly from social media

There is a line of argument that the style and approach to programming of the BBC offers a much needed antidote to the instant and depthless gratification offered by the TikToks of this world. When digital platforms take on infrastructure-like functions, their owners should be responsible for offering a higher level of protection and safety according to one view. In this case, there must be a question mark about whether the activities of the BBC are enough. Only recently have schools have started to limit the use of smartphones by children, and it could be argued that the world has been playing catch-up when it comes to the inroads that digital has made on the attention economy.

Good for all?

One way of tying together some of the above arguments draws on the growing interest in the economics of wellbeing. Since the 1980s a growing number of economists have argued that national income (GDP) is often a poor proxy for how well citizens are doing and so other measures should be used (Anand, 2016). Since 1990 the UN monitors a Human Development Index (HDI) comprising indicators of income, health, education, and on its website gender equity. In May 2011 the OECD launched its Better Life Index relating to eleven dimensions of wellbeing in life and included an indicator relating to subjective wellbeing. These approaches both emphasise the view that income is a means to human ends which includes agency, our real freedoms to choose, and how we subjectively feel about ourselves. If this approach to economics is right, and I think it is, then the economic arguments for the BBC would include a focus on the extent to which it improves our agency by knowing stuff that is true and important or developing skills.

There is some current interest in developing a hybrid funding model, comprising a free core with subscriptions for additional services. So long as the core was substantial, its public interest ethos were not diluted, and users not confused by a mix of free and paid services there might be little reason to oppose such a move, if indeed it were necessary.

References

Paul Anand (2016) *Happiness explained: What human flourishing is and what we can do to promote it,* Oxford: Oxford University Press.

Barrie Gunter (2024) *The BBC and the Public*, London: Palgrave Macmillan.

Clare Sumner (2021) 'Benefits for everyone: Making the case for a universal BBC', London: BBC Media Centre, 25 February.

About the contributor

Paul Anand is professor of Economics, Decision Sciences, and Philosophy Emeritus at the Open University, and participates in a health economics group in Primary Care at Oxford University. Among his other publications are *Foundations of Rational Choice Under Risk* (OUP), and a recent report for the UN on AI and Human Development.

Chapter 5

Streaming in numbers

Streaming in the UK is big. **Janine Chandler** explains exactly how big

Who's watching what in the UK?

The UK is a mature streaming market where around 68 per cent of UK households now subscribe to at least one streaming platform. Most households have multiple subscriptions.

- Netflix: 17.4 million UK households; 59.2 per cent penetration
- Amazon Prime Video: 13.4 million households; 45–47 per cent penetration
- Disney+: 7.3 million households; approximately 25 per cent penetration.
- Apple TV+: 2.6 million households; approximately 9 per cent penetration.
- Sky (satellite): 11.8 million households; approximately 40 per cent penetration.
- NOW (Sky streaming): 1.8 million households; approximately 6 per cent penetration.

Global growth and market size

- The global subscription video-on-demand market is projected to grow from US $117bn in 2024 to US $207bn by 2029.
- The broader subscription economy (including media, e-commerce, software) could reach US $1tn by 2028.
- Streaming platforms invest huge sums:
    - Netflix spent over $17bn on content in 2023.
    - Disney committed more than $30bn across its platforms.
    - Amazon invested heavily in prestige content (for example, US $465m for season 1 of *Lord of the Rings*).

Churn, loyalty, and what keeps users subscribed

- Churn (customer cancellation) for streaming platforms ranges from 5 to 10 per cent monthly.

- 46 per cent of users in the UK say they've cancelled a service in the last year.
- The biggest reasons for cancelling are cost, lack of new content, and switching between platforms.
- Loyalty is driven by:
    - Original content (especially series)
    - Exclusive access
    - Ease of use
    - Perceived value

Who's winning and why?

Netflix

- Dominant in scale, global brand recognition, and original series.
- Success built on habit. It's the default app in most households.

Amazon Prime

- Part of a broader Prime bundle (shipping, music, books). Hard to cancel without losing value elsewhere.
- Prime Video is a retention tool for retail customers.

Disney+

- Built on franchise loyalty: Marvel, *Star Wars*, Pixar.
- Strong family appeal, massive library, and high production values.

Apple TV+

- Small but growing. High-quality prestige content (for example, *Ted Lasso*, *The Morning Show*).
- Often free or bundled with Apple devices.

Sky/NOW

- Strong sports and entertainment offer.
- Transitioning from satellite to flexible streaming models.

Streaming isn't the future—it's the now. Everyone's in. Most people subscribe to more than one service. But the real winners won't just be the biggest players. They'll be the ones that matter. Because this isn't just about tech. It's about trust, storytelling, and belonging.

And this is where the BBC still has a shot — if it dares to evolve.

Chapter 6

Can the BBC be saved from itself?

Robin Aitken calls for an overhaul of the BBC's internal political culture

In March 2025 the BBC's Director-General and its Chairman were briefed by the Corporation's Head of News about what are somewhat euphemistically referred to as 'low trust issues' among supporters of the Reform Party. Deborah Turness laid out to the top brass a pretty devastating set of polling results which found that 85 per cent of Reform voters don't trust the BBC. That, to put it bluntly, is disastrous for an organisation that proclaims 'trust' to be at the heart of everything it does. When the supporters of the most popular party in the country blow you a big raspberry in reply you know you have a problem. The question is what can be done about it?

There was a time, not so very long ago, when the BBC might have sloughed off a problem like this with a shrug of its haughty institutional shoulders: the Corporation has in the past treated the complaints of the *sans culottes* with an insouciant disdain. For decades the BBC radiated a scarcely concealed contempt for anyone who criticised its news output on the grounds of bias. I know this from personal experience because it is eighteen years since I published my book *Can We Trust the BBC?* and the Corporation's collective response then was to comprehensively ignore all my criticisms, the fruit, let it be said, of my 25 years as a BBC reporter. They made it plain they couldn't care less what I thought, but now times have changed and the carapace of iron-clad self-confidence in the absolute rightness of BBC progressive groupthink is beginning to fray.

Times have changed

There's a new nervousness at the BBC born of a realisation that complacent, long held assumptions about British politics can no longer be taken as axiomatic. The rise of Reform is scary for an organisation that has survived until now thanks to the support of liberal-minded centrist politicians of all parties who have been reliable upholders of the broadcaster's status quo. Ever since its earliest days in the 1920s the BBC has attracted the suspicions of right-wing people who viewed it then, and still view it today, as ineffably biased towards the progressive left. They are right to do so, by the way. But what kept the BBC afloat, immune from any effective reform, was a political coalition that crossed the party-political divide. It comprised the bulk of the Labour Party (not the far-left which hates the BBC) but crucially it included the One Nation wing of the Conservative Party. Unlike their brethren on the right that grouping always happily went along with the Corporation's campaigns on behalf of progressive causes. These are the Tories who once upon a time welcomed the liberal reforms of Labour governments of the 1960s and 1970s on the easing of divorce laws, the introduction of abortion on demand, the de-criminalising of homosexuality, etc. More recently the One Nationers have enthusiastically signed-up to the net zero dogma and trans-rights.

Reform has upset that particular political apple cart. The outlook for the One Nation wing of the Conservative Party now looks very uncertain; the rise of Nigel Farage and Reform has destroyed the illusion that a broad church Conservative Party must be an eternal feature of the British political scene. Because Reform has outflanked them on the right the Tories are now experiencing a profound identity crisis which means they must define themselves anew if they are to survive. A Conservative Party dominated by MPs who could just as easily sit as Liberal Democrats (which is the unkind but truthful description of many One Nation Tories) will not be able to offer any kind of challenge to Reform with its visceral understanding of what conservative-minded voters actually want. But under Kemi Badenoch the party has a leader who is genuinely right-wing (her voting record shows her to have been among the most consistently right-wing MPs in Parliament) and her instinct will be to regroup on ground significantly to the right of any Tory leader of the past forty years. That will leave the One Nationers out in the cold.

And there's another important thing about Mrs Badenoch which is that she has formed a very negative view of the BBC; she has come to agree with Dominic Cummings who in a January 2004 blog described the BBC as the 'mortal enemy' of conservatism. This political realignment has not yet settled but potentially it means that the BBC is now in a position it has not faced before; if my analysis above is correct the Corporation will in the future find itself relying solely on the support of centre-left parties including Labour, the Lib Dems, and the Greens. Stripped of party political support from the right the future of the BBC will become another of those wedge issues that define our politics. And that, for an organisation that claims it speaks for all, will be a disaster which would have particular salience in the run-up to the BBC's Charter renewal in 2027.

The BBC's problem in a nutshell is this: it is being squeezed by technological changes which mean many once-loyal viewers and listeners have moved to other providers; at the same time it becomes ever clearer to an ever-growing number of the politically aware that the BBC is profoundly hostile to a right-wing world view. This greater clarity is a reflection of our more polarised politics but it was the BBC's naked partisanship for Remain during the 2016 Brexit convulsions that brought the issue into sharp focus. For the BBC to continue more or less as it is, a new funding mechanism will have to be found because it will be politically unsustainable to go on charging people for the licence fee to pay for an organisation they dislike and mistrust and for which replacement services can easily be found. As Tancredi famously remarks in Guiseppe di Lampedusa's novel *The Leopard*: 'if we want things to stay as they are things will have to change'. That is why so much cerebration by so many media bigwigs is going into devising new ways of funding the BBC; but whatever is devised will be on unstable foundations unless a broad political coalition in support of the Corporation, including significant elements from the right, can be put together. A funding arrangement supported only by Labour and the Lib Dems will always be at the mercy of the outcome of the next General Election.

Time for internal reform

So what is to be done? The answer now is the same as it has been ever since I started pondering this question thirty-odd years ago: internal reform. The great, often unacknowledged, truth about bias at the BBC is this: it is there in plain sight, obvious to millions, obvious even to some senior people in the BBC itself. They know that BBC story selection on major issues like Gaza, immigration, Brexit, trans rights, climate change, and indeed every other important issue consistently gives the game away. The polite term for this within senior BBC circles who discuss it is 'revealed preferences' — by which is meant that you can intuit what the BBC collectively believes simply by analysing the tone and content of BBC news output.

It is sometimes argued that no kind of empirical analysis can be done on the BBC's news output because 'it's all a matter of opinion', but that is complete nonsense. It would be very simple to do it; one could easily trawl through a week's news output on the major bulletins and filter out all the stories about a particular topic. One could then score each story; is this positive or negative or neutral and in which direction.

Does this seem a far-fetched or objectionable proposition for an organisation that has fetishised impartiality? I would argue that it's exactly the kind of measure, carried out at the journalistic coal face, which would reveal to BBC journalists themselves exactly where their 'revealed preferences' lie. It would of course challenge the ingrained prejudices of many BBC journalists who would be confronted with the uncomfortable facts of their own biases. But will it ever be done? That is the question and, depressingly, the prospect of such a reform seems very remote indeed. This is despite the fact that Tim Davie, Director-General, said on being appointed in 2020, that restoring the BBC's reputation for impartiality was his first priority. In June 2025 after five years of hard slog his message was unchanged: "I came into this role with impartiality as my number one priority. Our goal is fact-based journalism and everything else comes second". Which just goes to show how resistant the BBC is to real change because it doesn't really matter what the top man says — what matters is what the Corporation's front-line journalists think and feel and that cannot be changed on the DG's say-so.

If there has been change in the BBC it is clear that it's not apparent to millions of people. Despite the defenestration of individuals like Gary Lineker and the *Newsnight* presenter Emily Maitlis, both stars who were entirely open about their leftish politics, the Corporation's worldview has held steady: an unhesitating support for every issue which the left deems 'progressive'.

Keeping Reform happy?

Now to get back to where we started: Reform voters, by 85 per cent to 15 per cent, say they do not trust the Corporation's news output. The reference figure for the rest of the population is that 53 per cent overall do not trust the BBC in some degree (Gifford, 2024). The station that Reform voters do trust is GB News which gets 55 per cent approval. The figures for those identifying themselves as Conservative are also bad for the BBC so it is clear from these findings that the Corporation has a major task on its hands if it wants to regain the trust of these voters.

Unless the BBC does something it has never done before, which is to make a determined attempt to achieve real diversity of opinion within its ranks, the chances of one of the world's best known brands continuing for another 100 years look precarious. This political risk sits quite apart from the increasingly urgent need to decide on a new funding mechanism because there is a growing consensus that the licence fee has had its day. But whatever is decided on that score – be it subscription, or a household tax, or direct funding from the Treasury – it is difficult not to conclude that the BBC is going to undergo a period of radical change in the next few years.

It is too soon to assume the BBC will not survive in any form; it still has many influential supporters and there are underlying reasons why sincere conservatives should support it too. There is a profound instinct in conservatism (the clue's in the name) to conserve; and what conservatives should always want to preserve are those good things handed down to us by previous generations. These include landscape, buildings, political traditions, etc., but also institutions. The BBC, for all its faults, remains a highly professional organisation which is respected the world over (although, as President Trump amply demonstrates, the acclaim is not universal); to dismantle it would be an act of vandalism which would diminish Britain's much-lauded soft power and any British government will be cognisant of the fact.

There's another factor too: almost every country in the world has a state broadcaster. In fact the possession of such an entity might almost be considered a hallmark of nationhood itself. The BBC always bridles if the term 'state broadcaster' is applied to it; BBC people will hotly dispute the phrase and point to its operational independence and its freedom from government control. This is not an absolute independence, of course, because the government of the day still has ultimate control over the cost of the licence fee as well as other ways of influencing BBC output (the FCO can usually rely on the BBC to faithfully promulgate its policy lines). However the crucial point to recognise is that any government of whatever political stripe will be loath to abandon such a powerful instrument of influence. When it is necessary — 'in the interests of the state' — so to speak the BBC has proved a willing accomplice to government.

The only way to restore the trust of Reform voters and others is to effect a real change in the Corporation's internal political culture. In an ever more savvy information age, where people have access to the whole range of opinion, it is inevitable that they will come to understand better where on the political spectrum the BBC sits. Long ago it became crystal-clear to me where my employer's political heart lay; what has happened in recent years is that millions of my fellow citizens have come to the same conclusion. The current BBC Director-General has talked the talk but has yet to walk the walk; unless he does so, and visible change results, political bias will remain the Corporation's Achilles heel.

Reference

Dylan Gifford (2024) 'Who do Britons trust to tell the truth?', YouGov, London, 6 September.

About the contributor

Robin Aitken is a former BBC news correspondent on *Today*, *The World Tonight*, and *Breakfast News*. He now writes columns for *The Daily Telegraph* mainly on media matters.

Chapter 7

Held in memory, lost in structure

Ben Tuff offers a provocation and a call to action

The BBC doesn't need a rebrand. It needs a centre — one idea to unify its sprawl, earn attention, and make people feel that time with the BBC is time well spent

Brands as old as time

White Rabbit sewing needles dating back to China's Northern Song Dynasty carried instructions: 'Note the white rabbit at the front door'. A mark of origin. A promise of quality. A brand. It established identity, communicated ownership, and created recognition in a crowded field.

That core role of a brand still matters. A brand includes tangible elements such as logos, colours, and product design, and intangible elements such as reputation, values, personality, and emotion. Brands are multifaceted and are kept alive in what people feel, recall, expect, and experience of them. A brand's success lies in closing the gap between promise and delivery.

Brand BBC has a brand identity issue

That is a challenge the Brand BBC is fighting with. Brand BBC emerged in a time of very limited choice. Founded on a mission 'to act in the public interest [...] to inform, educate and entertain'. (First articulated by Lord Reith but long since incorporated into its mission statement.) This was a structured space that existed for decades, one where the BBC set the agenda. Then the world changed.

Brand BBC now exists in a world of near infinite choice. TikTok, Netflix, YouTube dominate. Points of view are available freely in mainstream to niche locations. They change rapidly and are no longer dictated by print deadlines or news timelines. Brand BBC is no longer the box in the corner, but one of many always-on solutions, available in a multitude of locations.

New rules

In this new game competitors have carved out distinctive identities, provide instant utility and single points of entry. They match the original BBC mission:

Netflix educates

TikTok entertains

Disney+ informs

And all do the others, equally well.

Brand BBC fought a differentiation battle, simultaneously seeking a higher ground rooted in its mission, whilst also segmenting itself and fragmenting. This muddle has not created anything distinctive that consumers can rally around. As examples, Radio 1 has multiple streams, as does Radio 5 Live. BBC One (not 1) exists in multiple locations. Touchpoints veer from linear TV to Sounds to iPlayer. Each has its own identify, colour palette, logo, tone. Brand BBC has followed the linear model into the streaming age.

Meanwhile, multiple competitors are rooted in a distinctive logo, sound, and access points. These brands have developed distinct single identities with libraries of content. And whilst there are nuances in terms of target bullseye, these brands, and many of the other competitors, have landed on a single position, a single access point, recognising that success lies in delivering entertainment to a broad audience.

With Brand BBC there is the strong whiff of consultantspeak: "Be all things to all people, create solutions (stations) for all your audiences." Radio 1 Dance, Radio 3 Unwind, Radio 5 Sports Extra 3, Bitesize, BBC Three appear to be cures but are symptoms of an ongoing lack of distinctiveness.

The search for a golden thread

Brands are stories. A golden thread should weave its way through Brand BBC, connecting the parts so it has a logical beginning, middle, and end. Instead, engaging Brand BBC is like engaging with a series of specialist shops with even more specialist offers. Competitors play in the space of department stores. They have built a single identify, one store, in which everyone mills whilst seeking content relevant to their need.

Brand BBC is performing as a House of Brands whilst aspiring to play as a Branded House. What is missing is a compelling thread that links the different components in the branded house. The corporate mark is not enough – indeed, it is barely used. Instead consumers engage through weak sub-brands that carry no cohesion: Sounds (red/orange), iPlayer (pink/purple), Sport (yellow), channels/stations – again, all a mix of logos and colours.

In the fight for attention Brand BBC must be easy to recall. It must be easy to access if Brand BBC is to move more top of mind. Whilst there are always going to be individual Brand BBC-led cultural moments – *Line of Duty*, *Traitors* and so forth – consumers curate. Brand BBC needs to be part of that conversation. Sliced-up offerings means each must compete as a brand on its own, internally against its brothers and sisters, and externally. With no clear distinctive Brand BBC identify, recognition is weakened.

Weak brands carry no premium

This creates a further challenge. Where the licence fee used to feel like a fair trade providing a return, it increasingly feels to consumers like the tax it ultimately is. Strong brands carry their price. People feel what they pay for. The balance between promise and delivery is achieved.

With no golden thread, if there is no whole, the brand becomes invisible. It is no longer top of mind in the consideration set. That is where Brand BBC sits now. Not because the content is weak, but because the brand does not connect to the content to the consumer. Consumers don't like paying for what they don't connect with.

A new centre

In a world of platforms with purpose and edge, the Reithian ideal is now table stakes, the bare entry requirement to get in the game. The solution is therefore not a new logo. Brand BBC does not need a new positioning. However, the individual 'shops' need simplification. Brand BBC must become easier to navigate. It must create stronger pathways in consumer minds. Brand BBC as a top of mind solution, why they should engage with a logical flow of what is where. Brand BBC needs a point of distinctiveness running through the core assets in the new world of Vision and Sound.

A distinctive brand sound.

A brand colour taxonomy.

A reduced, consistent set of logos.

A single place to engage.

A single vision.

A compelling centre needs to put Brand BBC back at the heart of UK lives, UK media habits, an ongoing emotional part of the UK landscape. Make it as instantly recognisable, easily accessible, mentally and physically. A modern brand system but not a new brand.

Be the challenger it now is

Brand BBC has legacy, but no longer dominates. It is now the challenger to global behemoths, no longer the first screen. But it doesn't appear to admit it. It is compensating, not challenging. A true challenger, comfortable in its own skin, behaves differently. They know what they stand for, make choices. They're brave enough to stand by it. This means asking harder questions:

- What makes us matter in a world that scrolls past?
- How do we show up in a way that sticks — not just once, but again and again?
- How do we become part of the entertainment environment, without disappearing into it?

Strategically, Brand BBC must:

1. Create desire and difference.
   Not every engagement needs to sell something. But every engagement needs to be worth remembering. Lead with feeling.
2. Choose unique neighbours.
   Relevance doesn't mean looking sideways. Play in unexpected places. Partner with surprise. Don't always sit next to the usual suspects.
3. Disrupt in mass media.
   Use existing (perceptual) scale. Shift the tone, not just fill a space. Brand BBC has the reach. Be bold. Be brave. Carry a tone. Make people stop and feel, not scroll past.
4. Make sacrifices.
   Being known for something means not chasing everything.

   Not every BBC platform needs its own voice. Not every audience needs its own stream. Choose where Brand BBC matters most. Then matter more there.

Above all, Brand BBC needs to be consistent with a thread that weaves through, creating a reason to be and a call to action and use.

Time well spent

Focus and simplification reduces the sprawl. Value, not volume emerges, Brand BBC takes on a presence, creates desire, is not just available as an option divided across a myriad of touchpoints. This thread creates a centre of gravity, a common pulse that runs through every engagement a consumer has with Brand BBC:

They no longer listen on Sounds, they *listen to the BBC.*

They no longer watch on iPlayer, they *watch the BBC.*

They no longer read on Sport, they *read on the BBC.*

And this brand needs to be matched with product delivery.

One place. Mentally, Brand BBC becomes top of mind. The place to go and, once there, physically easy to access. No longer fragmented, Brand BBC becomes a single, distinctive whole. It is not frustrating because it is connected. Time with Brand BBC becomes Time Well Spent. A connected experience with a cohesive brand system built around that single-minded promise delivered across vision, sound and text, all adding up to the same thing.

Brand BBC finally moves back to fulfilling its original remit but is ready for the landscape of today. Not segmented products, but a broad entry point. Less specialist, less constricting. One expression, one promise. Brand BBC becomes a promise of quality for all. A brand.

About the contributor

Ben Tuff is a senior leader in brand strategy, with over 25 years experience shaping and structuring brands internationally. He has worked across sectors including technology, hospitality, and consumer goods, guiding organisations in defining their identity and building frameworks that support growth. Ben's career includes leadership roles, both agency and client side, in Asia and the UK. His expertise in brand architecture focuses on helping businesses organise products and services clearly, enabling stronger connections with audiences and lasting value for organisations.

Chapter 8

'To lose one presenter, Mr Davie, may be regarded as a misfortune; to lose more looks like carelessness.'

After Lady Bracknell,
The Importance of Being Earnest

Is the BBC presenter talent pool running on empty? **John Mair** looks at the exodus of talent from the Corporation

BBC Director-General Mark Thompson was adamant. Back in 2010 he opposed publishing the salaries of the best-paid presenters. He said revealing individual wages would be wrong. Parliament, though, dictated that salaries above £178,000 a year should be declared in the Corporation's annual report. They have been since 2017, firstly in broad ranges and later more specific amounts. Catnip for the anti-BBC right wing press. The poaching and leeching of talent has been relentless, especially in factual genres. On-air talent is precious and restless. Ego and pocketbook dictate destinations.

Before statute there were isolated examples. Matt Frei went from BBC to Channel Four news in May 2011 saying, "I'm looking forward to the editorial creativity and the opportunities across the channel that come with working for a broadcaster with a remit for challenging, fearless news." Robert Peston jumped ship in October 2015 from the BBC to ITV News to be political editor saying ,"I sort of feel that I wouldn't mind another big change".

Shelagh Fogarty left BBC 5 Live in July 2014 for LBC but not before a row over the BBC announcement which implied she and others from the presenter lineup had been dismissed: "None of us had been sacked. We all decided to leave, with heavy hearts and great love for 5 Live. But clearly the press release gave that impression very strongly."

Post-statutory declaration in 2017 a real star of the BBC radio firmament Eddie Mair, who presented the *PM* programme on Radio 4, left after an alleged disagreement over money. He too went to LBC saying he would "miss the smell of Director-General Tony Hall's after shave" but not miss emails from an unnamed executive "whose emails are so witless, badly written and contradictory that for years I've had them diverted straight to my junk mail so I never have to read them." He retired from LBC in 2022.

On the music radio presenter front Chris Evans left BBC Radio 2 in December 2018 and started hosting Virgin Radio's breakfast show in January 2019. While he does host *The Chris Evans Breakfast Show* on Virgin Radio every weekday he doesn't seem to attract the media attention he once did when at the BBC.

Simon Mayo, the afternoon star of both BBC Radio 5 Live and BBC Radio 2 left in February 2019 for Greatest Hits Radio for a more professional reason. He had been forced to share his teatime show with Jo Whiley for reasons of gender balance. Neither enjoyed it; he left. His parting shot: "I'll be remembered as one who sacrificed himself for a noble cause – for better daytime radio!" After another thoughtful pause and with an enigmatic smile: "I hope they're grateful" (Collins, 2019).

In 2020 Times Radio, just set up, came harvesting talent. John Pienaar, the deputy political editor, left after nearly three decades with the Corporation to join them in February 2020. In April Aasmah Mir joined him from BBC Radio 4 saying it "was time for something new". She left Times Radio in December 2024.

Meanwhile LBC was busy converting itself from the London Broadcasting Company to a national talk station 'Leading Britain's Conversation'. First a big scalp in 2021: Andrew Marr, the former BBC political editor and presenter of BBC One's flagship Sunday morning programme *The Andrew Marr Show*. He was paid £400,000 at the Corporation and is thought to have increased that in his deals with LBC and Classic FM. Marr also wanted to "get my own voice back" and be able to be partial on major issues. He had served twenty years in the BBC impartiality cage after the freedom of print journalism.

He was followed to Leicester Square and Global Radio by a mini tsunami of on-air talent in February 2022. *Newsnight* presenter Emily Maitlis defected after twenty years. She had found herself on the BBC corporate naughty step too many times, finally being 'ticked off' by bosses for lambasting Dominic Cummings for his sight-testing trip to Durham during the Covid lockdown in her opening monologue on the 26 May 2020 edition of *Newsnight*. Global tempted her with a daily podcast called *The News Agents*.

She was joined in that enterprise by Jon Sopel, formerly the BBC North America editor. In May 2025 he told the Hay Festival: "the 'both sides-ism' I found at the BBC was one of the things that drove me out after many, many years [...] I thought that in our Brexit coverage, we just got it very, very wrong, to say, 'On the one hand ...', 'On the other ...', 'Only time will tell ... Jon Sopel, BBC News, Westminster.' I didn't think that was journalism; I thought it was cowardice." *The News Agents* was first broadcast on 30 August 2022 where Maitlis and Sopel were joined by former *Newsnight* policy editor Lewis Goodall as the presenting team.

2022 was not a good year for the emptying-out of the BBC talent pool. In May Dan Walker left BBC One's *Breakfast* to become the anchor of Channel

Five News but with a positive message: "I've got nothing but nice things to say about the BBC". Dan is a practising Christian.

In July 2022 Vanessa Feltz jumped into her own lifeboat. On her exit to TalkTV she was scathing about the ageism that she felt precipitated her BBC Radio 2 demise: "It seems to be a casual culling and jettisoning of proper broadcasting adornments […] and it feels as if that casualness and that callousness is applying not just to the presenters but to the audience. It's like, 'Oh, we don't need you and we don't want you. You're too old, you're too staid, you're too middle-class, you're too middle-aged'."

In August 2022 Roger Bolton was relieved of his job as presenter of *Feedback* on BBC Radio 4 with little ceremony after two decades in that hot seat. The BBC thanked him for his service but did not provide a reason for the change, saying it would be seeking a new presenter [Andrea Catherwood] and production company [Whistledown Productions] for the programme.

Bolton accepted the sack: "Traditionally, however, the BBC is not a sentimental organisation. For whatever reason, it can be, occasionally, quite cold." Bolton had been in and out of the BBC for more than fifty years including a spell as editor of *Panorama* and being sacked and reinstated for the programme's Northern Irish coverage. Today he produces a podcast — on BBC issues.

More BBC Radio 4 departures. In September 2022 Fi Glover and Jane Garvey joined Pienaar at Times Radio saying, "We're not leaving *Fortunately* [their BBC podcast] in a massive strop, but we have talked about ourselves as much as we want to, and we found the offer of a return to solid journalism appealing."

And then a big fish was hooked by commercial radio. Ken Bruce dominated BBC Radio 2's mid-morning with his folksy style and the hit music quiz *PopMaster*. By 2023 he had been with the Corporation for 45 years. But he jumped ship in March 2023 to join Simon Mayo at Greatest Hits Radio. The Corporation's farewell present to the long serving Bruce? They took him off-air early to stop him plugging his new broadcast home but he took *PopMaster*, whose rights he had been nifty enough to acquire, with him. That is now a centrepiece of the GHR morning schedule and More4's evening schedule.

2024 brought more big fish out of the BBC talent pool. Mishal Husain was a fixture on the Radio 4 flagship *Today* programme for eleven years as well as anchor on BBC One's evening news. She was also the go-to interviewer for big TV election events. The glue that kept her stuck to the BBC came unstuck in November 2024 when she jumped ship to Bloomberg Television with her own weekend interview show. One of her first guests was Elon Musk.

In March 2025 another on-screen heavyweight, Stephen Sackur, was eased out as his BBC News programme *HARDtalk* was canned after nearly four decades of interviews with the powerful worldwide. He did not leave quietly calling it a "depressing day for the BBC [...] *HARDtalk* is unique: a longform interview with only one mission — to hold to account those who all too often avoid accountability in their own country." In June 2025 Sackur joined Times Radio's *The Times At One* presenting team, along with Jo Coburn, another BBC talent loss after thirty years political reporting with the BBC.

One is only really able to highlight talent who work for BBC public service who by law have to declare their income. Since 2018 the BBC's commercial arm BBC Studios has been making programmes for the BBC's national and international markets. The remuneration of talent working for them does not have to be publicly declared so some stars hide completely or partly behind that arrangement. The only way of discovering what they're paid necessitates searching the accounts of their personal service company (PSC).

The churn out of the BBC in recent years has been concentrated in the factual areas. Other genres like light entertainment are used to talent flipping off to pastures new all the way from Morecambe and Wise in the 1970s to Thames TV and Jonathan Ross to ITV in 2010. Football pundits like Ian Wright and Micah Richards take the freedom of freelance life seriously. They are here, there, and everywhere. Pushed out of *Match of the Day* by the BBC for Instagram transgressions in May 2025, Gary Lineker will no doubt find an equally well-rewarded berth when the 2026 World Cup takes place. Talent will out on new platforms.

So, one of the major challenges for the national broadcaster is to grow onscreen and on-air talent, build them an audience, but also to keep them inside the tent. The BBC has not been good at that in the last decade. Lady Bracknell was right.

Reference

Andrew Collins (2019) '"It was an awkward, stressful few months": Simon Mayo reveals what went wrong at BBC Radio 2', RadioTimes.com, 8 February.

Chapter 9

Is the BBC the world's most influential news organisation?

Richard Addy considers just who is the world's most trusted and authoritative news organisation

International news providers are making competing and confusing claims about their global reach, reputation and influence. However, a new analysis based on how journalists behave across the world confirms the BBC's leading position.

Twenty years ago, when I became chief advisor to Deputy Director-General Mark Byford who held responsibility for all BBC journalism, the BBC was recovering from the Hutton crisis, described as 'one of the most damaging episodes in the BBC's history' (BBC.com, 2025). The organisation's response at a global level was to ensure that BBC's journalism was 'the world's best-known and most respected voice in international news' and that it would 'provide the most trusted, relevant and high-quality international news in the world' by embracing the multimedia revolution, changing the mix of services, and investing deeply in the training and development of journalists (BBC, 2009).

Since then the world has become more polarised, misinformation and disinformation have proliferated, and the battle for international news dominance has intensified with more players growing in prominence including Bloomberg, CGTN, CNBC, DD India, DW, Euronews, France24, NHK World, RT, and TRT World.

Conflicting influence claims from international news providers

In this hyper-combative space the leading international news providers have made bold and competing claims about their desired and actual reach, reputation, and influence. A review of some of the claims from the BBC, CNN, Reuters, AP, and *The New York Times* makes the point.

In June 2025 Rebecca Glashow, chief executive of BBC global media and streaming, said, "We see the BBC as the world's most trusted global news brand, and we have heard that time and time again" (Savage, 2025). Meanwhile, the BBC's 2025/26 annual plan, published in March 2025, states that 'BBC News remains the most trusted news provider in the UK and is the world's most trusted international news provider, reaching more than 400 million people globally on average each week' (BBC, 2025). These claims were probably underpinned by a new 2025 survey amongst 'mass audience' and 'influentials' in twenty countries, which confirmed 'the BBC's position as the #1 trusted international news provider' (BBC and Tapestry Research, 2025). So game, set and match to the BBC? Not quite.

For many years James Earl Jones bellowed that CNN was 'the most trusted name in news' (Joyella, 2023). In 2023, a CNN Worldwide factsheet stated that 'CNN Digital is the #1 online news destination, with more unique visitors than any other news source'. This claim to online supremacy was reiterated in 2024 in a CNN pressroom blog stating: 'Globally, CNN Digital also was the #1 digital news outlet in February with 138 million multiplatform global unique visitors, ahead of #2 BBC by 2.5 million' (CNN Communications, 2024).

Others make competing claims: in spring 2018 Reuters marketed itself as 'the world's largest multimedia news provider [...] read and seen by more than 1 billion people worldwide every day' (Reuters, 2018), and more recently laid claim to be 'the largest network of journalists in the world'. Not to be outdone, AP asserts that 'AP today remains the most trusted source of independent, nonpartisan and factual news in all formats' and that 'four billion people see AP journalism every day' (AP, 2025).

Meanwhile *The New York Times* recently became the first news organisation in the world to pass 11 million subscribers (Robertson, 2024) and in June 2025 was vying with the BBC and CNN for the top spot in global Google searches for news organisations (Google Trends, 2025).

Tackling the influence confusion

With all these competing claims is it possible to make an objective, quantitative assessment about which international news providers are the most influential? The current measures of influence rely either on surveys from a subset of the world's countries or on blunt reach-based tools. So, frustrated by all the claims and counterclaims, my consultancy, AKAS, set out to develop an impartial and objective way of assessing the influence of news providers across the world.

Over the last three years we've built a Global News Media Database of the world's leading 5,000 news providers across 197 countries. We did this through a combination of manually building lists using the brands appearing on the Reuters Institute *Digital News Report* questionnaires, reviewing BBC News' country profiles and full media guides, and SimilarWeb's news media lists, and online desk research using Google search (BBC News, 2012).

With this database we can now track which news websites are most hyperlinked to by other news websites, as well as by governments, academia, think tanks, NGOs, consultancies, international institutions, and business. Our approach analyses the hundreds of thousands of decisions made by tens of thousands of journalists every day in every country around the world. It's a new hyperlinking analytical approach that has even been recommended to practitioners in intelligence services (Rohr, 2024).

Global peer hyperlinking

We could call this approach 'global peer hyperlinking' as it captures when a journalist decides to hyperlink from their articles to another news provider's website, creating a digital connection between stories. Technically, this is called being a referring domain. For example, if CNN links to an article on the BBC, CNN is a referring domain for the BBC. Such links act as a measure of a news site's influence, especially if the linker is a reputable source. It's similar to journalists citing each other to support a story — each link is a sign of trust and relevance in the digital world. Analysed at scale, this approach allows us to understand the implications of every leading journalist's and news organisation's linking decisions to reveal the most influential news brands in the world, globally and regionally. (Country-level analysis is possible but is beyond the scope of this chapter.)

To make this influence analysis manageable we decided to investigate which of the world's most visited English-speaking news brands are the most influential. To do this we used SimilarWeb's list of the world's 50 most visited English-speaking news providers, which is published every month by *Press Gazette* (*Press Gazette*, 2025).

Rank	News Provider	All
1	BBC (UK + Global)	51.7%
2	The New York Times	47.2%
3	CNN	47.2%
4	The Guardian	46.9%
5	Reuters	46.5%
6	Daily Mail	42.4%
7	The Washington Post	41.8%
8	Bloomberg	41.3%
9	Forbes	41.0%
10	The Wall Street Journal	38.6%
11	APNews + AP.org	38.2%
12	The Telegraph	37.7%
13	The Independent	36.8%
14	Business Insider	36.3%
15	ABC News	34.7%
16	CNBC	34.3%
17	NBC News	33.2%
18	CBS News	32.7%
19	RT (Russia Today)	32.4%
20	Fox News	32.2%

Figure 1: Global peer hyperlinking - proportion of the world leading c5,000 news organisations hyperlinking to leading English language news brand

Source: AKAS, 30 June 2025

Figure 1 shows the proportion of the world's leading c5,000 news organisations that are linking to the top 20 of the leading 50 and reveals the BBC to be the only news organisation linked to by the majority of leading news organisations across the world: nearly 52 per cent of the 4,936 news organisations from 197 countries were linked to BBC content as of 30 June 2025. *The New York Times* and CNN were joint second with 47.2 per cent, ahead of *The Guardian* on 46.9 per cent. In fact, this approach shows how powerful a role the UK's news media plays globally: four of the top six news brands in terms of peer hyperlinking are headquartered in the UK – the BBC, *The Guardian*, Reuters News Agency, and *Daily Mail.*

Figure 2: Brexit: What you need to know about the UK leaving the EU (2016 to 2020) Source: https://www.bbc.com/news/uk-politics-32810887

One story that brings to life the BBC's influence is a constantly updated piece called 'Brexit: What you need to know about the UK leaving the EU', which explains all aspects of Brexit. Of the 920,000 news and information pages from across the world that mentioned Brexit in their title, the international version of this BBC article was the most hyperlinked-to by any website, with the article's domestic version being the second most hyperlinked-to (BBC News, 2020).

Although this may not be surprising, what is fascinating about this BBC story is how frequently the world's leading news providers and universities have kept hyperlinking to this story – essentially seeing it as the definitive guide to Brexit. For example, yahoo.com hyperlinked to this story 19 times, and *The New York Times* and *The Guardian* six times each. Beyond the media, both the UK

Government and US Senate hyperlinked to the article, whilst Ivy league universities Columbia, Yale, and Berkeley all hyperlinked multiple times.

Regional peer hyperlinking

Figure 3 shows the hyperlinking rankings at a regional level and for the world's largest news media market, the USA. It demonstrates that across Asia, Europe, MENA, North America, South America, and Sub-Saharan Africa, the BBC is the most hyperlinked-to news brand by other news brands. Only in Australia and Oceania, and the USA is the BBC eclipsed by Reuters, and *The New York Times* respectively.

Rank	News Provider	Asia	Australia and Oceania	Europe	MENA	USA	North America	South America	Sub-Saharan Africa
1	BBC (UK + Global)	1	2	1	1	2	1	1	1
2	The New York Times	4	6	3	6	1	3	3	3
3	CNN	5	5	4	2	9	2	2	5
4	The Guardian	3	4	2	4	16	4	4	4
5	Reuters	2	1	5	3	18	6	6	2
6	Daily Mail	7	8	6	5	26	10	8	9
7	The Washington Post	9	15	7	7	2	5	10	7
8	Bloomberg	8	12	8	9	9	9	5	6
9	Forbes	6	10	9	10	18	8	9	8
10	The Wall Street Journal	10	9	11	13	9	11	12	12
11	APNews + AP.org	12	12	13	14	13	7	11	10
12	The Telegraph	14	11	10	11	13	21	13	11
13	The Independent	13	12	12	11	13	22	22	13
14	Business Insider	11	18	14	15	22	23	16	13
15	ABC News	17	15	15	17	2	14	14	19
16	CNBC	15	18	16	18	6	19	21	17
17	NBC News	22	15	21	21	6	12	17	18
18	CBS News	24	18	20	23	9	15	22	20
19	RT (Russia Today)	31	43	26	7	43	16	6	25
20	Fox News	23	27	21	20	18	17	18	26

Figure 3: Global and regional peer linking - proportion of the world's leading c5,000 news organisations hyperlinking to a news brand by region

Source: AKAS, 30 June 2025

The regional breakdown also highlights other previously unknown patterns. Whilst SimilarWeb shows *RT* to be the forty-first most-visited English-language news website in April 2025, our hyperlinking analysis shows it to be the nineteenth highest linked-to news website by other leading news websites overall. The regional analysis shows it in seventh place in the Middle East & North Africa, and sixth in South America.

What does it all mean?

In a world where international news providers make multiple and sometimes overblown claims about their influence and impact, the global peer hyperlinking analysis provides clarity based on actual behaviour. The analysis confirms that, according to the actions and preferences of journalists in the world's leading 5,000 news providers across the globe, the BBC can confidently call itself the world's most influential news provider.

References

Associated Press (2025) *About AP,* available at: https://www.ap.org/about/ (accessed 4 July 2025)

BBC (2025) *BBC Annual Plan 2025/2026*, London: BBC.

BBC.com (nd) *Iraq, Gilligan, Kelly and the Hutton Report – 2003*, History of the BBC, available at: **https://www.bbc.com/historyofthebbc/research/editorial-independence/hutton-report/** (accessed 4 July 2025)

BBC (2009) *BBC Annual Report and Accounts 2008/2009*, London: BBC Trust.

BBC and Tapestry Research (2025) *Global Influence & Impact Research*, available at: **https://www.bbc.co.uk/aboutthebbc/documents/bbc-global-impact-and-influence-research-2025.pdf** (accessed 4 July 2025)

BBC News (2020) 'Brexit: What you need to know about the UK leaving the EU', 30 December, available at: **https://www.bbc.com/news/uk-politics-32810887** & **https://www.bbc.co.uk/news/uk-politics-32810887** (accessed 4 July 2025)

BBC News (2012) 'Country Profiles', 9 November 2012 onwards, available at https://www.bbc.com/news/world-20048811(accessed 4 July 2025)

CNN Communications (2024) 'CNN Ranks in Top 5 Most Watched Networks in All of Cable in March and Q1 2024', Press release, 2 April.

CNN Pressroom (2023) 'CNN Worldwide Fact Sheet', August 2023, available at https://cnnpressroom.blogs.cnn.com/cnn-fact-sheet/ (accessed 4 July 2025)

Google Trends (2025) Searches for the BBC, CNN, and *The New York Times*, June 2025,

Mark Joyella (2023) 'CNN Boss Chris Licht: We Have To 'Restore Our Reputation As The Most Trusted Name In News'', *Forbes*, 30 January.

Press Gazette (2025) Monthly audience data, available at: **https://pressgazette.co.uk/media-audience-and-business-data/media_metrics/most-popular-websites-news-world-monthly-2/** (accessed 4 July 2025)

Reuters (2018) *Reuters: The Facts*, Spring 2018, available at: **https://www.thomsonreuters.com/content/dam/ewp-m/documents/careers/en/pdf/reutersfactsheet2018.pdf** (accessed 4 July 2025)

Katie Robertson (2024) 'New York Times Passes 11 Million Subscribers', *The New York Times*, 4 November.

Ian Rohr (2024) 'Backlink Analysis Tools: A Nontraditional Resource for Intelligence Practitioners', *Security and Intelligence*, Volume 9, Number 1, March.

Michael Savage (2025) 'BBC to start charging US-based consumers for news and TV coverage', *The Guardian*, 26 June.

About the contributor

Richard Addy is a co-founder of the international audience strategy consultancy, AKAS (www.akas.london). He is an award-winning global expert in strategy, media, comms & media. In 2024 he was named a top 100 media expert. He has over thirty years' experience working as a strategist and government economist, advising C-suite executives, third-sector leaders, and government ministers. Previously he was the Chief Adviser on strategic and audience issues to the BBC's Deputy Director General who headed up BBC journalism, locally, nationally, and internationally. He currently sits on the boards of theguardian.org and Africa No Filter.

Chapter 10

Is the BBC losing its balance over Israel and Reform UK?

Raymond Snoddy examines claims made for and against the Corporation's coverage

The future of the BBC as a universal, public service broadcaster will ultimately depend on whether a means can be devised to fund it that is both socially and politically acceptable. It's an issue that is extensively addressed in this book. Yet there is another issue just as important and that is whether BBC news and current affairs retains relevance, trust, and a reputation for impartiality — if that is the appropriate target in an increasing divisive world of information.

The BBC has to continue to entertain and offer wide sports coverage although it could find that increasingly difficult in the unequal battle against international entertainment giants such as Netflix now being joined by the likes of Apple and Amazon. Without trusted news, nationally and internationally, the BBC might just as well become yet another voluntary subscription service.

Trust in BBC news

On the whole the news about BBC news is good. It is largely a trusted service in the UK, and probably even more so internationally through the World Service. The 2025 *Digital News Report* from the Reuter's Institute found that trust in Britain's news outlets is stable with the BBC the most trusted of all, although overall levels of trust remain 15 percentage points lower than before the Brexit referendum in 2016. BBC News had a 60 per cent trust level followed closely by Channel 4 and ITV News on 56 per cent. The right-wing GB News has improved its trust score but still languishes on 29 per cent, although that is higher than both the *Daily Mirror* and the *Daily Mail*, and 12 percentage points ahead of *The Sun*. The BBC also leads the usage charts with 47 per cent using BBC TV or radio at least once a week and 36 per cent using BBC news services at least three days a week.

Despite having many distinguished editors and correspondents it is perhaps the BBC's coverage of the Middle East crisis that generates the sharpest complaints with allegations that the BBC is either pro-Israeli or anti-Semitic. Some factual light was shed on the issue in a massively detailed report on BBC Gaza coverage by the Centre for Media Monitoring (CfMM), a project of the Muslim Council of Britain. The study looked at more than 32,000 broadcast segments and nearly 4,000 articles, and found that the BBC on a per-fatality basis gave Israeli deaths 33 times more coverage in articles and 19 times more on TV and radio as Palestinian deaths. There are limits to how much such counting of deaths versus coverage can tell us. As Israeli deaths are more rare they may attract more coverage although editors should perhaps rethink what their news values are actually saying.

Other aspects of the study including use of language is more disturbing. The analysis found that BBC use of emotive language such as 'massacre' or 'barbaric' was used four times more for Israeli dead than for Palestinian victims. At the same time the BBC pressed 38 interviewees to condemn Hamas's 7 October 2023 murders while 'equivalent questioning to condemn Israel's actions took place zero times, despite Israel's actions resulting in tens of thousands of Palestinian deaths'. The report also says it has documented more than 100 examples of BBC presenters shutting down interviewees' genocide claims even though a number of international rights organisations have concluded that genocide is indeed taking place in Gaza and that war crimes are allegedly being committed.

Investigative journalist Peter Oborne, who says he loves and respects the BBC, concluded, 'This thorough and fair-minded report documents beyond reasonable doubt that the BBC has failed professionally and morally in its reporting from Gaza' (Oborne, 2025). He added that the BBC coverage had dehumanised Palestinians, failed to challenge Israeli lies, and constructed a framework where Israeli suffering was more newsworthy and tragic than Palestinian.

The BBC has said it would consider the questions raised, as indeed it should, but added that it had questions about the use of AI in compiling the report. The CfMM said it used AI to process transcripts, label speakers, and structure the content but that all AI-generated classifications were reviewed by human experts.

From Gaza to Glastonbury

There was more Gaza-related embarrassment on 28 June. First, Channel 4 picked up a documentary that the BBC had decided not to broadcast, *Gaza: Doctors Under Attack*, which examined allegations that Israel forces have been targeting hospitals and healthcare workers in breach of international law. The BBC dropped the documentary, a decision reportedly taken by the Corporation's Director-General Tim Davie, over concerns that it 'risked creating a perception of partiality'. The decision by Davie, whose background is in marketing rather than journalism, divided his own staff and provoked outrage among some of them.

Louisa Compton, Channel 4's head of news and current affairs, who acquired the documentary said that after fact-checking and verification the Channel would be showing 'a duly impartial view of a subject that both divides opinion and frequently provokes dispute about what constituted a fact' (Compton, 2025). Channel 4 said it believed the documentary met both its own editorial standards and the broadcasting code of media regulator Ofcom.

The same day another Palestinian row broke out involving everyone from the right-wing press to Prime Minister Sir Keir Starmer with this time the BBC being accused of being pro-Palestinian — by default. The BBC did virtually nothing to intervene at the Glastonbury Festival when obscure punk band Bob Vylan led repeated and noisy chants of 'Death, death to the IDF', a reference to the Israel Defence Forces. The duo also led chants of 'free, free Palestine' and 'from the river to the sea - Palestine will be free', something seen by the Jewish community as a call for the elimination of the state of Israel.

The BBC managed a warning caption but did not pull the live coverage of the band, although it added there were no plans to make the Bob Vylan set available on demand. The response seems weak and the consequences could yet be serious. Ofcom has asked for explanations and the BBC admitted that, in retrospect the coverage should have been pulled or the cameras switched to another stage. Unsurprisingly there have been calls for Davie to consider his position.

More than 20 years ago the then BBC director of news Richard Sambrook asked a senior BBC executive Malcolm Balen to investigate whether there was any truth in allegations that there was an underlying anti-Semitic bias in the BBC's coverage of the Middle East. Scandalously, the 20,000 word report has never been published on the rather spurious ground that it was largely a work of journalism intended for internal use and therefore beyond the reach of the Freedom of Information Act. Perhaps it is time for a new Balen report but one where the findings are published.

Another great gulf in trust in BBC journalism, and the main television news bulletins in particular, dates back to the 2016 Referendum campaign. The BBC has never fully accepted, nor shaken off criticism, that it was guilty during the campaign of 'false equivalence' – giving equal prominence to both sides even when Leave lies were being spread without factual challenge. Polls showed that more than 90 per cent of economists, including Nobel prize-winning economists said they believed the UK economy would be harmed by Brexit. Their collective fears were 'balanced' by comments from a single maverick economist, Professor Patrick Minford of Cardiff University. Worried economists were also balanced by Leave campaigner Boris Johnson, who studied classics at university, denouncing such fears as 'nonsense'. Predictions that the UK could lose up to £40bn a year in lost output, attacked at the time as 'fear-mongering', have just been judged to have turned out to be largely correct by the Office of Budget Responsibility.

Bending over backwards for Reform?

In a similar vein the BBC has been criticised for creating the public persona of Nigel Farage, in an echo of the way the US networks helped to create the Trump phenomenon, not least through 39 appearances on *Question Time* over the years mainly because he was seen as box office. Following its surge in the polls critics argue that the BBC is even now giving disproportionate cover to the latest Farage political vehicle Reform UK. A June 2025 Ipsos poll had support for Reform at 34 per cent, something that would result in a Reform government majority were a general election to be held. In many bulletins Reform with five MPs seems to take precedence over the Lib Dems with 72 MPs. There is a legitimate discussion to be had on whether the currency for television prominence should be the fixed point of seats in Parliament or the possibly much more ephemeral polls which can fall as rapidly as they rise.

There was yet more controversy over the 26 June 2025 edition of *Question Time* from St Andrews in Scotland which included a Glasgow Reform local councillor Thomas Kerr but no representation from the Lib Dems even though the local MP was actually a Liberal Democrat, Wendy Chamberlain.

Rather more seriously *Byline Times* got hold of the minutes of the 6 March 2025 meeting of the Editorial Guidelines and Standards Committee in which BBC News chief Deborah Turness gave a presentation discussing plans to alter 'story selection' and 'other types of output such as drama' to try to win the trust of Farage voters. Serious questions were immediately raised. Does the BBC think of tailoring its news story selection to please supporters of Labour, the Conservatives, or the Greens? There is an important underlying issue: that those who say they would vote Reform tend to be disaffected with traditional politics in their entirety and most would be unwilling to trust the BBC whatever it did or said.

Nothing but breaking news

There is a further problem which has nothing to do with bias — more about the style of journalism preferred and the move away from 'built' detailed reporting in favour of 24-hour breaking news. In part this is because the BBC is under intense financial pressure and breaking news, of which there is no shortage at the moment, is cheaper to produce.

There are two well-known examples which are emblematic of the way news coverage is changing. One was the decision to close down the experienced reporting teams on *Newsnight* and turn the programme into what critics have called an up-market chat show, albeit one with effective presenters. Perhaps even more dramatic was the Turness decision to close *HARDTalk*, the BBC's in-depth television interview programme and make its distinguished interrogator Stephen Sackur redundant.

Turness made her priorities clear in an email to staff. She spoke of the need for closures and, redundancies and then added that the plan was to 'focus on continuous live and breaking output on our News Channel, and do more to use and promote the high-impact interviews and important conversations that are happening every day across our platforms' (Maher, 2024). Sackur, who did not go quietly, described such breaking news as 'churnalism'. Observers have noted that the Turness move towards a greater emphasis on continuous live and breaking news seemed to run counter to one the most striking current trends – the rise of podcasts where time and space is given to consider serious issues.

The BBC will never satisfy everyone with its news coverage but there have been marked improvements in many areas such as an increase in fact-checking through BBC Verify.

There is still a fundamental issue to address, one that applies not just to the BBC but to all journalism: how to cope with the rise of populists from Trump to Farage and beyond? Simple impartiality of a traditional nature is unable to cope with those who either deliberately lie or who have only a casual acquaintance with the truth. Perhaps the goal in future should be objectivity rather than impartiality. Either way there are a few questions still to be answered about the future of BBC news and currents affairs before its next Royal Charter.

References

Adam Bienkov (2025) 'BBC Bosses Draw Up Plans to Win Over Reform Voters by Changing News and Drama Output', London: *Byline Times*, 9 June.

Centre for Media Monitoring (2025) *BBC on Gaza-Israel: One story, double standards 2023-24*, London: CfMM, June.

Louise Compton (2025) 'Gaza : Doctors Under Attack – Op Ed by Louise Compton', London: Channel 4, 28 June.

Bron Maher (2024) 'BBC News to close Hardtalk, Click and Asian Network news service in latest round of 185 job cuts', London: *Press Gazette*, 15 October.

Nic Newman, with Amy Ross Arguedas, Craig T Robertson, Rasmus Kleis Nielsen, and Richard Fletcher (2025) *Digital News Report 2025*, Oxford: Reuters Institute for the Study of Journalism.

Peter Oborne (2025) 'Reviewer comments', in *BBC on Gaza-Israel: One story, double standards 2023-24*, London: CfMM, June.

About the contributor

Raymond Snoddy OBE is the former media editor of *The Times* and the *Financial Times*. His publications include: *The Good, the Bad and the Unacceptable: the Hard News about the British Press* (1993), *Greenfinger: the rise of Michael Green and Carlton Communications* (1996), and *It Could Be You: the Untold Story of the National Lottery* (2001). He is now a freelance writer.

Chapter 11

BBC Studios: The piggy bank that does not keep giving?

John Mair looks at the mixed record of the BBC's commercial arm

BBC Studios is the dirty commercial side of the BBC, the moneymaker for the public service pure BBC. But is it becoming the piggybank that delivers less and less?

Studios was set up in 2018 as a for-profit organisation. The public Corporation, the BBC, is not designed to do that — to make and broadcast programmes domestically and worldwide using income from the licence fee and other sources but not to be profit-making. BBC Studios took over part of the old Television Centre in White City and the functions of BBC Worldwide, buying and selling BBC content all over the world. In the not-too-distant past that arm laboured under the oxymoron BBC Enterprises. It infrequently justified that. Tim Davie was the CEO first of BBC Worldwide and then of BBC Studios when that was set up. Now he is the seventeenth BBC Director-General.

Since its inception, Studios has become a behemoth. Many BBC production departments from Natural History to national events to documentaries are now subsumed under it. It is the home of many of the Corporation's crown jewels such as *Strictly Come Dancing*, royal weddings, funerals and coronations, the national treasure that is Sir David Attenborough, his output and much more. One huge advantage it has over BBC Public Service is that the onscreen talent in their programmes do not have to make their remuneration public. Who knows the wage packet of Tess Daly for *Strictly*?

It sells BBC programmes and formats abroad — worldwide hit *Strictly Come Dancing* is sold to forty-three territories —arranges co-production deals with foreign broadcasters such as Disney+ for *Doctor Who* to give a huge boost to BBC Public Service budgets. Co-production can turn a promising BBC drama into an international success. *The Bombing of Pan Am 103*, first broadcast on BBC1 in May and June 2025, a joint production by World Productions [part of ITV Studios], Toluca Pictures, Night Train Media, Netflix, and MGM Television, had big budget written all across the screen. The corollary is that the series had eleven executive producers!

Bluey shows the way

The biggest success story for BBC Studios is *Bluey*, an international hit for children's audiences. It is Australian in origin and the BBC describes it in very non-Reithian language as 'Bluey follows the adventures of a lovable and inexhaustible six-year-old Blue Heeler puppy who lives with her dad, mum and four-year-old little sister, Bingo'.

The secret? It is full of the joy of play for young children and the hidden lessons of that. Children worldwide have adopted it in droves. The franchise has expanded to include a feature film, stage shows, a YouTube channel, rides at Disney theme parks, and much more.

Bluey was initially commissioned by the Australian Broadcasting Corporation (ABC) and the British Broadcasting Corporation, with BBC Studios holding global distribution and merchandising rights. Disney came in on the deal later. Brand Finance estimates the net worth of the entire *Bluey* franchise to be around US$2bn.

The divisions

BBC Studios encompasses programming made across the Scripted, Factual, Global Entertainment, and Kids & Family genres; global franchises; and production bases around the world, for a wide range of global customers, as well as financing, distributing, and licensing content and formats on a world-wide basis. Seven of the top ten performing shows in the UK across 2023 were made by Studios. But the international market is now much about selling formats. The big independent companies have often retained their intellectual property. Think *Big Brother* and Endemol, *Traitors* and Studio Lambert. The format rights are not for BBC Studios to sell.

BBC Studios was the top UK distributor in 2023's *Broadcast* survey, accounting for 42 per cent of all UK TV exports globally with landmark natural history programming dominating the top five programmes. For the BBC, content highlights reaching audiences in the year included the third series of factual landmark *Planet Earth*, which was seen in over 100 territories around the world while *Mammals* aired on BBC One.

The elements of the company mix

During the year 2023-24 the organisation merged three areas of its formats' business to create a new Global Entertainment division, comprising BBC Studios' popular formats and brands in the UK and internationally through its network of production bases in the US, France, Germany, the Nordics, Spain, India, Australia, and South Africa.

Global Entertainment also includes BBC Studios' specialist Live Events teams, which had a busy 2023, leading on the King's Coronation and Concert, Eurovision, live coverage of Glastonbury, and culminating in Elton John's 'last ever' UK live appearance, with the Festival's biggest-ever overnight audience, and a peak of 7.6m on BBC One.

Major drivers of expansion include the successful transition to a commercial basis of the BBC's UK television production arm, producer of, inter alia, *Strictly Come Dancing,* Natural History Unit landmarks such as *Planet Earth* and *Blue Planet*, *EastEnders, The Weakest Link, Casualty*, and *The One Show.*

In scripted, the second series of Jimmy McGovern's *Time*, made by BBC Studios for BBC One, saw Bella Ramsey, Jodie Whittaker, and Tamara Lawrance taking on the British legal system and winning critical acclaim. Cop comedy *Black Ops*, from BBC Studios Comedy Productions for BBC One, immediately won awards, whilst *Here We Go,* starring Alison Steadman and Katherine Parkinson, returned for a second season and a Christmas special on BBC One.

Commercial it may be, successful in bolstering the finances of the BBC mothership it is not. The most recent BBC annual report points to a revenue of £1.8bn in 2023-24 with just £199m returned as EBIDTA (accountancy shorthand for earnings before interest, taxes, depreciation, and amortisation) to the BBC — a figure that has dropped £50m plus from the previous year. The annual report blames that on 'a backdrop of very challenging operating conditions, with softness in the commissioning and advertising sales markets, as well as the phasing of revenues from multi-year partner'.

The various income streams

How does BBC Studios make its money? According to the annual report: 'It is a diversified global business with a strong pipeline of content and relationships with global brands like Disney'. What does this look like in actual figures? Here's how the annual report summarises it.

	Sales £m		**EBITDA £m**	
	2023/24	**2022/23**	**2023/24**	**2022/23**
Content Studio	**1,354**	1,612	**114**	146
Global Media & Streaming	**549**	535	**85**	107
Group adjustments	**(66)**	(57)	**3**	(1)
Total BBC Studios	**1,837**	2,090	**202**	252
Total Commercial	**1,859**	2,115	**199**	252

Source: BBC Group Annual Report and Accounts 2023/24

EBITDA was also lower after making strategic investments in the business to support long-term sustainable growth, principally in UKTV Play and BBC.com There was a deemed gain on disposal of £202m following the acquisition of the other 50 per cent of BritBox International; this represents the change in accounting for the business as a subsidiary, rather than a joint venture, now it is wholly-owned.

Building up an empire of independent production companies

ITV Studios set the bar high on this. They buy in whole or part small production companies and provide accelerator capital for them. It distances them, not totally, from the ITV brand but gives them heft. They can sell more easily to the BBC and international broadcasters. The list is international — more than 60 companies, including Apple Tree Productions (Denmark), Armoza Productions (Israel), Cattleya (Italy), Windlight Pictures (Germany), Leftfield Pictures, Tomorrow Studios, Blumhouse Television (US), Mammoth Screen, Happy Prince, Poison Pen Studios, Quay Street Productions, Word Productions (UK). Their global distributions business sells a catalogue of 90,000+ hours to broadcasters and platforms around the world.

BBC Studios has followed their example with the acquisition of UKTV and premium scripted production companies including House Productions' *Sherwood*, Sid Gentle Films' *Extraordinary*, Baby Reindeer's *Clerkenwell*, Firebird Productions' *The Jetty*, and Lookout Point's *Happy Valley*. This sub-brand is winning increased share of work-for-hire orders from global streamers with shows including *Prehistoric Planet* for Apple Studios and investment in production companies Expectation, Mothership, Tumbler, Moonage, and VAL (Various Artists Limited).

BBC Studios is assembling a portfolio of what it hopes will be profitable indies under its umbrella.

This does raise several questions of why BBC Studios is creating some of its own 'independent' companies within the production companies they fully control or even within some of the large BBC departments which do not fall under its remit. They are essentially creating competitors for work in the market for BBC production companies.

The possible folly of investing in potential competitors can be demonstrated by the then BBC Worldwide and new production company Left Bank Pictures. BBC Worldwide took a 25 per cent equity stake at a cost of £1m for first-look distribution rights. Left Bank went on to make programmes for British terrestrial channels but, most importantly, the monolithic series *The Crown*: sixty episodes over six seasons about the British royal family. From 2016 this was sold to and shown on Netflix, firmly establishing it as the streamer of choice in the UK and farther afield. Left Bank Pictures made huge profits from a show they admitted the BBC would never have bought. In 2012 Left Bank was partly bought for £40m by Sony Pictures Television and in February 2025, in an ironic twist, they poached BBC Director-General Tim Davie's Chief Content Officer, Charlotte Moore, to head up the company.

Conclusion

So BBC Studios was set up at arm's length to make money for BBC Public Service. It has the best broadcasting brand name in the world in its armoury to open doors and wallets. It has succeeded in some markets but not all. The BBC brand may not have the salience it once did.

It seems to me the major failure is that the piggy bank when shaken does not produce many coins. How to resolve that is one of the big conundrums of the next Charter period. Its subsidies to public service BBC will be vital more than ever.

Reference

BBC (2024) *BBC Group Annual Report and Accounts 2023/24,* London.

Chapter 12

The tempest within? South Asian perspectives on funding the BBC

Prof Barnie Choudhury considers alternatives to the licence fee which could lead to a better deal for viewers of colour

Humble beginnings

No one doubts that south Asians have come a long way since the early 1960s when their parents and grandparents came en masse to the UK. Back then the government realised that it needed to teach these uneducated, illiterate foreigners not only how to speak English but how to learn the British way of life. Forget that it had colonised India for more than 200 years, and that the sun had recently set on its empire. In 1965 the BBC, with its public service remit, created programmes such as *Make Yourself at Home (Apna Hi Ghar Samajhiye)*. Three years later we had *Nai Zindagi Naya Jeevan* (*New Life, New Life*) – something I remember watching every Sunday morning when I first arrived here in 1969. And so it went on. A drip, drip, drip of meagre offerings to placate the south Asian licence fee payer. The corporation based its Asian Programmes Unit in Birmingham. This produced programmes such as *Network East*, *East*, and *Bollywood or Bust*, hosted by Sanjeev Bhaskar (Cottle, 1998). The BBC closed the department in 2008. In 1989 alongside the unit the BBC even set up an Asian Network, using the medium wave frequencies of BBC Radio Leicester and BBC WM. It became a 'national' station ten years later. The station still exists in some form. Since the pandemic its news was brought by Radio 1's *Newsbeat*, and last year the BBC decided south Asians no longer needed its own news service. And why should they? After all, the programme is aimed at 15 to 30-year-olds – the audience which eschews the appointment to listen. Go figure.

White peaks

Let's face it, if an alien from another planet were to land on earth and watched the BBC, it would see the monocultural programming it is today. Look at the programme schedules on BBC 1, 2, 3, and 4, and the little green men would be hard pressed to dig out factual programming other than for the white face. I have long argued that I don't get value for my licence fee. It is not that I don't enjoy drama, sport, or entertainment – mind you it's been a while since I listened to or watched a BBC output for its music. I have written about the window-dressing of more faces of colour on screen and on air. I have written about the lack of senior leadership, commissioners, and editors of colour.

That's why I have a problem with the way the BBC portrays and reflects communities of colour, especially south Asians. It is all too superficial, all too stereotypical, and it is all too patronising. If we don't have to explain what Christmas is to south Asians, why does the BBC feel it needs to explain Diwali, Eid, or Vaisakhi to those living in London, Leicester, Birmingham, Bradford, Manchester, Glasgow, or Cardiff? While the numbers of Christians are going down, the numbers of Hindus, Muslims, and Sikhs are climbing. Perhaps you begin to understand my frustration with the world's best news organisation.

Brown pound

I'm a news junkie. That's why I pay my licence fee. Anything else, the chances are I'm binge-watching on Sky, Netflix, Amazon Prime, Disney+, or Paramount. My wife, and hundreds of thousands like her, subscribes to the Indian channels. It used to be that we paid for Zee and Sony – Indian channels – separately. But we don't any longer. They come with our Sky subscription. And that's the point. Sky realised it made business sense to capture a lucrative and underserved market. Even Netflix and Prime know the value of the brown pound. They too have Bollywood movies, soaps, and documentaries from India. *The Fabulous Lives of Bollywood Wives* and *Indian Matchmaking* are the go-to for the two most important women in my life. So, why am I wasting £174.50 per year when my family and I are paying for streaming services?

Public service

The problem is that public service is expensive, and it is the other programmes the BBC makes – *Strictly Come Dancing*, *Eastenders*, Agatha Christie mysteries – which pay for it. Otherwise do what the former head of BBC religion, now visiting professor at the University of Greater Manchester, Aaqil Ahmed, speaking in a personal capacity, suggests: 'contestable funding' (Ahmed, 2025). "It's not about giving that money to the BBC, and that might mean that less money is collected," he said. "It's more about saying are we able to give this money to other broadcasters, whatever they may be, it may be Netflix for that matter, and they make programmes with prominence, in the schedule, where there's a contestable funded element for programming that is public service broadcasting – religion, arts, culture, children's, et cetera, all things performance, documentaries of a high end nature, etcetera."

Contestable funding would certainly focus minds. Ahmed said although it would mean a smaller BBC, it would ensure that public service programming would not be denigrated to times on the schedule when no one watches it. For too long programmes meant for communities of colour were exiled to the wee small hours of the morning as the schedulers filled slots, ticked their boxes, and satisfied the broadcast regulators and the charter renewal police. No one really cared – just as the BBC doesn't really care about racial diversity and inclusivity, even though it says it does to anyone who will listen.

Inexperience

Many south Asians argue that we must keep the licence fee because we are more than just brown people who want to watch just brown programming. They argue that we are now so much part of the fabric of Britain's history that what mattered to our parents no longer matters to our grandchildren. I get that, I really do. But that would mean we have assimilated and become a beige, homogenous, nation. My view is that we are far from that goal, if indeed homogeneity could be thought of as our nirvana. For others, such as Romail Gulzar, founder and director of Pukaar Group, a multinational media and events company based in multi-cultural Leicester, the BBC does not need a licence fee (Gulzar, 2025). His view is that if ITV and Sky News rely on advertising why can't the BBC? After all, he argues, the corporation already has a commercial arm, BBC Studios. In its defence, the BBC would argue that any money it makes from selling its products is ploughed back into content production. But BBC Studios is bloated, badly organised, and badly run. Gulzar went further: "I think at the moment the BBC doesn't have people who have the required experience to run a business. I will offer my services to the BBC for three months for free. Get me on the commercial team, and I'll give them the outputs, and within three months they will get the money they need."

Choices

In January 2025 the culture secretary told the BBC that there was 'a range of alternatives' when it came to funding the corporation (Youngs, 2025). The BBC already has a commercial arm. People inside and outside the BBC have told me that everyone knows the licence fee is no longer an option. It will have to produce adverts even though its chair, Dr Samir Shah, has ruled this out (Thomas, 2024). But I see no other option, even though this will put ITV, Channel 4, Channel 5, and Sky in danger. It will become the survival of the fittest.

Now to my ideas. Firstly, it seems to me that the BBC has some choices to win me over. Create more factual content which appeals to me and people who look and think like me, who are fed up with lazy, superficial content. I'm not concerned about on-screen or on-air representation any more. In news, we appear to have prominent south Asians. I just want the next generation who can replace the Rajans, Husains, and Chakrabartis. And please may we have more choice of south Asian talent? No, I'm more worried about behind the scenes in decision-making, budget-controlling positions. Create content which pays more than lip service to communities who look like me. Create content which reflects the changing face of Britain – and no, the odd Eid celebration or drama with a south Asian cop in Bradford ain't going to cut it. In other words, the BBC must hypothecate some of that advertising revenue to its public service remit. Let's face it, a fraction of commercial earnings from popular drama, entertainment, and Attenborough docs is the sugar to the BBC's medicinal public service remit.

Second, if we south Asians are willing to pay for streaming services, and the streamers get that, then it is not too far beyond anyone's imagination to think that the industry knows how to chase the money. The BBC has the biggest streaming services in the country in iPlayer and BBC Sounds. It is forbidden through its charter to monetise these. But the country is now willing to pay for video and sound on demand. In the very near future the BBC will have no option but to charge for this – and create what the listener and viewer wants. I also endorse Ahmed's suggestion of 'contestable funding' – but with a twist. If the government allows the BBC to charge for its streaming service, it must make sure that a percentage – say 25 per cent – must be public service content. And within that 25 per cent, 25 per cent – so one-sixteenth – must be content which specifically targets south Asian and other communities of colour with a remit of revelatory journalism. I would then make it the Media Select Committee's specific remit to crunch the data and investigate annually whether the BBC is fulfilling that mandate. The Committee currently invites the Director-General and Chair to appear before it. But rarely does it dig deep into the racial impact of the service the BBC provides. For three reasons: the lack of expertise on the Committee; the lack of inclination; and the lack of civil service back-up to truly investigate what the BBC does, whether it really provides value for money for communities of colour.

I did toy with the idea of getting south Asian billionaires to invest in the BBC – for all of one second. Then I realised that they got rich because they hold on tightly to their wallets. Try getting money for good causes out of rich south Asians. The first thing they ask is, "What's in it for me?" And the second weakness in this idea is that they would want editorial control. Mind you, I'm pretty sure there are some tax benefits to buying and running the BBC brand.

But for my third and final idea, here's something completely barmy. What if the government were to give the BBC a one-off £100bn loan golden handshake? That's 20 years of secure funding. But because this would be a loan what could the government expect, what would be the return on its investment (ROI)? The latest report from the British Private Equity & Venture Capital Association suggests that, since 1980, ROI has been 14.5 per cent per year (BVCA, 2025). Since 2014, it's been 17.8 per cent. So, let's be conservative. Let's say through shrewd investments and selling content the BBC earns £10bn. It's not as far-fetched as you think. According to the NASDAQ, in December 2024 Netflix posted a turnover of US$10.25bn. At today's dollar-sterling rate, that's £8bn. If the BBC learned from Netflix, rather than Sky, it could give £4bn to the government and keep £4bn. That four per cent is a better ROI than sticking the money in the bank.

Conclusion

I have never argued against the utility of the BBC. If you cut me open, I bleed BBC. The problem I have is that BBC output is too white-centric. It no longer reflects the changing face of Britain with any depth or authenticity. It no longer digs as deeply as it should into communities of colour. It is failing to serve its licence fee payers of colour. Whatever the BBC's future funding model we need three fundamental changes: a clearer understanding of its public service remit fully paid for upfront and hypothecated; a clear and legally binding commitment to accurately reflecting and authentically portraying communities of colour; and a watchdog with real teeth to sanction the BBC should it fail to do so.

References

Aaquil Ahmed (2025) 'What alternatives are there to the BBC licence fee for communities of colour?' Interview by Barnie Choudhury, 28 February.

BBC (2018) *One of us? Make Yourself at Home* [online] Available at: https://www.bbc.co.uk/historyofthebbc/100-voices/people-nation-empire/make-yourself-at-home [Accessed 9 March 2025]

BBC Studios (2024) *About BBC Studios* [online] Available at: https://www.bbcstudios.com/about-us/about-bbc-studios/. [Accessed 19 March 2025]

BVCA (2025) *Industry Performance* [online] Available at: https://www.bvca.co.uk/research/industry-performance.html. [Accessed 19 March 2025]

Simon Cottle (1998) 'Making ethnic minority programmes inside the BBC: professional pragmatics and cultural containment' *Media, Culture & Society*, Vol. 20, Number 2, April. Available at: https://journals.sagepub.com/doi/abs/10.1177/016344398020002008. [Accessed 16 March 2025]

Romail Gulzar (2025) 'What alternatives are there to the BBC licence fee for communities of colour?' Interview by Barnie Choudhury, 2 March.

Pebblemill.org (2015a) *Nai Zindagi-Naya Jeevan: Multicultural Programmes from BBC Birmingham* Available at: https://www.pebblemill.org/tag/nai-zindagi-naya-jeevan/. [Accessed 9 March 2025]

Pebblemill.org (2015b) *50 Years of BBC Asian Programmes* [online] Available at: https://www.pebblemill.org/blog/50-years-of-bbc-asian-programmes/ [Accessed 9 March 2025]

Daniel Thomas (2024) 'BBC chair rejects ads or subscriptions as options for future funding', *Financial Times*, 10 September.

Ian Youngs (2025) 'Culture secretary rules out funding BBC from taxes', BBC News online, 17 January. Available at: https://www.bbc.co.uk/news/articles/cp3wwkdnddzo [Accessed 19 March 2025]

About the contributor

Prof Barnie Choudhury is an award-winning journalist who worked for the BBC for 24 years, and is now an editor-at-large for *Eastern Eye*, Britain's number one south Asian national newspaper. The University of Buckingham appointed Barnie its first professor of professional practice in communications, and he now lectures in journalism at the University of East Anglia. He specialises in diversity and inclusivity, data journalism, and investigations.

Chapter 13

American public broadcasting: A cautionary tale

American public broadcasting was launched with great fanfare with the expectation it would address the many market failures of the commercial networks. **Lana Wrightman** argues that political interference and a lack of independent funding ensured it never lived up to its promise

Researching American public broadcasting I asked one of my interviewees why Public Broadcasting Service (PBS) has never had the cultural or political impact of the BBC. The former PBS station exec replied, "That's simple. Richard Nixon. There you go. Research done." If there is never a truer word spoken in jest, this is surely case, point, and example as President Nixon is undoubtedly the pantomime villain of US public service broadcasting. As part of his assault on PBS he placed it on a commercial footing and ensured it never fulfilled its promise to serve the entirety of the American public. How did he do this, and what are the terrible consequences of his actions?

A brief history of American public broadcasting

Public broadcasting in the United States is an outlier in so far as it was only launched after commercial broadcasting was well and truly established. It soon became clear, though, that commercial broadcasting was doing little to serve the public interest. Rather, it only produced what was interesting to the public, and too often this consisted of mindless game shows, Saturday morning cartoons, formulaic comedies, and news programming that followed the dictum 'if it bleeds, it leads'. Newton Minow, chairman of the FCC in the early 1960s, famously described American television as a 'vast wasteland'.

In response, campaigners advocated for an American public service broadcaster. Advocates began championing an American version of the BBC back in the radio era as GIs returning from Britain were struck by the difference between advertising-driven American commercial radio and the rich array of programming on the other side of the Atlantic. While their efforts to reform radio were largely unsuccessful, television's advent provided a new opportunity. In 1965 the Carnegie Foundation assembled a commission to explore the possibility of an American public broadcaster. The resulting report, *Public Television: A Program for Action*, articulated commercial broadcasting's many failures and called for the establishment of an American public broadcaster that would not be beholden to commercial imperatives. The report formed the basis of the 1967 Public Broadcasting Act, a key part of President Lyndon Johnson's Great Society plans.

A broadcaster born of compromise

The proposed public broadcaster was met with widespread support amongst both Republicans and Democrats. An array of dignitaries, intellectuals, and campaigners testified to the necessity of a new type of broadcaster that could address issues important to the citizenry, would broadcast challenging programming that wasn't necessarily aimed at just achieving high ratings, and children's programming that was educational and non-commercial. The bill swept through both the Senate and the House and was quickly signed into law by Johnson.

The only problem is that the act did not provide for an independent source of funding. The Carnegie Commission proposed a tax on television sets to fund the proposed broadcaster. Powerful lobbying groups working on behalf of commercial broadcasters and television set manufacturers ensured the proposition was never incorporated into the Act. There were further suggestions to tax corporations for the use of government-launched satellites. These proposals also came to nothing. Ultimately, public television's advocates and US lawmakers agreed to pass the bill minus any independent funding provision and to address the issue later. In the meantime, public television would be funded through congressional appropriations.

Only former CBS president Fred Friendly sounded the alarm. Testifying before Congress in April 1967 he cautioned independent broadcasting would be jeopardised if public television was beholden to Congress for its funding. His prescient words were largely ignored amongst the many other public television advocates queueing up to testify for the need of a public broadcaster.

Public television strikes at the heart of power

When it was launched in 1971 public television operated on a shoestring budget. Many of the pioneers recall egg crates being used to soundproof studios, and using student volunteers to get programmes on air. Despite these challenges public television's news and current affairs programmes were altogether different to those seen on the networks. The network aired documentaries challenging the government's narrative that the Viet Cong was suffering from poor morale and that American victory was at hand. Other programmes highlighted the safety issues of cars and consumer goods. One documentary was especially provocative: broadcast on 9 November 1970 *Banks and the Poor* revealed that many lenders were engaging in 'redlining' practices that ensured ethnic minorities were unable to buy in desirable neighbourhoods favoured by the white middle class. The documentary then ended with a scrolling list of US representatives and senators who sat on the boards of the banks named in the documentary.

PBS's provocative programming was particularly infuriating to Richard Nixon who had come to power just as public television debuted on American airwaves. Nixon had a notoriously contentious relationship with the press, but in his dealings with public television he realised he had the advantage. Although the appropriations bill for further funding sailed through Congress gathering bipartisan support Nixon vetoed it on the basis that the broadcaster was 'anti-administration'. The move sent shockwaves through Congress and the media but the message from the White House was clear: rein in the news and current affairs programming or funding will be cut. A revised bill was eventually passed after many of the programmes the White House found objectionable were axed from the schedule. The Nixon administration also made further funding conditional on public television raising two and a half dollars for every dollar of federal funding.

Serving funders, not the public

The consequences of this latter proviso were especially dire. In the absence of an independent funding source, public broadcasting had to go cap-in-hand to viewers and corporations to plug the funding gaps. The idea of an independent broadcaster which was not beholden to commercial interests and which could serve marginalised audiences would simply not be possible.

Viewers of public television were soon asked to donate to their local station. Pledge drives aired at regular intervals throughout the year asking viewers to make generous contributions in exchange for PBS-branded merchandise or items donated by local businesses. The programming mix often pivoted during the drives to ensure crowd-pleasing entertainment-based programming filled the primetime hours.

By and large the people who donated to public television skewed towards well-educated professionals. Viewers were under no obligation to make donations but the ones who did tended to be more affluent and were rarely from minority ethnic groups. Public television took note. To ensure the dollars kept rolling in public television programming morphed into shows that were more likely to appeal to this demographic. PBS's programming reflected the tastes of 'viewer checkwriters' rather than the entirety of the American public (Lashley, 1992: xvi). In place of documentaries which challenged the status quo were classical music concerts broadcast from Lincoln Center. Many of the BBC's and ITV's dramas based on classic English literature made their way onto PBS's primetime schedule. Julia Child introduced French cuisine to an eager audience of gourmets.

Working class voices, programmes aimed at minority audiences, and controversial documentaries were aired at unsociable hours or were quietly shelved altogether. Any programme with a hint of controversy not only endangered PBS's federal funding but also proved problematic for local station managers. In the Deep South programmes which showed people of different races intermingling, were critical of established religions, or portrayed gay characters in a positive light proved problematic with local audiences (Lesser, 1975: 196). Viewer checkwriters threatened to withdraw future donations if public television stations continued to air such programmes. The station managers implored PBS's executives to avoid such subjects, thus ensuring that public television faced pressure from both within and outside the organisation. In April 2023 the Heritage Foundation published Project 2025, a mammoth wish list of right-wing public policy proposals one of which was the complete defunding of public broadcasting. Deeming it too risky PBS pulled a February 2025 documentary featuring a transgender video gamer as it was due to air soon after a congressional hearing on future funding. Only after public protest was the documentary put back on the schedule (Engber, 2025).

Sponsor credits

While advertising is still prohibited on public television, commercial representation is evident virtually everywhere thanks to sponsor credits which air ahead of programmes. In the 1970s Mobil Vice President Herb Schmertz realised the opportunity commercial sponsorship on PBS represented. With the oil companies suffering a growing public relations issue during the oil crisis Schmertz began sponsoring PBS's *Masterpiece Theatre* which primarily aired British-produced dramas. The Mobil Oil brand became synonymous with the programme to the point where PBS was jokingly referred to as 'Petroleum Broadcast System'. The sponsorship gave Mobil the sheen of respectability and generosity to the corporation's target audience of affluent automobile owners. The sums involved were large and PBS became increasingly reliant upon Schmertz's largesse.

Schmertz was fully aware of the power he wielded and soon began making editorial demands despite public television's own guidelines which prohibited such interference. He instructed his staff to source new potential programmes for *Masterpiece* that would appeal to Mobil Oil's target consumers (Engelman, 1996: 194-195). On a trip to Britain Schmertz's wife began watching *Upstairs, Downstairs* and Schmertz suggested it to *Masterpiece's* producers on the couple's return. PBS executives dismissed the programme as a 'soap' but when Schmertz threatened to withdraw future sponsorship, executives reversed their decision. It set a dangerous precedent.

When funding became scarce PBS was increasingly willing to bend its own rules. Ideologically-minded foundations offered to sponsor documentaries focused on conservative subjects including a 1980 ten-part series on Milton Friedman's free market principles *Free To Choose*. Dow Chemical sponsored a documentary series on agriculture which heralded the positive changes pesticides and fertilisers had made to the industry. Public broadcasting also engaged in self-censorship to avoid offending donors. It originally offered funding for a documentary film exploring how the Koch Brothers had influenced elections by funding powerful super PACs. Funding was subsequently withdrawn when the local New York station raised concerns given that David Koch sat on the station's board and the David Koch Foundation was a generous donor (Mayer, 2013).

A cautionary tale

Today American public television is at a crossroads. Its impoverishment has meant that it struggled to compete with the networks. Its audience was eroded further when cable television channels began airing programming remarkably similar to PBS's nature, cookery, and children's programming. In the Netflix era it finds itself culturally marginalised and in the crosshairs of the Trump administration. With government funding decreasing with virtually every appropriations bill and its audience ageing out it is struggling for relevance. Its very future is in danger with many predicting that its days are numbered.

It stands as a cautionary tale for the British government. Abolishing the licence fee in favour of direct government funding renders the BBC politically vulnerable. Making it a subscription service that viewers can opt for in lieu of or in addition to their Netflix subscriptions ensures that it will be beholden to the tastes of viewer subscribers rather than the entirety of the British public in all its diversity. With misinformation proliferating across social media and other corners of the internet, a well and independently-funded public broadcaster has never been more necessary. We only have to look across the pond to learn what happens when politicians fail to value public broadcasting.

References

Daniel Engber (2025) 'PBS pulled a film for political reasons, then changed its mind: a window into how the network is handling the new Trump era', Washington, D.C.: *The Atlantic*, 18 April.

Ralph Engelman (1996) *Public radio and television in America: a political history,* Thousand Oaks, CA: Sage.

Marilyn Lashley (1992) *Public television: panacea, pork barrel or public trust?* New York, NY: Greenwood Press.

Gerald Lesser (1975) *Children and television: lessons from* Sesame Street. New York, NY: Vintage Press.

Jane Mayer (2013) 'David Koch vs. PBS', New York, NY: *The New Yorker*, 20 May.

About the contributor

Lana Wrightman holds a doctorate from Goldsmiths, University of London. Her 2025 thesis, *From Great Society to Great Compromise: American Public Television's*

Struggle for Survival in a Neoliberal Era, explores how American public broadcasting has been commercialised and its values eroded over its 50 year history. She has worked as a lecturer and journalist, and is a highly regarded public relations consultant.

Chapter 14

In the new world of authority bashing

Any historical reverence the public had for the BBC is now under increasing threat. **Salil Pajwani** asks how the Corporation can hope to deliver impartial material. And what happens when it falls short?

I have no credentials to be writing this other than a long career as CEO of the innovation company ?What If! Limited. We were paid good money to challenge our clients to think differently about how they would navigate the dynamics of a changing world. Questioning the unquestionable became a key skill. But we sold that business to Accenture six years ago, so I'm a bit out of practice. I have since started up a new business called 2ndStage, which is in the process of buying up small companies who provide services and equipment for the elderly. So if you want to read something by someone who knows what they are talking about, you might want to look elsewhere. On the other hand, if you want a Zimmer frame or mobility scooter, then give me a call. But for what it's worth, here are some thoughts about where the BBC now finds itself, and how it got there.

My wife Sarah grew up in a fishing village in Cornwall. Her parents had big aspirations for her and her younger sister Kate. Education was a critical component and a lot of sacrifices were made so they could go to private school and, from there, to university and good careers. It wasn't a strict family but there was a sense of right and wrong — or 'appropriate for young ladies' and then 'inappropriate'. Watching the BBC was appropriate. ITV was not. Quite why no one has been able to explain to me. Maybe it just felt better. Fast forward many decades and I can now have nostalgic conversations with my wife about Peter, John, Valerie, and Lesley (if you don't know what I'm talking about here, ask anyone over 60). But she hadn't even heard of Jenny on *Magpie*. She talks animatedly about *Here Come the Double Deckers* (and the closing wave 'see you next weeeeeek') but looks blank when I mention my childhood crush, Marcia from *The Brady Bunch*.

Sarah's mother, Sheila, prided herself on 'doing the right thing'. She would go to church every Sunday, would dress up to see the doctor, and she organised the local Meals on Wheels rota. Like all the well-to-do in Cornwall she was a staunch Liberal Party supporter for most of her life. But her support was abruptly curtailed when stories emerged of 'Paddy Pants-Down'. A Liberal no longer, she became a floating voter. She passed away before the Jimmy Savile saga came to light. And if that hadn't shaken her respect for the BBC, then

Huw Edwards and Gregg Wallace would have destroyed any lingering BBC attachment.

But there's more to this than a simple 'sex scandal shakes brand belief' dynamic. Giving a rare interview on the 17 April 2025 edition of *The News Agents* Matthew Freud made an excellent point about the increasing public appetite to hear about the flaws in conventional figures of authority: "When I started in the 1980s defensive comms was a peripheral field. Very few people or organisations had press agents. They didn't need them because they were largely admired and having a good reputation was quite normal." He went on to say that the press now get much more excited about throwing dirt at targets who used to be regarded as 'beyond reproach'. Dirt makes for a much better story. Great news for Freud's PR business, but the implications for the conventional Establishment are quite profound.

So what caused the first cracks? I think it all started in the 1970s, when the London Broadcasting Corporation (LBC) launched the first participative phone-ins. For the very first time the public were broadcasting, commenting on the news and even making the news themselves. The gloves were slowly coming off. New, controversial, and unsubstantiated opinion was being given a platform.

The nightly phone-in became a nationwide phenomenon. I moved to Newcastle in the early 1980s, when the LBC-led format had spread beyond London. I became addicted to the Metro Radio version:

- Next on tonight is Jim. Hello Jim. What point do you want to make?
- I want to talk about that ghastly woman Prime Minister.
- And what do you want to say about Mrs Thatcher, Jim?
- She's rubbish. Totally rubbish. We need to get someone better doing that job.
- And why do you think that, Jim. What has she done to get you so annoyed.
- Everything. Everything she does is rubbish. We need a change.
- Can you give me an example?
- Everything she does. It's all rubbish. The whole lot.
- I'm just asking for one example, Jim. Just tell me one thing she has done that you think is rubbish. I'm not disagreeing with you. I just want an example.

- I've given you an example already. My example is everything. Everything she does. What more example do you need?

There haven't many times in my life when I've felt a twang of pity for Maggie, but this was one of them.

And so the journey of Establishment knocking gained momentum. The seeds of the Instagram era were sown, rising to an extent where everyone is now a broadcaster. And everyone is a target.

It gets worse — because the dynamic starts to feed off itself. If we are not going to respect the Establishment, why should the Establishment respect us? £350m a week? Who's going to know? Sounds like a big number. That will get them to vote to leave Europe. We all know the end of that story.

And then the spiral starts. The established media starts introducing the concept of Fact Checking. Hang on? So you are telling us that you broadcast stuff first and then later work out whether it is true or not? I'm not sure.

So who is going to struggle most in this world of authority bashing? Of course it's those who have presented themselves as the biggest authority. Any claims about neutrality or impartiality or even correct facts will come under greater public scrutiny and social media dirt-slinging. Maybe the days of resting on the benign centrepiece of truth and impartiality are now gone. Unwise in this environment to set yourself up for a fall. We have seen, to our great national cost, the appetite that the public has acquired for table-thumping and change. Regardless of your politics on a sheer energy level would you rather be part of a mission-driven team who want to 'Take back control', or would you prefer a clean-cut gentleman asking you to 'Remain please'?

Now might be a good time to challenge the unthinkable. Is impartiality the right mantra to take our great institution forward? Or do we need something with more edge and more energy, and more likely to survive modern media dynamics?

My late mother-in-law used to respect the local doctor, the bank manager, the priest, the head teacher, and the BBC. My kids think that our bank manager is a prize idiot (he is), the doctor doesn't understand medicine any better than Google, and they wouldn't know the priest if they bumped into him in the street. And the BBC's views are no more valid than anyone else's. And you have to pay a licence fee for these views, right? Maybe not.

About the contributor

After working in brand and marketing management at Procter & Gamble and Diageo Salil Pajwani then spent nearly twenty-seven years as global CEO of the innovation company ?What If! In 2019 he co-founded 2ndStage who undertake creative acquisitions for small businesses.

SECTION TWO: THE LICENCE FEE – THE ONLY WAY?

Introduction

Janine Chandler

The debate about how to fund the BBC has never felt more urgent, or more open. The licence fee has been both the bedrock of the Corporation and the lightning rod for every argument about its role, reach, and relevance. Now, as we approach the end of the current Charter period in 2027, the question is no longer when the model will change, but how.

This section of the book brings together a powerful set of perspectives, from former insiders and creative practitioners to media economists and cultural commentators. It begins with a big-picture framing of the issues, then travels through the past, present, and possible futures of BBC funding. We explore what we might lose, what we might gain, and what it will take to secure a sustainable, independent BBC.

John Mair offers a brisk and brilliant tour through a century of licence fee history. From the ten-shilling radio licence of 1923 to the current £174.50 TV licence, he tracks the major milestones and political turning points. His conclusion is stark: 'For probably the first time in the BBC's century of existence there is a febrile debate about the very principle of the fee.'

Adam Sherwin asks whether the licence fee is sacrosanct. He explores the changing attitudes among politicians, the rise of viewers evading paying the licence fee, and the challenges of maintaining universality in a multi-platform world. His analysis reveals a widening gap between political rhetoric and public sentiment.

Patrick Barwise and Peter York take us into the data. They map the pros and cons of six funding models, from full commercialisation to full public funding via general taxation. Their verdict is sharp: most alternatives either damage the BBC's independence or its ability to serve all audiences. 'There is no perfect solution,' they note, 'but some are clearly worse than others.'

David Elstein doesn't pull punches. With a career spanning leadership roles at Thames, Sky, and Channel Five, he knows the business from the inside. But he's long been a vocal critic of the Corporation he never ran. In his view, the licence fee's days are numbered. The BBC, he warns, is teetering on the edge of a cliff – with half a million households having already cancelled their TV Licences. And this, he argues, isn't a blip but a gathering wave. If that number continues to rise or even accelerate, then 'the pressure to abandon the licence fee system would become irresistible.'

Roger Bolton has earned his BBC stripes. From editing *Panorama* and *Nationwide* to hosting Radio 4's right to reply programme *Feedback* for over twenty-three years, he's been both BBC insider and listener advocate. But in a surprise twist, he proposes a radical rethink. Why not a Beebflix? 'I think we need to consider a two-tier form of funding: a reduced licence fee which delivers a basic public service and subscription for a more mainstream offering, prioritising drama and comedy, with the proviso that its programmes would be eventually shown on free to air, perhaps with a six or twelve month delay.' Think delayed access, not diminished ambition. It's definitely not the official line but a pragmatic voice in a world of shifting media habits.

Daniel Freeman introduces a hybrid funding model. Combining a core of publicly funded content with a layer of paid extras, it aims to square the circle between universality and sustainability. Freeman sees this as a way to evolve rather than dismantle the BBC's DNA.

Maggie Brown sees the bigger picture. A sharp-eyed chronicler of UK broadcasting, she zooms out from the BBC to consider the health of the entire public service ecosystem in the UK. That might be achieved through 'improved funding, either through tariffs on streaming income or tax relief for producers'. Key to that process, which could include 'the creation of an independent panel to set licence fee levels', she argues, is that it must remain 'separate from the government of the day and put viewers before politics.'

Daithí McMahon makes the boldest proposal in this section: iPlayer+, a global subscription streaming service built on the BBC's back catalogue and its trusted brand. He sets out the numbers, the strategy, and the international potential. His message is clear: 'The current model is no longer sustainable. The time for action is now.'

Peter Kosminsky brings a creator's perspective, focusing on the risks to high-end drama. He warns that commercial pressures are already shrinking the space for ambitious British storytelling. Without secure public funding, he argues, the pipeline of global-class British drama will dry up.

Nick Manley adds another lens: wildlife programming. He reminds us that blue-chip natural history is both expensive and uniquely valuable. It embodies the BBC at its best: educational, awe-inspiring, global. Lose the licence fee, and we risk losing the scale and ambition that makes these programmes possible.

In my own contribution that follows, I explore the world of subscriptions — not just as a funding model, but as a cultural movement. Subscriptions are growing, but they're not just about unlocking content. They're about identity, trust, and belonging. If the BBC is to explore this path, it must do so with care, creativity, and a commitment to its unique role in our shared lives.

Taken together, these contributions don't land on one answer. But they do make clear what's at stake. This is not just a technocratic argument about revenue models. It is a cultural reckoning. What kind of BBC do we want? Who is it for? And how much are we, as a society, willing to invest to keep it alive, independent, and meaningful?

This section invites you to reflect, argue, and imagine. The BBC is more than a broadcaster. It is part of the UK's cultural infrastructure. And that means the question of how we fund it is not just economic. It is civic.

So, read on. This is not just about how the BBC gets paid. It's about what it's for. And what we're willing to fight for.

Chapter 15

A short history of the BBC licence fee

John Mair explores the history of the BBC licence fee from 1923 to 2025

Today a TV licence costs £174.50 per year. One hundred and two years ago, when the BBC radio licence was first invented to pay for the radio service, it cost ten shillings (50 pence). The 2022 licence fee settlement guaranteed it would rise in line with inflation every year until 31 December 2027, the end of the current ten-year Royal Charter period. For probably the first time in the BBC's century of existence there is a febrile debate about the very principle of the fee and suggestions for its improvement or amendment or abolition abound.

As history always helps us to understand the present let's see how we got from 1923 to 2025.

The major moments

It started life as a BBC radio licence. The BBC brand was on the sets, the money was collected by the then General Post Office (GPO), and was largely passed on to the British Broadcasting Company, a Corporation from 1927. It stayed at ten shillings a year from then (£37.39 in today's money) until after the end of the Second World War (£18.69 in today's money).

From this income the BBC was expected to fund all services including various television experiments before 1939. In 1946 radio licences were set at £1.00 (£36.28 in today's money) and TV black and white licences £2.00 (£75.25 in today's money). It crept up gradually.

The radio licence remained until 1971. One can trace the changing of the electronic guard through the numbers of television and radio licences issued. Crossover, where the number of TV licences exceed the number of radio licences, came in 1958. By then the UK had a second, commercial, television channel, ITV, regionally-based and financed entirely by advertising. The BBC took a while to adjust to competition.

The biggest and most significant jump in the fee came with the coming of BBC Two. After regular colour broadcasting in the UK was launched on BBC2 on 1 July 1967 viewers were required to purchase a colour licence from 1 January 1968. That cost £10 (£153.25 in today's money), a black and white one £5 (£76.62).

By 1999 the cost of a TV colour licence had gone over the £100 a year mark (£191.95). By April 2018 that had risen again to £150.50 (£196.67) for colour and £50.50 (£60.54) for monochrome. It was a criminal offence not to have a licence and an enforcement operation was developed, detector vans and more, to take offenders to court if found without one. The then Conservative government consulted on decriminalising licence fee evasion. That produced 154,737 responses. On 21 February 2021 the then Secretary of State for Digital, Culture, Media and Sport Oliver Dowden offered a written statement making clear their take on those responses: 'A significant number of people oppose the criminal sanction with some highlighting the considerable stress and anxiety it can cause for individuals, including the most vulnerable in society, such as old people' (Dowden, 2021). The BBC, though, warned that decriminalising non-payment would cost it £1bn plus and that would mean big cuts to programmes and services. It fought off the idea then as it has all attempts to change the universal licence fee before and since. That argument is losing currency.

In 2022 the then Culture Secretary Nadine Dorries, a firm non-believer in the licence fee, froze it at £159 for two years. In April 2025 it only went up by £5.00 to £174.50, though you can still buy a black and white licence for £58.50.

There have been significant budget cuts at the Corporation as a result. Between 2010 and 2020 the Corporation lost 30 per cent of its budget in real terms. Programme trims, salami-slicing, and simple removals have become the order of the day. No major services have been lost. Yet. There is now in place a £500m budget cut per year for the foreseeable future. Public service broadcasting staff numbers have gone down by 1800 in the last five years to 17,700.

How many licence fee payers?

As the UK population has increased over the last century and as radio and then TV broadcasting came into every home so too did the number of licence fees bought. In 1927 2.3 million were issued. In 1946 10.4 million. The zenith was in 2018 when 26.2 million were issued. Some of those were concessionary free licences to householders aged over 75. That was largely withdrawn in 2021. Since then gross numbers have dropped off as the number of refuseniks has increased. In 2022 the percentage of evaders was up above ten per cent (see below).

How much income does the BBC get directly from licence payers?

In 2022/23 TV licence fee revenues were £3.74bn, which was lower than the 2020/21 figure of £3.80bn in cash terms. The decrease in 2022/23 on the previous year was attributed to flat licence fee pricing and a decline in paid-for licences.

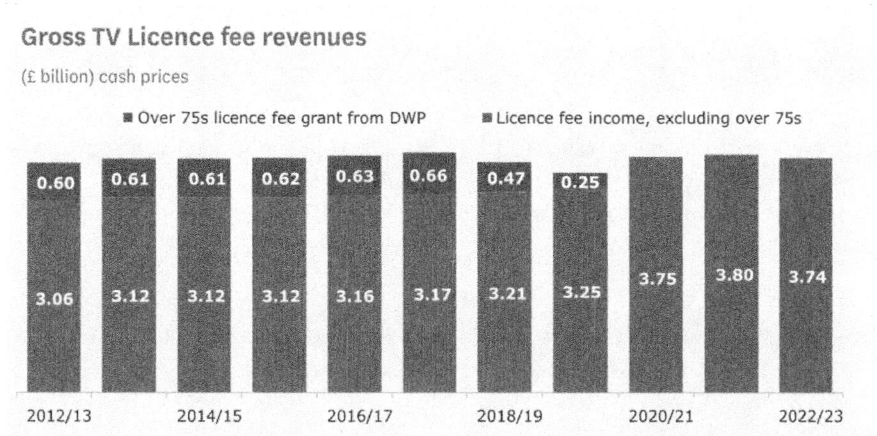

Source: House of Commons Library Briefing Paper, December 2024

But, significantly, the number of refuseniks, licence fee payment evaders, has increased. It has nearly doubled in the last decade to 10.31 per cent. For some, it has become socially acceptable, for others a political gesture to refuse to pay the BBC licence fee. The zeitgeist on the matter has shifted. In 2018 using the BBC iPlayer or watching on a computer screen or similar became feeable.

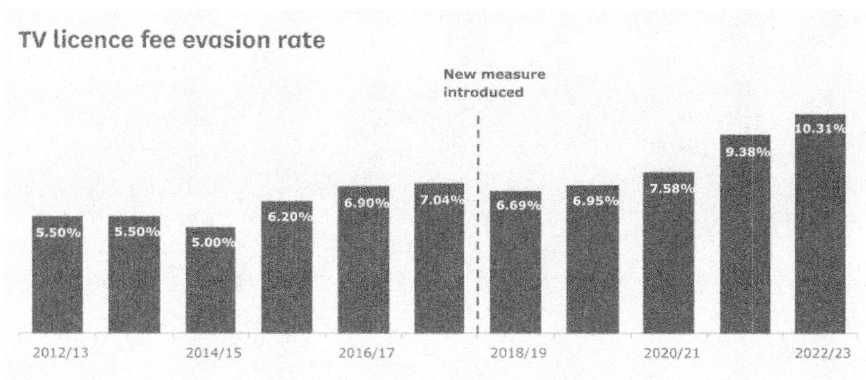

Source: House of Commons Library Briefing Paper, December 2025

The total income of the BBC group in 2023 was £5.5bn including £1.86bn from commercial activities, mainly BBC Studios. Yet the net contribution from the latter to the public service element was just £350m.

The future of the licence fee and BBC public service funding

The BBC itself is fond of saying 'other funding models are available'. Some are under active discussion; all are discussed in this book. They include a hybrid system in which core public service elements such as news are provided free, while high-end TV would sit behind a paywall using the iPlayer for conditional access. Direct payment by government from taxation, a household tax, and levies on streaming services are also in the mix. Big decisions are there to be made for the post-2027 BBC.

Note: all 2025 values for historical sums quoted here have been adjusted using the Bank of England's Inflation Calculator.

Reference

Oliver Dowden (2021) 'Written statement to Parliament', House of Commons, 21 January.

Chapter 16

Is the licence fee sacrosanct?

Adam Sherwin examines the alternatives

Should BBC viewers pay a £10 supplement to watch *The Traitors* early? Would adverts during *Strictly* ruin enjoyment of the samba?

The Government is promising 'radical' options to reform the £174.50 licence fee in the BBC Charter Review consultation, now formally under way. Nothing is off the table at this stage, allowing officials to float ideas such as asking wealthier viewers to pay more. Director-General Tim Davie is open to a reformed, progressive charge – as long as it ends the cycle of 'begrudging cuts' and delivers a secure pipeline of rising investment, a big ask for ministers when the cost of living crisis shows little sign of receding.

The temperature of the debate is different under a Labour Government. The BBC is still struggling to stem the viewing drift to deep-pocketed streamers. But there is no longer any question of abolishing the fee (the ambition of former Tory Culture Secretary Nadine Dorries) which brings in £3.66bn a year. Yet there is concern that 500,000 licences were cancelled last year, raising questions about the ongoing legitimacy of a mandatory charge.

Ministers want a funding solution that will future-proof the broadcaster without political opponents being able to accuse the Government of imposing a new 'TV tax' on hard-pressed voters. Despite its resources, inflationary pressures and a licence fee which has lost 30 per cent of its value over a decade have forced the BBC to make drastic cuts to its news operation, shedding hundreds of jobs. Flagship drama productions are being paused because producers cannot raise the finance alone to begin shooting.

Meanwhile, there are Whitehall whispers that the DCMS could be abolished altogether with responsibility for broadcasting parcelled off between the Business and Science departments.

The next reshuffle could see Lisa Nandy made the latest victim of the carousel of Culture Secretaries if Downing Street briefings are true.

So when the talking stops, which of the options are ministers most likely to land on when the current Charter, which oversees the BBC's governance, ends in 2027?

Means-tested licence fee

Licence fee evasion now stands at 10 per cent. Women make up 76 per cent of those prosecuted – an excessive number, which ministers say must be tackled. Changing the flat rate charge to make wealthier households pay more would allow people on lower incomes to pay less. Former Director-General Greg Dyke has said people on benefits could get free licences under a truly progressive system.

Chance of success

BBC boss Tim Davie says he is open to a progressive tax, which also meets the Labour Government's fairness test. It is likely to be a recommended option, allied with extra support to help families struggling to pay the fee. Ministers could explore using council tax bands to set licence fee levels.

'Netflix tax'

The latest Whitehall briefing suggested that subscribers to streaming platforms including Disney, Netflix, and Amazon Prime who say they do not watch any BBC programmes could be forced to pay for the BBC licence.

Currently, a licence is only required for people who watch live broadcasts online, whereas the vast majority of viewing on streamers is on-demand.

However the streaming giants are increasingly moving into live programming like sports, with Amazon buying rights to Premiership football and tennis.

Chance of success

With people opting out of paying the licence fee, raiding the subscriptions of the 20 million and rising UK households who voluntarily pay for streaming would secure a new long-term revenue stream for the BBC. But the idea of a 'Netflix TV tax' to pay for shows they do not watch would prompt fury and be opposed by streamers.

Subscription

Licence fee critics such as Nigel Farage say the charge should be abolished and replaced by a voluntary monthly subscription, forcing the BBC to compete with Netflix et al. Others argue for a reduced annual licence fee to cover core essential services like news and current affairs which the market cannot deliver, with viewers paying a top-up subscription for entertainment, drama, and sport.

Chance of success

The BBC argues that hit dramas like *Happy Valley* demonstrate the licence fee is delivering value for all viewers. It allows the BBC to create creative risks instead of commissioning by algorithm. Ministers could ask the BBC to test the waters by experimenting with subscriptions for events that superserve some audiences, such as a digital pass to watch every Proms concert live.

iPlayer charge

Charging UK viewers to use iPlayer is among the draft proposals being considered, according to reports. The BBC already has the log-in details of millions of users which could be used to create a paywall. iPlayer could remain largely free but with viewers paying extra for early exclusive access to programmes or to view shows from the archive.

Chance of success

Viewers could object to paying extra for programmes they have already funded by paying the licence fee. With the BBC shifting from linear TV channels, where viewing is declining, to iPlayer, charging for access to the app would effectively turn the broadcaster into a subscription service. The BBC is unable to charge international iPlayer users since it does not own individual rights to most of the programmes on the platform.

Advertising

Advertisers would jump at the chance of reaching the ten million viewers who watched the latest series of *The Traitors*. If breaking up programmes is deemed too intrusive for viewers, dramas such as *EastEnders* could be sponsored, bringing in vital revenue to support production costs.

Chance of success

Letting the BBC charge for advertising would decimate the business model of ITV and other public service commercial broadcasters. But the BBC is selling adverts on some of its podcasts on Apple and Spotify and charges a premium fee for some podcasts internationally. Increasing the BBC's commercial activities, reducing reliance on the licence fee, is central to its future. Last year BBC Studios, which owns rights to *Bluey* and *Strictly*, returned £1.9bn to the BBC in profits and income.

Taxation

Funding the BBC from general taxation would solve the evasion and prosecution problem overnight. It would provide the BBC with a secure funding mechanism and end anguished debates over whether the licence fee is fit for purpose. Reports suggested this model was being considered by culture secretary Lisa Nandy.

Chance of success

Government sources moved swiftly to kill off this option, raised at a time when the Treasury is having to damp down fears of new tax rises. The BBC is opposed to any mechanism that might threaten its independence. Government funding would make the BBC vulnerable to the whims of ministers. However, shifting the licence fee to a broadband tax, added to monthly utility bills, would benefit the BBC since the number of UK households is set to increase thanks to rising net migration levels.

Rundfunkbeitrag

A catchy name for the German system which pays for public service broadcasting by levying a tax on every household and every business. The BBC would save the £137m it spends on licence fee collection if there was a consensus that funding the national public service broadcaster is a national good.

Chances of success

Who will make the case for paying for TV programming many people won't watch? And why should the BBC get the whole pot? Support is wavering in Germany. An increase in the fee, which funds 17 TV channels to the tune of €18.94 per month between 2025 and 2028 has been delayed.

Those are the options ministers are most likely to consider to replace the licence fee. But what about those options that are off the table, the no-gos?

Radio tax

Listeners to the BBC's radio stations could be made to pay extra, a *Bloomberg* report suggested. Monitoring the nation's listening habits would make this extremely difficult to enforce.

Streamer levy

Wolf Hall director Peter Kosminsky has said streamers such as Netflix should pay a 5 per cent levy on their UK subscription revenues to support public service broadcasting in the UK. However, Culture Minister Chris Bryant has said "we haven't got any plans" to follow other European countries and introduce a streamer levy. Netflix argues it has spent more than £5bn making TV shows and films in the UK since 2020, boosting the creative economy and showcasing national locations on series like thriller *Black Doves*.

What do the Government and BBC say?

The DCMS said: "The forthcoming Charter Review is a key opportunity to set the BBC up for success long into the future. As we address these vital issues about the future form of the BBC, we must also ensure that there is a sustainable funding model that is fair for those who pay for it. The Government is keeping an open mind about the future of the licence fee, but we are clear that the BBC's funding and its operation are inseparable."

A BBC spokesperson said: "The public cares about the BBC and this year, we will launch our biggest ever public engagement exercise so audiences can help drive and shape what they want from a universal and independent BBC in the future. We look forward to engaging with government on the next Charter and securing the long term future of the BBC."

And the outcome is . . .

For all the talk of 'ripping up' the 'unsustainable' licence fee, it wouldn't be too surprising if the final outcome retains the principle of a universal charge, with some 'progressive' tweaking, alongside a collection mechanism pegged to household bills that curtails the expense and anger caused by licensing enforcement officers knocking on pensioners' doors.

Adam Sherwin has adapted and updated his original 30 January 2025 *i Paper* story for this book.

About the contributor

Adam Sherwin is the arts and media correspondent for *The i Paper.*

Chapter 17

BBC funding models: Options, pros, and cons

Prof Patrick Barwise and Peter York ask what are the pros and cons of the licence fee and the alternative BBC funding models, and what's the best option for the next BBC Charter

That so much of the debate about the BBC is about funding is a tribute to its enemies' success in making a mountain out of a molehill. The TV licence costs £174.50 per year with a range of easy payment options, equivalent to £3.35 per week. This is trivial for the great majority of households that have to pay. And it's free if the licence payer or their partner is aged over 75 and receiving Pension Credit. The average British adult still consumes the BBC's TV, radio, and online services for two hours a day — far more than any other product, service, or media brand. The average cost per user — again excluding those paying nothing — is just 10p per hour for adults, with kids for free. And at the national level, the BBC's £3.7bn licence fee income — none of it from HM Treasury — is loose change.

Given the BBC's popularity and the low financial stakes, why all the fuss about its funding? We think there are three reasons:

1. The BBC is so much part of most people's everyday life that they take it for granted, underestimating the value they get from it - until they're deprived of it: after nine days with no BBC, 70 per cent of those who'd said it was poor value for money changed their minds (MTM, 2022)
2. The attacks are just part of the wider 'war' against it by its right-leaning enemies (Barwise and York, 2020)
3. Like every funding model, the licence fee has some disadvantages — seized on and much exaggerated by the Beeb-bashers.

In 2015, the Commons DCMS committee discussed the licence fee's pros and cons. They said its advantages were that it was simple, secure, and predictable; associated in people's minds with funding the BBC; protected its commercial and political independence; and enabled its services to be universally available. None of these is seriously contested. They listed three disadvantages, saying it was 'regressive'; compulsory (including for households that 'do not use [BBC] services'); and 'expensive to collect', with a 5.5 per cent evasion rate. Let's consider these:

1. 'Regressive': the licence fee is the same for rich and poor families and, therefore, a higher proportion of poor families' income. That's true for

all paid-for media - and, at £3.35 per week, it costs much less than most. The basic Netflix package, with advertising, costs £7.99 per month (£1.84 per week) — but most subscribers pay £18.99 per month (£4.37 per week) for the ad-free premium version, while also paying for broadband and a smart TV. Most Sky subscribers pay at least £10 per week. And BBC consumption remains huge, especially among poorer, older people. So the licence fee's 'regressiveness' has been greatly overstated — including, hypocritically, by the same right-wingers who bang on about 'benefit scroungers'.

2. 'Compulsory': like all taxes, the licence fee is compulsory. But the number of households that pay but get no direct benefit is negligible. No one knows the exact number, but it is tiny. In 2015, the last time this was measured, 99 per cent of households consumed at least some BBC services in a single week, never mind a whole year (BBC, 2015).

3. 'Expensive to collect': collection costs increased after the BBC, forced to take over responsibility for the over-75s' free TV licences, limited them to households with members receiving Pension Credit. But they are still only 3.8 per cent of licence fee revenue. The evasion rate has increased more, partly because more households are watching only online and claiming they 'never watch live TV', but also encouraged by campaigns like the 'grassroots' - or Astroturf - #DefundTheBBC (Barwise and York, 2020: 272-5). By 2023/24, evasion was 11.3 per cent, making a total collection and evasion cost of 15.1 per cent (3.8 per cent plus 11.3 per cent) of licence fee revenue. This is higher than at the time of the Commons report but still, as discussed shortly, significantly less than the equivalent costs for advertising and, especially, subscriptions.

What are the alternatives? The DCMS committee discussed four: advertising, subscriptions, a revised licence fee (or another earmarked tax), and general taxation.

You can rule out advertising

Advertising is a non-starter. It was rejected by the 1984-5 Peacock Committee commissioned by Margaret Thatcher, who had initially favoured it, as had Professor Peacock at the start of the review. The committee gave two reasons for rejecting it, saying it would (a) damage other advertising-funded media, and (b) distort the BBC's incentives. These disadvantages are even greater today, with most commercial media under pressure and the BBC facing more competition than ever.

Two further disadvantages – completely missed by Peacock – are that audiences dislike interruptive commercials and, less obviously, that broadcast advertising has large hidden overhead costs: 20-25 per cent of advertisers' campaign expenditure (Barwise and York, 2020: 171) - well above the 15 per cent combined licence fee collection and evasion costs. No serious stakeholders still advocate BBC advertising and it is opposed by all the newspaper groups.

What about subscriptions?

The most widely touted alternative is subscriptions. There are many options: single- or multi-tier, 'pure' or 'hybrid' (partly tax-funded), etc. They should all be rejected because of their inherent disadvantages:

- They all require every device used to access the BBC's subscription services to have 'conditional access' technology to exclude non-payers. It's unclear how long it would take, and how much it would cost, to achieve this for BBC TV (and for radio, it's impossible)
- Once this technical barrier has been overcome - say, in the late 2030s - the BBC would have a financial incentive to prioritise the programme preferences of those best able to pay
- Crucially, it would no longer be a universal public service, shared equally by all. John Reith's famous claim 'There is no first and third class' would be history (Knight, 2022)
- Finally, to maintain the BBC's content investment, the average subscription price would need to be much higher than the licence fee, for two reasons. First, not everyone would subscribe, so those who did would each need to pay more to generate the same revenue. Second, less of the revenue would be available to invest in programmes because, as with advertising, subscriptions involve large overhead costs (marketing, customer service, technology) – about 35 per cent of revenue, much higher than the 15 per cent equivalent for the licence fee.

It gets worse. These two factors — non-subscribers and higher overheads — would create a vicious circle: because less of the revenue would go into programmes, reducing value for money, fewer households would subscribe, further reducing the revenue, and so on. No one knows the eventual outcome. But to maintain the BBC's content investment, the average subscription would likely need to be at least 50 per cent higher than the licence fee.

General taxation

General taxation, apparently favoured by culture secretary Lisa Nandy, is attractive in principle, but the results have been mixed in countries that have switched to it. Ringfencing the funding and ensuring it covers several years (the model in Finland, Norway, and Sweden) offers public service broadcasters some protection from political interference and funding cuts. Countries such as Denmark and Canada, where the public service broadcasting has to compete for government funding in the annual budget round, have found it harder to keep it politician-proof (Steemers, 2020; Tamas and Waddell, 2020).

The DCMS committee rejected this model because of the likely threat to the BBC's political independence, concluding that the licence fee, perhaps with some modification, was the 'least worst' short-term option, while the best long-term one would be a different hypothecated tax.

We agree. In particular, a universal household levy, with exemptions — as in Germany since 2013 — looks like the best long-term option. The German system, now also adopted by Austria, is a universal flat fee — €18.36 per month, about 20 per cent higher than the UK licence fee — paid by every household, with some exemptions and discounts. (It is also paid by companies and public institutions, although it would take a brave politician to propose that here.) An independent expert panel, the Kommission zur Ermittlung des Finanzbedarfs der Rundfunkanstalten (KEF), recommends the multi-year fee level, which then has to be agreed by Germany's 16 state governments. In October 2024, the states rejected the recommended 3.2 per cent increase. The case is now with the country's Constitutional Court.

A progressive levy?

A more progressive levy could be, say, a fixed percentage supplement to electricity and/or broadband bills so that bigger, richer households paid more than smaller, poorer ones — cheap to administer and with minimal evasion. However, switching to any standalone progressive system that generates the same revenue as the licence fee would be politically difficult as there would be losers as well as winners.

Which model should the UK government adopt?

Although the licence fee's disadvantages have been much overstated, the evasion rate is now over 11 per cent and the arbitrary link with whether anyone in the household ever watches live TV is unsustainable.

Among tax-based models, the Finnish version (multi-year ring-fenced funding) is better than the Canadian one (annual funding out of general taxation). But even the Finnish model would be risky here, with our more polarised media, society, and politics and the continuing 'war' against the BBC, although there's a strong case for reinstating ring-fenced government funding for the BBC World Service.

A universal household levy is the best and least risky alternative to the licence fee. That still leaves a choice between a progressive levy based on utility bills (which would, arguably, be fairer, but would require facing down objections from bigger and better-off households) and a flat one with exemptions and/or discounts, as in Germany, which would be politically easier. Given the trivial cost for most households, the simpler option — a flat universal household levy, with exemptions for those least able to pay and everyone else paying the same – is, in our view, the best practical option. But either would be better than the alternatives.

Who should decide the BBC's funding level?

Finally, we need to ensure that the BBC has the resources to deliver its remit. To protect it from hostile politicians, that means handing future funding settlements to an independent body transparently administered by Ofcom at arms' length from the Government, similar to the KEF in Germany. The new UK body should start with the Charter: what are we asking the BBC to do? It should then look at projections of household numbers, evasion, industry costs, continuing efficiency savings and commercial revenue, and set the recommended levy accordingly. The Government should be required to follow this recommendation or, if not, explain its reasons and defend its decision in the media and in Parliament.

Fortunately, unlike in Germany, the settlement would not need agreement by 16 state governments with wildly differing politics. In fact the German system would, we think, work rather better here than in Germany!

Why this matters

As we've seen, BBC funding is financially trivial – a coffee a week for the whole household, excluding those with free TV licences, and a rounding error in UK GDP. But in societal terms, ensuring proper BBC funding is massive. In a difficult world, the BBC is one of Britain's shining successes. And its public purposes beyond pure entertainment (*The Traitors* and all that) — trusted news, countering disinformation, supporting citizenship and cohesion, promoting learning, stimulating creative excellence, representing the UK and its nations and regions, bringing the UK to the world and the world to the UK, and helping the country adapt to new technology — could hardly matter more. So, despite the low financial stakes, getting this right will be hugely important.

References

Patrick Barwise and Peter York (2020) *The War Against the BBC*, London: Penguin.

BBC (2015) BBC's response to DCMS green paper: BBC charter review, Audience appendix, London.

House of Commons DCMS Committee (2015) Future of the BBC: fourth report of session 2014-15, 26 February.

Sam Knight (2022) 'Can the BBC survive the British Government?' New York: *New Yorker*, 11 April.

MTM (2022) *Deprivation study: What is life like without the BBC*? London: MTM.

Jeanette Steemers (2020) *The Funding of Public Service Broadcasting in Europe – Funding Systems and Decriminalisation – Selected Territories Information Briefing 30 March 2020*, London: King's Research Portal.

David Taras and Christopher Waddell (2020) *The End of the CBC?*, Toronto: University of Toronto Press.

About the contributors

Prof Patrick Barwise is emeritus professor of management and marketing at London Business School, chairman of the Archive of Market and Social Research, and co-author with Peter York of *The War Against The BBC* (Penguin 2020). After an early career at IBM he joined LBS in 1976 and has published widely on management, marketing, and media.

Peter York is a capitalist tool by background, as a market researcher and management consultant. In parallel he is a social commentator, journalist, occasional television presenter, and author of twelve books, ranging from *The Official Sloane Ranger Handbook* to *Authenticity Is A Con*. His most recent publication is *A Dead Cat On Your Table* (Byline Books 2024).

Chapter 18

Can the licence fee survive?

David Elstein asks the fundamental question

BBC Charter review is under way. It started under the previous government (I was part of an advisory panel on funding), paused for the July 2024 election, then landed in the lap of Lisa Nandy, the unexpected appointee as Secretary of State for Culture. The designated candidate, Thangam Debonnaire, had lost her Bristol constituency to the Greens.

There is a perpetual chicken-and-egg tension about these reviews. Which should be decided first: the BBC's purpose or the means of financing it? Typically, the issues are resolved separately, but in parallel, not least because hitherto the only financing option under consideration was the licence fee.

The last review, under John Whittingdale in 2016, provided the option of subscription as a supplement to the licence fee, but the BBC has simply ignored that. So the political decision was reduced to setting the level of the licence fee, almost irrespective of the BBC's purported purpose, along with the duration of the fee agreement, and the arrangements for adjusting the level of the fee (historically, only ever upwards) during that period.

Since the 2016 review much has changed for the BBC. Most notably, the value of the licence fee has been sharply eroded by a combination of freezes in level and inflation, to the tune of a 30 per cent real terms decline. The BBC has adjusted to this straitening of its finances by — essentially —steadily reducing its quality of output, though it stoutly rejects any such accusation, and would point to its healthy wodge of awards at the May 2025 BAFTAs.

But the truth is that, however slow the process of dilution, it is continuous. These days the BBC can rarely, if ever, venture into production of the most expensive of high-end dramas, especially as an hour of it now costs £2m — enough to fund, for example, a whole season of 50 hours of *Pointless* (a series which is also readily repeatable).

Moreover, the BBC remains massively over-staffed, with 17,000 employees. Its claims to be efficient are risible: the figure of 5 per cent of its income that the BBC claims is spent on overheads has been exposed as fantasy. In broadcasting there are two types of outgoings: the cost of actual programmes, commissioned externally or made in-house; and everything else – rent, rates, utilities, distribution, marketing, engineering, promotion and presentation, development, finance, HR, non-programme staff, telephony, travel and so on.

Typically, these will constitute around 40 per cent of all expenditure. Ofcom's 2017 study calculated the correct figure for the BBC was 44 per cent.

And the BBC remains bitterly opposed to any idea of replacing the licence fee with a subscription system.

Universality rules?

Much of this opposition is expressed as a defence of universality, a so-called principle which has very little basis in the BBC's history where for long periods entire services were only physically available to a minority of households. That subscription services are in practice universally available (but with no compulsion to pay for them, unlike the licence fee) is a fact that seems to have escaped the ideologues of Broadcasting House.

The BBC has no qualms about the compulsory element of the licence fee system. However, even though the number of prosecutions for non-payment has dropped from a pre-Covid annual peak of over 150,000 to around 30,000 currently, the demonstrable unfairness of the way the law is enforced is a source of embarrassment. Overwhelmingly, those who are caught out by the TV Licensing officers are single mothers, the unemployed, and the disabled — those most likely to be at home when the doorbell is rung.

The Single Justice Procedure (SJP), under which licence non-payment penalties are these days enforced, has made matters worse. Vulnerable groups are those least likely to be able to respond to a court notice within the 21 days allowed, or to know how to plead mitigation, let alone ensure the magistrate ruling on conviction ever sees any plea of mitigation. Even some magistrates are uncomfortable about the rubber-stamp element of SJP. Lisa Nandy is not the only culture minister to have flirted with the idea of decriminalising licence fee evasion, a measure that the BBC estimates would cost it hundreds of millions each year.

A regressive tax

The other unfairness, which does cause the BBC some discomfort — even though it has been integral to the system for 100 years — is that, with a flat rate, the poor pay the same as the rich. The BBC has strongly hinted, on more than one occasion, that a different and more progressive collection mechanism would be preferable, most obviously by adding the TV licence fee to council tax bills.

Superficially, one can see the attraction. The banding system makes council tax relatively progressive, even if the compression of the bands means that increases in house values only affect the lower bands. Band H covers everything from about £1m in value to £20m or more.

In effect, requiring the £3.7bn generated annually by the licence fee to be delivered by council tax would mean adding a surcharge of 8 per cent to bills.

Given that far more people are in council tax arrears — 1.6 million, with accumulated arrears of over £6.6bn — than fail to pay the licence fee, the BBC might easily lose not just control over its overall finances but any reliability of cash flow. Indeed, the imposition of a surcharge would inevitably make collecting council tax even harder, increase arrears, and no doubt incentivise councils collectively to resist such a move. Some councils — in the Midlands or the North-East, for instance, where the BBC spends little of its billions — might even ask why they should shoulder the burden of collecting money to pay high salaries to hundreds of BBC executives living in Camden, Dulwich, or Barnes. Some, for instance in Scotland, might choose to challenge the BBC's editorial as well as financial policies.

Beyond that, the modestly progressive structure of council tax could lead to the replacement of perceived unfairness by organised resistance. A typical band H home would be paying £256 for what previously cost £174-50. For the one million people who own second homes, £170 would become £512. For those of them now being charged a 100 per cent second home premium, the total would be £768.

Voluntary subscription

Two possible consequences flow from such calculations. First, a substantial constituency could well be created of people who believed the cost of paying for the BBC was far too high. Such a grouping might join, or lead, a campaign to force the BBC to operate on the basis of voluntary subscription. Netflix, reasonably, charge just one subscription, however many homes you might have, as you can only watch their service on one screen at a time.

Secondly, many might join the exodus from live television altogether, thereby obviating the requirement to have a television licence, and so presumably exempting them from paying the council tax surcharge. And as councils would not benefit in the slightest from the surcharge, they would have little interest in checking whether live television was being watched.

At that point it is conceivable that the BBC would simply lobby ministers to make the payment a BBC tax, not connected to any device or screen or behaviour, payable irrespective of whether you owned a TV or radio, or watched or listened to any live broadcast. Such a draconian outcome is very unlikely to be electorally popular, and even a Labour government might baulk at the prospect.

Rather more importantly, a potential Reform UK government — already committed to abolishing the licence fee as it stands — is sure to oppose any such iron-cladding of the BBC's finances. Indeed, for the BBC not to have contingency plans for a potentially swift abolition of the licence fee after the next election, in the event of a Reform UK victory, would be a gross dereliction of duty.

Changing ways of viewing

The looming threat of Reform UK is sharply visible. Less obvious is the rapid shift in viewing habits and household technology which may undermine the licence fee from within. Ten years ago, much of the resistance to replacing the licence fee with subscription was based on the fact that millions of people were out of reach of broadband. Today, fast broadband is available to 99.7 per cent of UK households, and over 70 per cent have connected their television sets to it. Eighteen million homes subscribe to the likes of Netflix and Sky. Another 14 per cent of households have broadband, but have not yet connected their TV to it (Ofcom, 2024).

The remaining 14 per cent of households are within reach of broadband but have yet to take advantage of its availability, most likely on account of unfamiliarity with matters digital, or lack of interest, or cost, though suppliers such as BT offer social rates below £20 a month. Typically, these households comprise adults who are alone, and older and poorer than the average: 90 per cent are over the age of 55, and 80 per cent are in the C2DE demographic.

In parallel with the spread of streaming services and smart TVs there has been a steady shift of viewing away from live TV to on-demand. Fifty per cent of all TV viewing is still linear, but official forecasts say it will drop to 30 per cent within five years, and then continue the downward trend.

So the BBC now stands at the edge of a steep precipice. In recent years, half a million homes have cancelled their TV licence. The BBC believes that the rate of exit is no more than 1 per cent of eligible households a year, which is below the level by which the cost of the licence fee, and thereby the BBC's income, rises each year as long as it remains inflation-proofed. That trade-off, it thinks, would be survivable, if uncomfortable.

The viewing audience is not a solid block. Like a glacier, whole chunks can break off very rapidly. Currently, in a typical week, a majority of 16-24s watch no live television at all. Based on current consumer behaviour the figure for households abandoning the licence fee seems likely to continue rising, and even to accelerate. Were it to reach 20 per cent, let alone 30 per cent, the pressure to abandon the licence fee system would become irresistible.

Twenty years ago there was an expensive transition from analogue terrestrial broadcasting to digital terrestrial transmission (DTT), in order to make more efficient use of available spectrum. Whether or not the DTT system survives is not strictly relevant to the case for replacing the licence fee with subscription. But if DTT is indeed abandoned a voluntary subscription mechanism will be the only available option for funding most of what the BBC does, assuming the Treasury covers the cost of certain types of public service output that subscription would not support.

Given the inexorable trends in consumer behaviour, content provision, technology, and the looming shadow of Nigel Farage, the BBC's room for manoeuvre appears very limited. In the short term, decisions lie with Lisa Nandy, but an organisation as large and important as the BBC should surely not be substantially dependent for its future financing on what one of its most illustrious presenters once called a here today, gone tomorrow politician.

Reference

Ofcom (2024) *Connected Nations*, 5 December.

About the contributor

A distinguished programme maker, David Elstein was Director of Programmes at Thames Television from 1986 to 1992, Head of Programmes at BSkyB from 1993 to 1996, and the launch Chief Executive of Channel Five in 1997.

This is an edited version of a piece which originally appeared in the August 2025 edition of *The Critic*.

Chapter 19

Time for Beebflix?

Roger Bolton makes the argument for a two-tier BBC licence fee

It is getting harder and harder to defend the licence fee, and it is hardly the fault of the BBC, or its energetic Director-General, Tim Davie.

The Beeb has always had to ride and feed two horses at the same time, and now it is in danger of doing the splits and falling off. One horse is called 'Market Failure' and its chief strength is serving minorities who are in danger of being underfed. It is sometimes called 'elitist' but it does set standards and offers something different, particularly in the field of science, children, news, religion, and education. The other horse is called 'General Public' and offers something for everyone, even though much of what it does is increasingly replicated elsewhere.

As long as these two horses were well fed and winning races against fewer and weaker opposition, racegoers did not mind too much having to pay for both of them. But this is changing, and supporters of rival horses wonder why they still have to pay for their competitors as well as their own, and increasing numbers are not going to the broadcast races at all.

Precisely when the BBC horses needed to be at their fittest to face increasing opposition they have been increasingly underfed. This has not happened by accident.

It started with Thatcher

Forty years ago the then Prime Minister, Margaret Thatcher wanted to bring the BBC under control (her control?) and kill off the licence fee. She hoped making the Corporation take advertising would be the way to do it. Even her supporters told her that it could not be done. So she arranged for the BBC's Director-General to be fired, and a more sympathetic regime put in place, and then turned her attention to ITV and awarded their franchises to the highest bidders, helping get rid of such irritations as the current affairs series *This Week* and *World in Action*. (To declare an interest, I edited the former from 1986 to 1989.)

Still the BBC and ITV remained remarkably popular, kept winning prizes, and reinvigorated their journalism. Stalemate?

Her Conservative successors, egged on by supporters who thought their own horses should be winning races, decided to reduce the BBC's income, and indeed, over the last 15 years the value of its licence fee has dropped by almost

40 per cent in real terms. Both the BBC's horses are now severely undernourished.

It is still possible to make a strong case for the continuation of the licence fee, and yet to believe it is doomed in its present form.

What does the BBC provide?

It is not just a licence for TV of course. As well as providing eight national TV Channels (BBC1, 2, 3, 4, CBC, CBeebies, BBC News, BBC Parliament), and national and regional TV stations, it pays for ten pan-UK radio networks, six National UK radio networks, and 40 local radio stations. Then there are the online services, iPlayer, Sounds, and the BBC Website containing News, Sport, Weather, CBBC, Food, Bitesize, Arts, BBC3. Then there is the World Service — TV, radio, and online— S4C, and Local Democracy reporters.

All this for the price of a cappuccino a week!

We must be mad to consider getting rid of the licence fee. And yet I think, in its present form at least, it is doomed.

The death of the licence fee?

It is not just that more people are refusing to pay it, and that prosecutions for non-payment are increasingly unpopular, but also that there is a political and business attempt to kill it off.

Sir Paul Marshall, an evangelical Christian and hedge fund manager, who owns GB News, as well as *The Spectator* magazine and the Unherd website, recently called for the BBC to be 'broken up' and its fact-checking service 'shut down'. He said, "The BBC squats like a giant toad in the middle of the UK media landscape," and that "It is a propaganda arm of the state."

This will come as a surprise to former members of Conservative and Labour Governments who have had many stand-up rows with the Corporation about its independent journalism, and to those members of the security services and armed forces who have tried to silence its investigative journalists.

Nevertheless, the licence fee is losing support.

Big questions about the licence fee

Is there any viable alternative, or can it be reformed to make it more acceptable? I believe those are important but secondary questions. I believe that first we have to make the case for public service content, and only then discuss how best to deliver it and how to pay for it. This the BBC seems reluctant to do.

Over the twenty-three years in which I presented the Radio 4 series *Feedback* we had the greatest difficulty in getting senior executives to come on and explain themselves. Perhaps in the past they could afford to ride out the many storms but not now. Public service broadcasting is not whatever the BBC decides is in its own interest, it should be a publicly agreed concept.

I believe that the Corporation has to remake the case for its existence, not just as a great brand, respected worldwide, but as the best vehicle for commissioning, producing, and distributing public service content. It has to have a strategy for each of the key PSB areas and be prepared to spell them out.

The licence fee is becoming increasingly difficult to defend in its present form. It is regressive, everyone pays the same, regardless of income, and increasing numbers do not use its services, or at least think they do not.

Alternatives to the licence fee?

It is easy to dismiss some alternatives to the licence fee.

If the Corporation took advertising it would dominate that market and destroy many commercial competitors, and would diminish not increase competition.

Subscription, at least in the short term, say the next ten years, would mean switching off the transmitters, and in the process denying those not online access to any BBC services. The poor and remote would be penalised, and there are still several millions who are not online.

A direct Government grant or tax would hardly strengthen the Corporation's independence and might make it even more dependent on Government.

How about a BBC payment collected with the council tax, which would at least make it more progressive? This is an option which the BBC Chair, Samir Shah has gently floated. Possible, but, presumably, Government would have to set the tax rate and be prepared to prosecute non-payment.

What about using a digital services tax? Well President Trump and the US tech bros are implacably opposed to the UK's digital services tax which takes two per cent of all revenues from social platforms and search engines even if they are based outside the UK. I detect little enthusiasm in Government to raise BBC revenue this way.

Which leaves what?

I think we need to consider a two-tier form of funding: a reduced licence fee which delivers a basic public service, and subscription for a more mainstream offering, prioritising drama and comedy, with the proviso that its programmes would be eventually shown on free to air, perhaps with a six or twelve-month delay. This would satisfy the need for Public Service Content to be universally available, although with a time delay. The reduced licence fee would also have to pay for the BBC World Service since clearly the Foreign

Office, faced with tough spending decisions, tends to prioritise embassies and ambassadors above transmitters.

The mainstream offering (Beebflix or Britflix?) would be publicly owned, perhaps on a mutual model, but able to take some private investment, and would be self-funding after initial start-up costs. Given the British talent available, in many cases the best in the world, it should be possible to both make outstanding and profitable programmes but also, of course, to retain the intellectual property rights. Too many of those, at the moment, are winging their way to the other side of the Atlantic.

Pandering to populism?

There is another danger that the BBC must avoid in its attempt to justify the increasingly unpopular licence fee and catering to those who increasingly turn away from its programming.

Minutes from the BBC Board's Editorial Guidelines and Standards Committee meeting in March 2025 included this: 'The CEO, News and Current Affairs, provided the Committee with a presentation on plans to address low trust issues with Reform voters [...] Directors discussed how story selection and other types of output such as drama also had a role to play.'

It would, of course, be remiss of the Directors not to be concerned about licence fee payers becoming alienated from the output, but the BBC's first and main priority should be to tell uncomfortable truths and report the world as it is, not as we would like it to be.

Where do we go from here?

In conclusion, let us not argue about the licence fee, without arguing what it pays for. Let us not defend the BBC simply because it is the BBC. We must demand that there is a proper debate about the future of public service broadcasting and media, and convincing definitions of what that means in practice, and then discuss whether the BBC needs to be reformed to deliver it. Then, and only then, let us discuss how to fund it.

The status quo is untenable, but almost every other form of funding is flawed. Time for Beebflix?

About the contributor

Roger Bolton edited *Tonight*, *Panorama*, and *Nationwide* at the BBC. He was twice fired by the Corporation over coverage of Ireland. He then moved to *This Week* at ITV and once again encountered trouble when the British government tried to prevent the broadcasting of the 28 April 1988 edition 'Death on the Rock' about the shooting of unarmed IRA men by the SAS in Gibraltar. He presented *Right to Reply* on Channel 4 between 1994 and 2000, Radio 4's *Sunday* from 1998 to 2010, and *Feedback*, also Radio 4, from 1999 to 2022. He was fired from that too. He now curates his own podcast *Roger Bolton's Beeb Watch*.

Chapter 20

Between subscription and the state: A hybrid approach to BBC funding

Daniel Freeman argues the licence fee cannot sustain the BBC in the long term. Relying on a single replacement source of funding presents serious problems. The BBC should be split between a subscription and advertisement-funded mutual and a separate tax-funded news arm

Managing decline

The BBC today is in a position similar to the Church of England in the 1970s. Once a central part of national life, it has for many years been suffering from falling engagement, especially among the young, as Britons find other things to do with their time. This is not to say that the organisation is disliked; the majority of the public feel warmly towards the BBC (YouGov, 2025a). But, as with the Anglican Church, warm feelings are not enough to maintain its preeminent position, culturally or financially.

A large part of the problem is downstream of the BBC's reliance on the TV licence fee, which, since the introduction of the combined radio and TV licence in 1946, has grown to become its primary source of income (House of Commons Library, 2025). It is a hypothecated tax, that is a tax whose revenue is ring-fenced for a particular purpose, levied on anyone who watches live TV or uses the BBC iPlayer. There is no variation on price based on level of consumption or income with the vast majority of licence fee payers being charged the full fee of £174.50 which applies to anyone who watches live broadcasts even if they consume no BBC content.

This system is widely seen as unjust with polling conducted by YouGov in March 2025 finding that 63 per cent of the public consider the BBC licence fee to be unfair, compared with just 20 per cent who thought it fair (YouGov, 2025b). But worse than being unpopular, the current funding model tethers the BBC's income to a form of media consumption, broadcast TV, that is in rapid (and almost certainly irreversible) decline.

According to Ofcom, the British public spent 6 per cent less time watching broadcast TV in 2023 than in the previous year, and about a quarter less time than it did in 2018 (Ofcom, 2024). As late as 2018 nine-tenths of the public watched broadcast TV in a given week, but by 2023 only three in four did. The drop in interest is most pronounced among the young. Ofcom found that most British 16–24-year-olds now watch no broadcast TV in a given week, and average viewership for this age group is down 16 per cent year-on-year. This is not a trend confined to Generation Z. Millennials are also increasingly abandoning broadcast TV as a source of entertainment. In 2013 the average 25–34-year-old watched over three hours of TV per day. By 2023 they were watching just 64 minutes. Today it's highly likely that they are watching less than an hour.

This is already having an impact on the BBC's bottom line with the number of TV licences purchased in 2023/24 down by half a million on the previous year, which also saw a similar fall (BBC, 2024: 53). Numbers will likely fall further in 2025 as the licence fee freeze in place since 2021 comes to an end. In the medium-term the prognosis for the licence fee as a source of revenue is even more grim as younger generations with light TV viewing habits account for a larger share of households.

Alternatives to the licence fee

Perhaps the simplest of the proposals for replacing the licence fee would be for the government to directly fund the BBC from general taxation. However, this would present problems. Firstly, this would not resolve the issue of perceived unfairness, and would in some regards deepen it as even taxpayers without a television would have to contribute.

Secondly, the Treasury will be justifiably reluctant to accept financial responsibility for filling the £3.66bn hole in the BBC's budget left by the licence fee at a time when budgets across government are being squeezed. There are also reasonable concerns that giving the government such a direct control over the BBC's finances would put its independence at risk. Indeed, this was the concern cited by culture secretary Lisa Nandy who ruled out a general taxation funding model in January 2025 (Youngs, 2025).

With general taxation funding now off the cards another option would be to replace the licence fee with a standard levy indexed to inflation on broadband connections. This could keep the government at arm's length and could be incorporated into bills, significantly reducing the costs of collection and enforcement which currently run to £145m per year (BBC, 2024: 56).

However, a levy sufficiently large to replace the licence fee would have a grossly distortive effect on the home internet market. About 25 million of the UK's 28 million households currently have a broadband connection and each would need to be charged roughly an extra £12 per month to compensate for the loss of the licence fee. This would increase the average broadband bill by over 40 per cent. Such a sharp rise would likely lead to light internet users and those on low incomes cancelling their broadband packages adding to digital exclusion and the social costs this brings.

Subscription

A subscription model in which those who wish to pay for the BBC are given access to it has a lot to recommend it. It would eliminate the unfairness of a tax-based system which requires payment regardless of viewing habits while ensuring the BBC remains independent from government.

While subscriptions should play a role in the future of the BBC current technology makes it difficult to rely on exclusively. Freeview TV and radio broadcasts are non-excludable, meaning anyone with the required equipment can access content. If the BBC were to adopt a funding model based solely on subscription it would be forced either to switch off Freeview and radio broadcasts (no doubt politically contentious) or accept that there would be a substantial number of free-riders who would continue to access content on TV and radio without paying.

A hybrid model

I would propose a hybrid model in which the BBC is funded in part by advertising, in part by subscription with news and current affairs split off and funded by a small levy on broadband.

The majority of the BBC could be reorganised as a subscriber-owned mutual along the lines of the national trust or mutual insurance companies. Subscribers would have access to the BBC iPlayer, archive material and, in time, extra channels in return for a monthly fee. They could also be given a vote in elections to a board of trustees which would be accountable for the BBC's content. Booth (2019) goes into greater detail on how such a system could be implemented.

Broadcast TV and radio would remain available to non-subscribers but could include commercial advertising as a means of dealing with the free-rider problem. This would not be as unpopular as is sometimes suggested: polling consistently shows advertising during commercial breaks to be the public's preferred means of funding the BBC, beating the current system by a significant margin.

Keeping live broadcasts free to access with advertising would not only raise revenue but would also help drive people towards subscription as the public would be able to 'try before you buy' by watching programmes with adverts and would then be able to subscribe in order to access the content ad-free. In the case of the BBC subscribing would come with the bonus of being able to have a say in the direction of the organisation through having a vote in board elections.

However, this subscriber-owned model does throw up some problems when it comes to news and current affair content. As in the current system news would have to compete for resources with other, perhaps more popular, types of content and if responsible to subscribers the impulse to remain impartial may be diminished. Therefore it might be advisable to split off BBC news and current affairs into an organisation separate from the rest of the BBC, though likely retaining the BBC brand. It would continue to operate as now in terms of impartiality and at least initially the BBC subscriber mutual could be required to give it airtime. It could run its own news channel work with the BBC mutual to supply news content for the website, and perhaps have its own radio station. In terms of funding a broadband connection levy would be much more feasible if only required to fund this element of the BBC. In 2023/24 the BBC's entire budget for news and current affairs content was £321m. A broadband levy would only need to raise £1.07 per month per household in order to cover this provision, which would have a far less distortive effect on the household internet market than if it were required to finance the entire range of BBC content.

In terms of other policy objectives such as education which broadcasting could support, this could be achieved through a system of grants and sponsorships open both to the BBC and private broadcasters. For example, the Department for Education could offer a grant for a series of documentaries on the origins of the Industrial Revolution for which any broadcaster or online content creator could bid. This is a system already used by the Arts Council and there is little reason a similar system could not be applied to broadcast content. If the state is to use broadcasting to advance a particular policy objective it should be willing to fund those projects directly and work with the organisation best placed to deliver rather than relying on a single broadcaster.

Conclusion

Moving towards a hybrid model of funding will doubtless bring some trepidation on the part of the BBC. This is understandable but not unprecedented. When ITV was first established in 1955 it was in the face of fierce opposition. Lord Reith, the first Director-General of the BBC, claimed that permitting commercial competition would sink 'a maggot— a quite unnecessary maggot—into the body politic of England'. Regardless of what one thinks of ITV's output, today most people would acknowledge that these fears proved to be unfounded. The BBC benefited from the challenge competition brought and adapted to its new context. Moving to a hybrid funding model after 2027 will help the BBC rise to the challenge of new competition and provide a sustainable financial future where the licence fee no longer can.

References

BBC (2024) *BBC Group Annual Report and Accounts 2023/24*, London: BBC.

Philip Booth (2019) *New Vision: Transforming the BBC into a subscriber owned mutual*, London: Institute of Economic Affairs.

House of Commons Library (2025)'TV licence fee statistics', 18 June. https://commonslibrary.parliament.uk/research-briefings/cbp-8101/

Ofcom (2024) *Media Nations UK 2024*, 31 July, accessed 12 June 2025.

YouGov (2025a) 'BBC fame & popularity tracker', YouGov quarterly tracker, https://yougov.co.uk/topics/consumer/trackers/fame-and-popularity-bbc

YouGov (2025b) 'How fair is the BBC licence fee?', YouGov biannual tracker, https://yougov.co.uk/topics/politics/trackers/how-fair-is-the-bbc-liscence-fee

Ian Youngs (2025) 'Culture secretary rules out funding BBC from taxes', BBC News, 17 January, https://www.bbc.co.uk/news/articles/cp3wwkdnddzo

About the contributor

Daniel Freeman is the Managing Editor at the Institute of Economic Affairs.

Chapter 21

How to fund the BBC after 2027

Maggie Brown reflects on the BBC in her life then and now

When you woke up on Sunday morning 22 June 2025 what did you do? In my home we reached for the bedside radio and BBC News, to absorb the shock of Trump's attack on Iran's nuclear assets. Where else?

What needs to be appreciated as the BBC gears up for the rapidly approaching 2027 renewal of its Charter is the vital importance of avoiding damage to one of our great British institutions, which has clocked up a century of delivery. The BBC has earned a unique and special place in the lives of UK citizens over a century because it attempts to cater for everyone, from toddlers to the elderly. I think that trust continues despite the major changes taking place.

The BBC in a divided world

The antagonism that surfaced notably with Margaret Thatcher's election in 1979 has cooled, and though British media is rapidly transforming its methods of delivery from curated channels to online and streaming, the BBC's Director-General Tim Davie is correct in pointing out it is a 'really weird institution but it works'.

He points out that the world is polarising, that 75 per cent of the global population do not have a free press. So while the BBC's more than 21,000 employees and contributors are bound to make mistakes, it has a clear mission in its the Reithian motto: to inform, educate, and entertain. To aim at impartial news and current affairs. With conflicts raging across the globe the need for accessible documentaries to bring stories to the screen is essential. It has a built-in strength thanks to expert correspondents.

So, the mood music around the BBC has changed, dare I suggest, to affection. For example, consider the exceptional coverage it organised for the funeral of Pope Francis in Rome, and the commentary for his successor Pope Leo. The BBC drew packed audiences for Wimbledon in the summer of 2025, and continues to develop the Proms, which in 2025 included only the second-ever performance of Ravel's *Piano Concerto for the Left Hand* by an actual one-handed pianist. It also provides services to regions which are often overlooked, services such as radio and news geared to licence payers' interests without advertisements. Living partly in rural Wales I am one of millions of listeners who appreciate this.

The fact is the BBC takes great care to cater for everyone, from original children's programming to pensioners. There is also a growing ancillary concern that the World Service needs cherishing, not cutbacks. We have a national broadcaster that can deal competently with key events and open up cultures beyond our own British borders.

Value for money?

So, given the monthly cost of streamer subscriptions, the £174.50 annual BBC licence fee is arguably reasonable for such a service. Though I accept that around 300,000 more people in the past year have cancelled their TV licence in favour of a streaming service and no live broadcasts, that means 23.9 million households are still paying. Culture secretary Lisa Nandy has ruled out, correctly, funding the BBC in future from taxes.

One source of financial self-help worth studying is the successful *Bluey* example, an animated puppy cartoon from Australian Broadcasting Corporation, designed for pre-schoolers but with older fans, and now in its third series. BBC Studios holds global and merchandising rights. It pioneered children's television in post-WW2 Britain and has never deserted that mission.

At a packed awards ceremony at Lambeth Palace in June 2025, organised by the Sandford St Martin Trust, to reward programming that enriches our culture (from religion through to children's content and outstanding drama), I was struck by a key theme. It was a clarion call to ensure continuity, and the emergence of an increasingly vocal lobby for protecting the supply of quality public service programming. Which means improved funding, either through tariffs on streaming income or tax relief for producers.

A lost generation

However, the biggest challenge for the BBC as it promotes its historic strengths and values is how to recapture the attention and support of younger people who are deserting it. Channel 4 commissioned research agency Craft to undertake a study in 2023-24. A total of 3,000 people took part in the survey which broke down to 2,000 13-27 year-olds, and 1,000 28-65 year-olds. The study found that trust in the BBC had dropped to 38 per cent among 28-65 year-olds, and to 43 per cent among 13-27 year-olds as they lavished their attention on social media posts and friends (Channel 4, 2025a).

The study observed that 'news consumption for Gen Z is delivered in bite-sized snippets via platforms including TikTok and YouTube'. Discussing this trend with children and young people has blown away the complacent acceptance that youth will grow up and morph into more traditional viewers who will come to value traditional public service programming.

One solution, which Channel 4 has reached for in the past two years, is to follow the audience, use the channels they use, and release relevant programming on YouTube. Channel 4 has set up dedicated and successful *Unreported World* and *Dispatches* websites (Channel 4, 2025b). The strategy appears to be working: in 2024 viewers accessed 3.4 billion minutes of Channel 4 content via YouTube.

The debate now facing the BBC is whether to follow suit. It would mean more prominent branding, say an attention-catching tag, on all such releases. TV experts in children's programming appear to be swinging behind this. But such a move implies a further dismantling of channels while encouraging expansion of the BBC's commercial studios arm.

Back to basics?

Another interesting development is that Netflix is striking a deal with TFI, France's largest broadcaster, to place programmes on its networks. This is a fascinating prospect, given that it represents a partnership of the new (Netflix) and the old (TFI). Might legacy or traditional broadcasting dogs have new tricks to teach the new kids on the block?

Whatever happens between now and the crucial 2027 date, the issue of funding the BBC should at the very least result in the creation of an independent panel to set licence fee levels, whose interests are separate from the government of the day, and put viewers before politics.

References

Channel 4 (2025a) *Trends, Truth and Trust*, London, January.

Channel 4 (2025b) *Report and Financial Statements 2024: Fearless, Funny & Free*, London, 21 May.

About the contributor

Maggie Brown was the media editor of *The Independent*, a *Guardian Media* writer, and *Observer* contributor. She is the Channel 4 historian.

Chapter 22

The BBC iPlayer+: A sustainable income stream for the BBC

Dr Daithí McMahon proposes the BBC's iPlayer be expanded into an international multi-media subscription service that would compete with the existing streaming platforms for audiences and establish a sustainable future for the BBC at home and abroad

Context

The world has experienced accelerated media conglomeration and convergence in the digital age, creating new media opportunities for consumers but in the process making it increasingly difficult for traditional media, with antiquated economic models, to compete. This is part of what Jenkins (2006) posits as convergence culture and involves control over media production and distribution being wrested from media corporations by increasingly powerful, and globally interconnected, audiences. This rapid shift has not just been driven by young audiences, what Prensky (2001) referred to as 'digital natives' who grew up with digital media, but by audiences of all ages as choices have been broadened beyond terrestrial media markets.

Audiences now expect much more from media outlets including: a wide choice of quality programming (vast media libraries); flexibility as to when to consume it (on-demand consumption); flexibility on where to consume the media (home and portable media devices); and flexibility of contract (monthly, cancel anytime, subscriptions). The shift to new patterns of consumption is a fundamental change and media corporations must understand and adapt to survive in the modern convergent culture. Viewers are much more active and willing to seek out, and most importantly pay for, the content they want. As a consequence, younger consumers are favouring media streaming services – video, podcast, music and, to a lesser degree, news – and shunning the traditional public service media and the statutory, licence fee, despite a video subscription costing roughly the same amount as a TV licence per month.

Of the fifteen countries that continue to use the licence fee model the UK had the fourth highest cost in Europe. Several European Public Service Broadcasters (PSBs), including Germany and the Netherlands, have launched their own media streaming services, and in France, Greece, Italy, Romania, and Sweden public broadcasters have their own platforms akin to the BBC iPlayer streaming service, yet 78 per cent of public service media (PSM) continue to be publicly funded so the taxpayer continues to bear the brunt (European

Broadcasting Union, 2024). This needn't be the case. Despite Director-General Tim Davie's rejection of a subscription model for the BBC, the 26 June 2025 unveiling of a paid subscription plan for users in the US (Thomas, 2025) is a clear sign the CEO has an appetite for international income for its productions via more sustainable subscription fees in large untapped markets.

What is abundantly clear is that the existing funding model with the television licence as a core revenue stream is no longer sustainable. The BBC needs to diversify from the licence fee and create new revenue streams to steady its finances and establish a more resilient and stable funding model for future generations. Allied to this the structure and costing model of the BBC needs to be completely reviewed.

Income and sustainable revenue streams

Although it offers its television and radio programming free-to-air for the domestic UK audience, the commercial arm of the corporation, BBC Studios, has successfully exported its media content internationally for decades via two avenues, both of which could be brought under one distribution platform. The first is syndicated news channels, the second is via its content production and distribution department which sells the rights to its programming to territories globally. The BBC has several other smaller streams alongside these which collectively generated income of £1.9bn in 2023-24 (BBC, 2024).

The corporation has some highly lucrative media products including *Top Gear, Doctor Who, Blue Planet,* and *Strictly Come Dancing*, the latter of which also has licenced locally produced versions running in various countries (BBC, 2022). Another successful example, *Planet Earth*, has been licensed in over 100 territories (BBC, 2024). The reality is the BBC has strong international demand for its titles (BBC, 2018).

Therefore, the BBC is not unaccustomed to striking deals that exploit their content and raise additional revenue. The organisation has proven potential to expand the commercialisation of their content and we should thus not assume the organisation is incapable of the change proposed here. The licence fee accounted for two-thirds of the corporation's income, hence the reluctance to consider axing it. However, licence fee income is in slow decline from £3.80bn in 2021-22 to £3.66bn in 2023-24 (Zayed, 2025): a new model is needed, and quickly.

Introducing . . . the BBC iPlayer+

The BBC needs to abandon their overreliance on the TV licence fee and put all of their content past, present, and future into a world-leading streaming site that will extract funds directly from audiences around the world – the BBC iPlayer+. The iPlayer+ would be a highly competitive multi-media platform with a potentially vast audience base and income, offering access to new programming and the vast back catalogue to world-leading, critically acclaimed drama, film, and factual products.

The current approach of licensing content to territories would be scrapped and the BBC would instead retain all of its titles on the BBC iPlayer+, thereby driving up subscription growth in its new platform. This proposal would provide savings by centralising distribution operations under one roof and removing the need for the duplication of contracts with multiple broadcasters in different countries.

With 23.9 million TV licences and an 11 per cent evasion rate currently, the BBC could potentially have around 26.5 million subscribers under the new subscription format. If, as a conservative number, they managed to secure a similar number internationally, the organisation could have 50m+ subscribers. At a competitive £10 ($14) per month, which is 30 per cent less than the current licence fee, the model could generate upwards of £6bn per annum, more than is generated in the current model and with further growth potential.

This may seem an ambitious figure, but Disney+, despite a difficult start in 2019, had subscription and advertising revenues of $10.4bn (£8.88bn) in 2024 from 117.6 million subscribers, an increase of 12.6 per cent on the previous year (Business of Apps, 2025). The BBC's charging $8.99 per month for US subscribers, offering access to news, features, and livestreams via BBC.com, is a price point that will attract an audience. A bundled BBC iPlayer+ premium subscription bringing all news, video, and BBC Sounds audio content together for $14 a month would therefore be attractive in the US and other lucrative markets. The current iPlayer has been a proven success domestically with 8.1bn streaming requests in 2023/24, a 10 per cent increase on the previous year which represents strong growth (BBC, 2024).

There will be lessons to be learnt from the BritBox venture which did not manage to capture a large share of the market (Ampere Analysis, 2024). On the contrary, it was not ambitious enough. The global streaming market is competitive with households already carrying several video subscriptions (Statistica, 2013), but in order to serve its Charter and remit the BBC only has to achieve income of roughly £6bn per annum to cover its running costs of £5.6bn, and it can reinvest the surplus in local, national, and international news and media.

Reinvestment in news and journalism

As a result of the decline in income for the BBC income the organisation has had to cut costs in recent years. This has resulted in the regrettable loss of a whole swathe of BBC local radio programming and output across the UK and there are signs this will continue. With the surplus income from the BBC iPlayer+ subscriptions the BBC could reinvest funds in core news and information programming and reinstate local media, including radio. The availability of independent, trustworthy (Reuters Institute, 2023) and high-quality journalism is central to a properly functioning democracy and more important than ever with the contemporary phenomenon of fake news dissemination via social media and other unregulated channels. To combat the misinformation UK PSM – BBC, ITV, and Channel 4 – must continue to provide impartial news via television, radio/audio, and online. This service should remain free to the British public as an essential public service under the proposed model. Should the government and the BBC decide to continue with their current structure beyond 2027, a PSM fund from the government that rises in line with inflation and is ring-fenced for news and current affairs programming would need to be introduced.

As the globalisation of news and media continues, where borders are blurred and trusted news is ever more important, public service media needs to be protected. The current funding model in the UK and across several European countries does not support the costs of producing news and journalism to the required standard, does not take advantage of the international market, and does not reflect contemporary, sustainable funding models which are based on a combination of subscription and sponsorship and advertising revenue. The time for action is now so the BBC must act and propose bold change in the next Charter.

References

Ampere Analysis (2024) *Unpacking the BBC's BritBox Deal*, Available at: **https://www.ampereanalysis.com/insight/unpacking-the-bbcs-britbox-deal**. [Accessed 20 June 2025]

BBC (2018) 'BBC Worldwide reveals its top rating shows internationally'.

Available at: **https://www.bbc.co.uk/mediacentre/worldwide/2018/bbc-worldwide-reveals-top-rating-shows**. [Accessed 28 November 2023].

BBC (2022) *BBC Group Annual Report of Accounts 2021/22*, London: BBC.

BBC (2023) *BBC Group Annual Report of Accounts 2022/23*, London: BBC.

BBC (2024) *BBC Group Annual Report of Accounts 2023/24*, London: BBC.

Business of Apps (2025) *Disney Plus Statistics* Available at: **https://www.businessofapps.com/data/disney-plus-statistics/** [Accessed 20 June 2025]

European Broadcasting Union (2025) *Funding of Public Service Media*, Available at: **https://www.ebu.ch/publications/research/membersonly/report/funding-of-public-service-media** [Accessed 20 June 2025]

Henry Jenkins (2006) *Convergence Culture*, New York: NYU Press.

Marc Prensky (2001) 'Digital Natives, Digital Immigrants Part 1', *On the Horizon*, Vol. 9 No. 5.

Nic Newman, with Richard Flecther, Kirsten Eddy, Craig T Robertson, Craig T Robertson, and Rasmus Kleis Nielsen (2023) *Digital News Report 2023*, Oxford: Reuters Institute for the Study of Journalism.

Statistica (2023) 'Average number of video streaming subscriptions users are willing to pay for worldwide in 2023, by country', Statistica. Available at: **https://www.statista.com/statistics/785597/online-streaming-video-service-subscriptions-worldwide/** [Accessed 2 December 2023].

Daniel Thomas (2025) 'BBC unveils paid subscription plans for US users', *Financial Times*, 26 June. Yago Zayed (2025) *TV Licence Fee Statistics*, London: House of Commons Library.

About the contributor

Dr Daithí McMahon is a critically-acclaimed and multi-award-winning audio playwright, director, producer, and Associate Professor of Media and Culture at the University of Derby. His research interests lie across media theory and practice; media sociology; digital cultures; and the critical political economies of the media industries.

Chapter 23

Saving UK-produced high-end drama

Between October 2024 and April 2025 the Culture, Media and Sport Committee conducted an inquiry into British film and high-end drama. In January 2025 **Peter Kosminsky** submitted written evidence to the Committee. He argued that were he to try to make *The Mirror and the Light* today he would not succeed

The problem

The Mirror and the Light was offered to each streamer in turn. Despite the fact that its first series had won a Golden Globe, they all turned it down. It was only possible to begin production when the producer, the writer, the director, and the leading actor all gave up a significant proportion of their fees. We had shepherded the series through a ten-year development process but, in the end, it was necessary for us to work for very little to get the show made.

Mr Bates and the Post Office, which altered the national narrative on an important issue, similarly teetered on the brink of not making it to the screen.

PACT has identified 15 further TV dramas that have been green-lit by the UK public service broadcasters (PSBs) but are currently unable to proceed. This is because the financial contribution a PSB can offer, together with a sales advance and the UK tax break, are insufficient to make high-end TV drama in 2024/5 – in the inflated cost environment created here by the streamers.

What do all these programmes have in common? Their subject-matter is of particular interest, perhaps of particular cultural significance, to a UK audience. But they are not seen to have 'legs' – not likely to appeal, in particular, to an American audience.

The streamers

Though there are exceptions it is not currently part of the streamers' general financial model to co-produce with UK PSBs. They prefer to wholly own a project. The UK public service tradition involves purchasing the right to broadcast from an independent company, leaving that producer free to sell their programme to overseas territories and to participate in its eventual success. If an indie makes a high-end drama for a streamer it generally has to hand over the whole intellectual property (IP). They work for a fee, removing the possibility of sharing in the programme's profits, reducing its creators to the status of freelances – hired by the streamer in the same way a production might hire a sound recordist or an editor.

Oddly, this was the status of programme-makers when I joined the industry in the 1980s. We worked for a flat fee, no more. Then came Channel 4 and, with it, the indie revolution. This was the UK's gift to the wider industry, mimicked across much of the western world, but it is now being steadily undermined by the streamers, who seem to prefer to turn the clock back.

The streamers pay little tax and, unlike the UK PSBs, have no regulatory obligations. I'm not suggesting adding such obligations, which would be hard to police for multinational companies. The streamers aren't like the PSBs. They think only commercially and internationally and have made some stunning programmes. But they have little or no interest in making the minority of high-end dramas that are of specific interest to a UK audience. And we need to ensure that, in pursuing their entirely legitimate business model, they don't drive UK-skewed, public service drama out of existence.

The UK is not the 51st state. We have our own culture, and public service drama is a part of that heritage, as well as being an important manifestation of free speech. We can't afford to lose it. Luckily, there is a solution – one that is already in use in most of our neighbouring industries.

The solution

Five per cent of each streamer's UK subscription revenue would be earmarked for a cultural fund, to be used exclusively for high-end drama of specific interest to UK audiences but which doesn't necessarily have cross-border appeal.

Seventeen other countries in Europe already do this. Five more, including Ireland, are considering putting similar structures in place. Netflix fought this initiative in the courts, first in France and then in Germany. It lost in both jurisdictions. On one of his rare visits to London, I asked Reed Hastings, co-founder and executive chair of Netflix, if he would similarly seek to fight it in the UK courts. "Not if it was a level playing field across all the streamers," was his reply.

As I understand it, the current percentage holdback for programming of particular local relevance is: France – 5.15 per cent (of French streaming subscriptions); Denmark – 5 per cent; Netherlands – 5 per cent; Germany – 2.5 per cent; Romania – 4 per cent; Poland – 1.5 per cent; Italy – 20 per cent; Spain – 5 per cent; Portugal – 4 per cent; Croatia – 2 per cent; Belgium – 2 per cent; Greece – 1.5 per cent; Switzerland – 4 per cent; and Czech Republic – 3.5 per cent.

The streamers will say that such a hold-back would reduce UK inward investment, which is currently at a high level. Of course they would say that. But I would argue, as someone who has worked in UK high-end television for forty-five years, that it will not. The streamers come to the UK because of:

- our generous tax breaks

- the common use of the English language
- our creative talent base: the celebrated writers, actors, directors and producers who work here
- our crew skills in depth
- our excellent modern studios
- our good digital communications
- our world-renowned post-production crews and facilities
- our long experience of visual and special effects
- our similar cultural reference points
- our stable political and financial climate, and
- the benign, compared with the US, union environment in our industry.

It is my contention a five per cent hold-back on subscriptions wouldn't affect how many programmes the streamers made in the UK at all. If the government follows the rest of Europe and brings in such a system, the streamers must make this contribution whether they shoot or post-produce a single programme here or not. The decision to produce in the UK will be made, as it always has been, on hard-headed considerations: relative cost; available facilities; artistic preference of key talent; and the other factors listed above. The creation of a creative fund wouldn't increase a streamer's actual cost of production in the UK by one cent.

From the UK's own point of view, as the streamers' success with our audience grows, this independent creative fund will simultaneously grow. And with it, the number, always a minority, of programmes of special interest to our audience that we can make using it.

How would it work?

We would set up a slim, free-standing body, call it 'British TV' or 'BTV'. It would be entirely self-financing, drawing its capped running costs directly from the sums received from the streamers. It would be staffed by a small group of people with extensive, hands-on experience of UK high-end PSB drama production. Its editorial panel would be made up of experienced people who can command industry-wide respect. Its members would serve for a limited period (say five years) to avoid creating permanent barons with the power to say yay or nay to programming.

Only producers would be allowed to submit programmes to BTV for funding consideration. Broadcasters couldn't do it. Panel members would be able to recuse themselves if a particular project presented a conflict of interest.

Each programme submitted would need to have UK PSB funding already attached, together with a realistic advance from a sales company. The fund's finance officer would need to be convinced that BTV's contribution would fill the funding gap, allowing the programme to go ahead for production. And the programme would need to be of particular interest to a UK audience, the kind of series a streamer wouldn't make.

The contribution from BTV would be a grant, not a loan or an investment. This would have several advantages: (a) It would avoid unpicking the investment structure already in place, by not requiring a change in back-end recoupment; and (b) it would remove the profit incentive for BTV, the need to make its money back. This would allow the editorial panel to make its decision entirely on the grounds of the merit of the project.

So, the panel would be assessing the project's:

- importance to the UK audience (must be high)
- likelihood of attracting streamer finance (must be low or zero)
- artistic/cultural merit (must be high)
- regional element (must be significant), and
- their confidence that the programme would get made if BTV agreed the requested grant.

The streamers are perhaps the ultimate manifestation of a free market in television. They have made some extraordinary, mould-breaking programmes – turning high-end TV drama into the medium of choice for A-List talent, partially usurping the feature film and breaking the unhealthy, snobbish divide between theatrical and television filmmaking. But an unintended consequence of this explosion of creativity has been a market failure, a failure to fund the kind of drama, such as *Mr Bates* or *Wolf Hall*, that is of particular interest to a UK audience. Whilst these programmes will always be a minority of our output, they are also an essential part of it. And we are losing it. Blink and it will be gone – and our audiences will not thank us for it.

A British TV, with its self-financing cultural fund, would be brought into existence entirely to address this market failure. Its criterion wouldn't be profit, it would be excellence. And our culture would be the richer for it.

About the contributor

Peter Kosminsky is a writer and director of television drama, with approaching 45 years in the UK industry. He has worked for all the UK public service broadcasters, has served on both the Bafta and BFI boards, and is a Fellow of the Royal Television Society. In 2015 he made *Wolf Hall*, the BBC TV adaptation of Hilary Mantel's two Booker Prize winning novels. In 2024 he directed *The Mirror and the Light*, completing the adaptation of Mantel's trilogy.

Chapter 24

Wildlife and high-end drama: Endangered species?

Wildlife and drama programming are at the core of public service broadcasting. **Nick Manley** asks if they will atrophy if the BBC gets smaller

A colleague had an interview for a highly-paid production role at the BBC. Sitting in the White City canteen they watched a BBC staff member come back for a second and then third heavily-subsidised breakfast thinking 'that's not what I'm paying my licence fee for' and decided not to take the job. Although this behaviour isn't policy or even generally accepted, perhaps it displays an outdated sense of entitlement that just wouldn't happen in a modern independent production office.

Wildlife means money for the BBC

The Natural History Unit (NHU) in Bristol is a specialist department within BBC Studios Productions and is generally considered to be the largest producer of natural history content in the world. At its inception the NHU was seen as a department that offered distinctive programming unmatched anywhere in the world. BBC Studios was created by a merger of the BBC's distribution and commercial sectors, including BBC Worldwide, in April 2018. It is an autonomous commercial entity which generated an income of £1,837m in the year 2023/24, according to the National Audit Office (NAO). From inception in 2018 to 2023/24 BBC Studios provided £1,906m in financial returns to the BBC through dividend payments and contributions made as part of its work as the BBC's main production and distribution partner.

The NHU makes money for the public service BBC network. It does so through co-productions with international partners including major streaming services. According to Tom Fussell, CEO BBC Studios, as of 2023 over 75 per cent of revenue came from sales to third parties such as Discovery, Netflix, and Apple TV. The BBC is aware it is behind the digital competition – as the NAO also concluded: 'the BBC has not been able to develop its product portfolio with the same pace and sophistication as that of rival media organisations' (NAO, 2024).

I worked as a freelancer and staff member for the BBC for over 30 years on a huge range of factual and drama programming. I spent many years on BBC science shows. Some old friends moved on to the NHU. I asked ex-colleagues how would the NHU survive. The clear response was 'very easily'. However, that will not come without a sea change in the editorial experience. With NHU production running at £3m and over per episode BBC Studios is keen to promote only projects that are seen as globally marketable. The NHU works on a loose model of one major series and three minor projects at an annual pitch to the head of sales and commissioning at the BBC. The current internal commissioning model allows continuity-potential as 2026 project proposals can be greenlit for production in 2028/29. The problem in this model is that short-term contracts are being offered to creative editorial staff with many directors and development producers on monthly or annual contracts rather than on a permanent staffing basis.

Wildlife without the licence fee?

The worry is that such contracts leave the door open for drastic staffing cuts should the 2028 licence fee settlement mean a radical rethink of budgets and project planning. The streaming service model requires viewing completion, that is, producing a series that will hold viewers across an entire season of episodes. The streaming model wants a viewer to watch all episodes: the series must have a link, an emerging theme, that will draw the viewer into repeat consumption of the product. A broad encyclopaedic description of the varied species of the Galapagos would be informative and educational but would not retain audience figures. The assumption is that potential viewers may be selective about which episodes they watch or just lose interest in a repetitive format. The immediacy of mass information and images via the internet has prompted programme-makers to look to how they entertain and retain audiences.

To achieve this, the streaming networks buy into series that have a narrative hook to get and hold viewing figures. Natural History struggles with this as it has always adhered to the Reithian model to inform and educate. When Disney/Pixar partnered with the NHU in 2009 there were staff sessions on narrative structure to promote the idea of entertainment in story construction. Shooting schedules included material to construct narratives. A scene such as the beautifully-edited baby iguana vs snakes in *Planet Earth 2* used reaction shots and cutaways in the narrative style of a Hollywood blockbuster. It is an incredible watch but works to very different genre conventions than the traditionally revealing, but more informational, wildlife approach.

The streaming model needs action, it needs narrative, it needs broad appeal through entertainment. What this will mean is that the funding will come with conditions that are currently not in initial editorial and commissioning meetings. The money will still come, there will be millions to support the output, but the sales suits will be in that meeting from the start.

For BBC staff that means a far more unstable career and a creative editorial process that must now include second-guessing the business model with sales targets and short-term deadlines. This is detrimental to creativity and bold decision-making. A staff employee who has the potential for a long career in the department will feel confident to promote new and diverse content. The employee on a six-month contract will worry about rocking the boat and be constrained by looking to secure re-employment.

Bake Off takes off

Historically the BBC has a global reputation for truthful representation of fact. In August 2023 the Reuters Institute described it as 'one of the most highly trusted sources of news'. The BBC itself claims a global reach of 400 million people. The sixth Ofcom Annual report on the BBC 2022/23 reported a 69 per cent positive audience view when they were asked to comment on the BBC's ability to help people understand what is going on in the world. The BBC should be looking to preserve the emerging talent that created small show formats like the original BBC2 *Great British Bake Off*. At its beginning, it ranked seventh on the BBC2 weekly viewing figures, twelfth on nightly ranking, and had an audience of 2.24m. Thirteen years later the show's producer, Love Productions, reported a turnover of £85m from the show while the BBC gained 35 international territory sales in 2021. Then Love fell out of love with the BBC's financial plans and took the show to Channel 4. BBC guidelines on how much of the licence fee it will pay had increased to £500,000 an hour, totalling £15m. That was £10m short of the Channel 4 offer of £75m over three years. BBC Arts Correspondent David Silletto commented: 'It's no wonder that a rival broadcaster swooped [...] it has something very few programmes an offer, five million viewers under the age of 34 [...] That demographic is marketing catnip.' (Perhaps the corporation's single biggest mistake came in 2007 when it gave away the iPlayer for free. Asking viewers to pay 48p a day for the iPlayer, offering global content on demand, seems far more palatable than £174.50 as an annual charge.)

Across the television industry there is a sense that editorial creativity generally feels hollowed out by purely profit-driven production. In November 2024 Steven D Wright asked, 'Are we watching the death of British television? With no one daring to risk new formats and 68 per cent of freelancers out of work, our world leading industry is in terminal decline'. To support this assertion he characterised the BBC's decision to spend £9m on a Danish dating show *Stranded On Honeymoon Island* in 2025 as a 'slap in the face for homegrown creatives'.

What has begun to emerge are leading independent producers of wildlife and natural history content. In 2012, after thirty years at the NHU, including five years as head, Alastair Fothergill left to set up Silverback Films with Keith Scholey. In April 2017 he reminisced about pitching the *Our Planet* series: 'That would have been hard to manage with the BBC'. He diplomatically said the Netflix budget compared 'very well' with the BBC offer. The BBC has a range of indicative prices for the supply of commissioned programming. The tariff for a BBC high-end factual is between £225 and 350,000. Fothergill did not disclose the value of the Netflix funding but if the entire budget for the BBC's most expensive documentary series ever, *Planet Earth*, was £16m, it's no idle speculation that *Our Planet*'s was greater by far. That could also be why Left Bank Pictures moved to Netflix. According to their own company financial statement season one of *The Crown* cost £11.6m an episode. That figure rose to £40m, as a running total, as it released the fifth series on Netflix in 2023 (Reid, 2023).

Turning a crisis into a continuing drama?

So where does television drama sit in a post or reduced licence fee model? In conversation with Selwyn College Cambridge master Roger Mosey on 6 February 2025 BBC Director-General, Tim Davie, asserted, "*Wolf Hall* wouldn't happen without the BBC". Wolf Hall's creator and director, Peter Kominsky, appeared on *Newsnight* on 21 March 2025 stating the opposite, claiming the 2024 second series, *The Mirror and the Light*, was nearly cancelled due to BBC budget pressures. (See chapter 23 of this book for Peter Kosminsky's account of the series' fraught history.)

In March 2025 Katie Razzall, BBC culture and media editor, and Tom Brooks-Pollock, *Newsnight* editor, quoted Jack Thorne, writer of *Adolescence*, and television adapter of *His Dark Materials, Skins,* and *National Treasure*, saying he thought traditional broadcasters like the BBC could have made the drama but they would have had to cut some of the most expensive scenes: "I could have done it, it just would have been very different. And truthfully, it probably would have needed co-finance from abroad." Could the BBC have produced other top dramas such as *Mr Bates vs The Post Office?* Patrick Spence, the executive producer of the show, told the BBC: "Not only would *Mr Bates* not get funding today, but I wouldn't have even started developing it".

In his January 2025 Crick Institute Lecture the BBC's previous Director General, Tony Hall, argued that, 'We first need to decide want we want a BBC to do – for all of us – for our country – for the world'. Yet who are the 'we' he refers to? What do people want from the BBC for the £3.74bn it received in licence fee revenue in 2022/2023? The viewing figures point to high-end outputs and news, not so much for regional content or solely UK-relevant issues. The much-quoted figure of 67 per cent of UK viewers looking to the BBC for factual output also shows 70 per cent of those choose to access the BBC online and to seek international issues.

Is the future independent?

Companies such as Bad Wolf Productions (*Wolf Hall, His Dark Materials, Red Eye*) which have high-end £1m to £2m an hour budgets will always have the option of co-funding as they have big name casts attached – actors such as Mark Rylance, James McAvoy, or Ruth Wilson – alongside a track record of international sales. Between 2015 and 2020 Bad Wolf spent £259m on seven seasons of television: *A Discovery of Witches* seasons 1, 2 and 3, *His Dark Materials* seasons 1 and 2, *Industry*, and *I Hate Suzie*.

But mid-range independent producers would be struggling to find collaborators. Very successful BBC returning series like *Death in Paradise* (Red Planet Pictures) work on a budget of about £900,000 an episode where around £400,000 comes from BBC Studios, Britbox, and the BBC. In addition €500,000 (£431,000) comes from Guadeloupe where the series is filmed. Red Planet also get a 30 per cent tax rebate from the French Government under their Tax Rebate for International Productions (TRIP) guidelines for shooting in France or a French territory.

Co-funding is a starting point before beginning commissioning talks with the BBC. Less well-funded series such as the UK-based spin-off *Beyond Paradise*, made for £400,000 an episode, may suffer. A series like that is also looking to find funding from the BBC, BBC Studios, and BritBox. The sales gap becomes a chasm for a mid-range series when looking for international sales when what sells is star names, and period, costume, and heritage drama. Hence *The Crown* had Netflix invest an estimated $130m (£97.65m) for the first two seasons (Seale 2019). That's around £12m an episode. What does that mean for the UK viewer? This comes back to the issue of BBC core values: does the BBC want to inform and educate? By educate does that mean it is prepared to encourage UK-based talent, jobs, and craft by subsidising UK-based and UK-focused programming? The potential financial alternative would be akin to the Channel Five drama model which works on a £275,000 per hour budget. At that funding level they cannot afford UK production wages and costs so they go abroad to find cheaper personnel and locations. The *BBC Commissioning Supply Report 2023/24* showed 39 per cent of productions were made by qualifying indies but only £1m of that is ring-fenced for small independent production companies.

International sales to 230 territories mean that it's very likely BBC Studios, as an independent funding source, would step in to fill any funding gap left by a BBC without the licence fee. Independent production companies likely to survive without a BBC licence-based commission could be the likes of The Forge who made *National Treasure*, *Roadkill*, *Help*, and *Becoming Elizabeth*; Sister Pictures and Noisy Bear who produced *Black Doves* (2024); Quay Street Productions who produced *After the Flood*, *Nolly*, and *Lazarus*; and World Productions, producers of *Line of Duty* and *Vigil*. But for the BBC to survive it may need to take a good hard look at how successful UK independents run their businesses and forgo the nostalgia of the licence fee model.

References

BBC (2024) *BBC Commissioning Supply Report 2023/24*, BBC: London.

BBC (2023) *BBC tariff range of indicative prices for the supply of commissioned television programmes*, BBC: London.

BBC (2023) 'BBC Studios hits £2 billion in sales', BBC Media Centre, 11 July.

Tim Davie (2025) *The BBC: Its future and how we fund it*, Selwyn College: Cambridge.

Tony Hall (2025) *The Crick Institute Lecture*, Voice of the Listener and View: Northfleet.

National Audit Office (2024) *BBC Departmental overview 2022-23*, NAO: London.

Rasmus Kleis Nielsen, Ann Schultz, Richard Flecther, and Craig T Robertson (2020, 2023) 'The BBC is under scrutiny. Here's what research tells us about its role in the UK', Reuters Institute: Oxford.

Ofcom (2023) *Ofcom's annual report on the BBC*, Ofcom: London.

Katie Razzall and Tom Brooks-Pollock (2025) 'UK TV industry in crisis, says Wolf Hall director', BBC: London.

Caroline Reid (2023) 'Sony spends a record $140 million on The Crown' *Forbes*, 28 January.

Saffery Champness/Nordicity (2021) *The economic impact of Bad Wolf: The first five years 2015-2020*, London.

Jack Seale (2019) 'From The Crown to Game of Thrones: what's the most expensive TV show ever?, *The Guardian*, 16 November.

Pippa Shawley (2017) 'Alastair Fothergill: How can you possibly care about the natural world if you've never seen it?', *Television*, 6 April.

David Silletto (2016) 'Why did The Great British Bake Off move to Channel 4?' BBC Media Centre: London.

Steven D Wright (2024) 'Are we watching the end of British television?' *The Times*, 27 November.

About the contributor

Nick Manley teaches at Falmouth University where he is practice lead for their postgraduate programme in film and television. Since the mid-1980s he worked in factual and drama production worldwide both as a freelance cameraman and BBC staff series director. Credited as director of photography he currently has over 40 hours of drama work on BBC iPlayer, BritBox, Netflix, and Prime TV.

Chapter 25

Not just a swap: Why subscriptions won't save the BBC (unless we do it differently)

Subscription is a much favoured successor to the licence fee. **Janine Chandler** tells the Corporation why this isn't a magic bullet

The subscription economy is booming. From TV to toilet rolls, the chances are your audiences are already subscribed to more things than they realise. But for you, it's not as simple as swapping the licence fee for a Netflix-style model. That idea might sound seductive but it doesn't stack up. Because this isn't just about payment — it's about purpose, trust, community, and value.

A short history of long-term commitment

Subscriptions aren't new. In seventeenth-century Britain authors like John Milton relied on subscribers to publish books like *Paradise Lost*. But subscriptions really took off with the arrival of cable TV in the mid-twentieth century and digital services in the 2000s.

Netflix started out in 1999, mailing DVDs to subscribers. By the early 2000s it pivoted to streaming, ditching late fees and queues at Blockbusters. It wasn't just the tech — it was the promise of convenience, freedom, and a bottomless pit of choice. Now over 17 million homes have Netflix in the UK; that's nearly 60 per cent of dwellings.

Sky took over British living rooms in the 1990s and is now in 12 million homes. Then Amazon Prime bundled entertainment with next-day delivery (13 million homes). Disney+ (7 million), Apple TV+ (2.5 million), and others piled in, offering exclusive worlds to loyal subscribers. This wasn't just a shift in format. It was a shift in power — from broadcasters to users, from schedules to on-demand, from mass to personalised.

The numbers are big — and getting bigger

The global subscription economy is expected to hit nearly $1 trillion by 2028 (Juniper Research, 2024). Some forecasts say $2.1tn by 2034 (Market.us, 2025). That's not just media — that's meal kits, razors, supplements, software, cars, clothes.

In the UK 81 per cent of households have at least one subscription box (Whistl, 2025). The average household monthly spend? £52 (Whistl, 2022). Even toilet tissue has a subscription market. Which only goes to show that if it's regular and predictable you can build a business around it.

But here's the rub: media subscriptions are among the most vulnerable to churn. When times get tight Netflix and Spotify are the first to go. Attrition rates of 5 to 10 per cent a month are common. So, for you, switching to subscriptions is not just about the revenue model. It's about understanding what makes people stay.

People stay for belonging, not just content

Great shows are vital but they're not the whole story. It's how they make audiences feel. People stay when they feel part of something. When they feel seen. When their values align with yours. When there's a sense of tribe. Look at the best brands in the subscription world: they don't just deliver a product. They deliver identity, surprise, delight, novelty.

The best brands don't just deliver content — they deliver identity. Think of a Patagonia newsletter. Or a Headspace reminder. Or Disney's themed watch parties. Or a Peloton leaderboard. They build community through shared values.

So what could BBC subscriptions actually offer?

If you're going to do this, you can't just copy-paste Netflix. You have to build something only you could build.

- Freemium access: the basics are free, funded by ads or public support. But subscribers get more.
- Tiered memberships: unlock archives, documentaries, behind-the-scenes content, early access, exclusive audio. Maybe even physical perks: books, events, merch.
- Community creation: clubs for drama lovers, history nerds, podcast fans. Think virtual salons. Live Q&As. Not just content delivery — conversation.
- Surprise and delight: special drops. Personal thank yous. Curated playlists. A gift in the post.
- Total flexibility: pause, cancel, upgrade at any time. Respect your users.

And crucially: lean into what only you have.

The BBC brand has what others don't

Credibility. Curiosity. Creativity. Cultural reach. Values.

People trust you more than any other media brand in the UK. Globally the BBC is a trusted brand. That trust is priceless. In a world of deepfakes, misinformation, and algorithms, this is the BBC's unique selling point.

But trust alone isn't enough. You need relevance. People won't pay for what they used to get for free, unless it feels new, better, and worth it. And that means offering something no one else can:

- Impartial news in an age of spin
- Curated content when the algorithm overwhelms
- Shared experiences in a fragmented world

This is where subscriptions can help. But only if they're designed to build loyalty, not just extract money.

Lessons from the big players

Netflix spends billions on original content. Amazon bundles everything to justify the price. Sky mixes satellite with on-demand. Disney has fandom on its side. Apple is playing the long game with elegance and exclusives.

Each has a hook. Each has churn. And all fight to stay on your card statement every month.

The BBC can't win on volume. You must compete — and win — on values.

A dangerous myth: that subscriptions replace the licence fee

Some say you should ditch the licence fee entirely and let the market decide. Put BBC content behind a paywall. But that means only those who can afford it get access. That's not public service. That's premium service.

If you are to stand for something — a shared cultural space, a trusted voice, a universal storyteller — it needs to remain accessible. Subscriptions should be an *extra* income stream, not a replacement, not exclusive.

Think *The Guardian*. Wikipedia. Headspace. Patreon. Voluntary contributions that feel personal and purposeful. That's the opportunity.

Don't forget you're a global brand

The BBC World service reaches 300 million people. In countries where media freedom is fragile you're a trusted lifeline. A global subscription model could serve diaspora communities, English language learners, and podcast fans worldwide.

This is a chance to connect the world — not just change it.

What's at stake

The BBC is at a crossroads. The subscription economy is here to stay. But success won't come from copying others. It'll come from doing what the BBC has always done best: innovating, informing, including.

So, let's stop talking about just 'swapping the licence fee'. Let's talk about *building belonging*. Let's ask: how do we create something people want to be part of? Because in the end, people don't subscribe to services. They subscribe to stories. To values. To each other. And that's where the BBC still has magic.

References

Juniper Research (2024) 'Subscription Economy to Be Worth Almost $1 Trillion Globally by 2028; Facilitated by Proliferation of Subscriptions into New Industries', Basingstoke, April.

Market.us (2025) 'Subscription Economy Market', New York, March.

Whistl (2025) '81% of UK Households Now Use Subscription Services', Marlow, February.

Whistl (2022) 'The Rise of the Subscription Model', Marlow, February.

SECTION THREE: THE BBC'S FUTURE?

Introduction

Andrew Beck

BBC crises might be like buses but in 2025 the Corporation was superserved by them in ways that public transport hasn't run since the 1960s. While some problems were simply a sign of changing times – audiences, finances, technology – many of the BBC's troubles were of the Corporation's making, due to its being unprepared for or ignoring crises.

In February 2025 the BBC had reason to feel good about itself: Enders Analysis reported a 3 per cent increase in 2024 total viewing hours, while ITV had fallen by 5 per cent, and Sky by 6 per cent. Where Disney+ viewing hours dropped, BBC iPlayer increased by 24 per cent. Despite ongoing rumblings in the wake of the Huw Edwards scandal, as well as public accusations about the behaviour of *MasterChef* co-host Gregg Wallace, many Corporation senior managers were focused on stemming the loss of young viewers as well as increasing return traffic to iPlayer.

But scandals wouldn't go away. That same month the BBC board of directors apologised after a review found they didn't take adequate action over concerns about DJ Tim Westwood's behaviour, who had displayed conduct 'entirely incompatible with BBC values'. In March the BBC made settlements to four female news presenters to avoid an employment tribunal: when the BBC News and World News channels were merged Martine Croxall, Karin Giannone, Annita McVeigh, and Kasia Madera lost out on jobs due to a rigged recruitment and selection process.

On 24 April BBC Two broadcast a longform interview of Gary Lineker by Amol Rajan. Lineker didn't hold back. A BBC insider thought it 'baffling' the organisation gave him a 'prime-time platform to embarrass the BBC'. Addressing the decision to pull *Gaza: How to Survive a War Zone* he felt the BBC 'just capitulated to lobbying that they get a lot'. A BBC insider stated there was 'anger that the BBC's highest-paid star has effectively said the chairman of the BBC is a stooge for Israeli lobbyists.' By 16 May pressure had grown to remove Lineker from the BBC team covering the 2026 World Cup when he reposted a Palestine Lobby post featuring an antisemitic rat trope on his Instagram account. By 19 May he was off World Cup coverage, his *The Rest Is Football* podcast had been dropped by the BBC, and he'd left the BBC altogether.

Internal crises over the Corporation's Gaza coverage continued. On 20 June the BBC announced that it would not screen *Gaza: Doctors Under Attack*, on hold since spring 2025. A BBC statement explained: 'We have come to the conclusion that broadcasting this material risked creating a perception of partiality that would not meet the high standards that the public rightly expect of the BBC.' The same day news broke that the editor of BBC1's *Breakfast* programme had gone on extended leave pending investigation of bullying charges.

Come late June the BBC concentrated much of its efforts on coverage of the 2025 Glastonbury festival. Worried that it could lose broadcast rights to US streaming giants, and with YouTube expressing serious interest in outbidding them, the BBC had increased payment for exclusive broadcasting rights. Having decided that Kneecap's set would not be broadcast live, and despite a 400-strong BBC staff and freelancer presence on site, no action was taken to prevent Bob Vylan's set being seen by a live TV audience. (See chapter 10 for more about this.) Characterised by one BBC insider as a 'shocking editorial failure', another pointed to the inconsistency in management decisions: "Tim Davie axed Gary Lineker for accidentally sharing an antisemitic tweet. What's the penalty for live-streaming an antisemitic rant to the whole nation?"

Meanwhile the *MasterChef* crisis continued: Wallace was sacked; the BBC's chair and Director-General faced a parliamentary select committee grilling about the Corporation's prior knowledge of *MasterChef* misconduct allegations; Lewis Silkin's report into the allegations upheld 45 complaints; the BBC announced that Wallace would never work for them again in any capacity; and Wallace's co-presenter, John Torode, was also sacked from the programme. BBC bosses had to address several questions: to show or not show the already recorded *MasterChef* series? to edit out or not edit out Wallace and Torode? to cause distress to the programme's amateur cooks by not showing it? The latter issue was further complicated by contestant Sarah Shafi saying the whole show felt like 'a boys' game' and should be axed in its entirety. While her contribution was completely edited out, the broadcast union Bectu still felt that inappropriate behaviour 'should not be rewarded with prime-time coverage'.

The end of July brought more troubles: news that free TV licences for the over-75s receiving Pension Credit cost the BBC £185m in lost income; a number of Ofcom reports one of which showed that YouTube was now the UK's second most-viewed platform after the BBC; Lineker revealing he was sacked from the BBC; and Radio 2 losing one million listeners, down to its lowest since 2003. August started with revelations about cocaine use on the set of *Strictly Come Dancing*; *Repair Shop's* former star Jay Blades being charged with two counts of rape; and, even though it was subjected to savage editing, the 6 August broadcast of the new *MasterChef* series left audiences feeling somehow complicit in the hosts' bad behaviour

All of this paints a picture of an organisation that lacked editorial oversight, looked incapable of crisis scenario planning and handling, was losing audiences and income, yet whose role as a reliable source of objectively reported news was more important than ever. This final section of the book looks at the BBC and how it might gear itself up for a long-term future, how it might address dwindling or lost audiences, how it might secure steady future funding, and what all of this means for public service media in the UK.

In the midst of any number of crises in May 2025 Director-General Tim Davie went to Salford's Media City to deliver a state of the nation speech about his aspirations for the BBC. We start this section with an edit of that speech 'The BBC: A catalyst for building trust'. Whatever Davie's ambitions for it, the speech attracted little media attention, making only seven brief paragraphs on page 15 of *The i Paper*. In 'A 5,000-word resignation letter' I work through Davie's objectives, assessing their practicality in terms of finance, organisational structure, staffing levels, and management expertise. His job security might simply be the sheer undesirability of it. As *Private Eye* has consistently argued in its *Media News* column, 'no one else in their right mind would want the job.'

One of Davie's ambitions for the BBC is to do better with local news. In 'Is Director-General Tim Davie series about local news?' Dr Liam McCarthy lauds Davie's ambitions but cannot see how they can be realised whilever the Corporation 'remains a top-down, London-centric organisation with the power residing within the M25. If Tim Davie is serious about his ambition to address failing local journalism ecologies he needs to rebuild the BBC – around a Local Digital First strategy.'

Lost young viewers and listeners are, and should be, a key concern for BBC management. In 'Threading the BBC into the lives of the next generation' and 'A BBC for the YouTube generation' Dr Martin Moore and Tara Conlan, respectively, address this issue. Moore proposes the BBC faces a 'fundamental challenge: how to make itself integral to the lives of the digitally native', concluding 'we cannot afford to let young people's relationship with the BBC fade away.' Taking a long, hard look at young people's viewing habits Conlan asserts 'Verified journalism is vital in a world of AI slop and bots'. The BBC must respond to the way young people consume media. It is more than fifty years since Stuart Hall first proposed a fundamental shift in the way people use media, from the adoring audience to the active audience. Today's digital natives are that audience writ large: 'Participation and flexibility are important for youngsters used to taking part in and uploading content on social media.'

While this book has featured contributions with criticisms, serious criticisms, of the BBC it has consistently included advice about how it might better address issues of lost audiences, lost finance, and new technology. In 'This is bigger than the internet: Why public service AI is the next great leap' communications, digital, and AI expert Peter Heneghan urges the BBC not to shy away from generative AI but rather to embrace it. AI, he asserts, 'isn't just a technological upgrade. It's a once-in-a-lifetime cultural and societal force. The

BBC must not follow Silicon Valley, It should lead by forging a new path for public-service AI, rooted in trust, inclusion, and purpose.'

That said, we should never lose sight of the scale of the challenges facing the BBC. In July 2025 Ofcom published *PSBs in the platform era: A YouTube case study Annex 1: Review of Public Service Media*. In our edited highlights of that report Ofcom paints a fascinating picture demonstrating that UK major public service broadcasters — BBC News, ITV News, Channel 4 News, 5 News, and STV News — have not been technological luddites but rather have been active on YouTube for at least ten years.

All good and well, but as most of the contributors to Section Two of this book argued, sometimes from an ideological perspective but often from a realistic one, it is difficult to conceive of the BBC licence fee surviving for much longer in its current shape. In 'After the licence fee: Rethinking the future of public service media' Deborah Wilson David considers three alternative funding mechanisms: subscription hybrid, user-directed voucher, and civic infrastructure. But her chapter does not limit itself to the Corporation's finances; it is as much about what a future BBC would look like. She argues it is losing trust, 'among younger audiences, marginalised communities, and creative sectors who see it as increasingly out of touch'. It needs to shake off an internal culture that 'often prioritises continuity over experimentation' as well as ditching an executive leadership that 'remains disproportionately drawn from narrow professional backgrounds.' If anyone for one moment doubted what's at stake in the UK, veteran investigative reporter David Cay Johnston portrays the horror show unfolding in the US, what he sees as nothing more than the evisceration of public service broadcasting. We have been warned.

If the existential dangers currently facing the BBC were not already crystal-clear Janine Chandler writes it a love letter – of sorts. Arguing that it must change or fade away she passionately argues that, while the media world around it has radically changed, the BBC is 'still clinging to a map that no longer matches the terrain'. To regain its relevance it needs 'to stop obsessing over protecting what it was, and start building what it could be.'

We close this section with edited highlights from another July 2025 Ofcom report – *Transmission Critical: The future of Public Service Media*. It does not make for easy or comforting reading for all UK public service broadcasters. Ofcom argue there is 'no silver bullet that will address the challenges that the sector is facing' and present a set of recommendations for how those challenges might be addressed. But it will take concerted efforts from all concerned parties: the broadcasters, social media, video sharing platforms, government, and Ofcom itself. The stakes are high; nothing is guaranteed. Read on.

Chapter 26

The BBC: A catalyst for building trust

In May 2025 BBC Director-General **Tim Davie** addressed what he saw as the key issues facing the Corporation. This is an edited version of that speech

Today I want to speak about one thing: trust. Trust in each other, trust in our institutions, trust in information, and trust in the UK. The glue that holds us together. The essential ingredient of a secure, cohesive society. The enabler of a creative and competitive UK.

I want to go further. I want to talk about how the BBC, the world's leading Public Service media organisation, of which I am so proud, can become even more precious and valuable. An institution that builds social capital and stimulates growth in the online, AI age.

Why the BBC?

Disinformation is thriving. And free reporting and impartial content has never been under greater pressure. The World Economic Forum has singled out disinformation as the biggest short-term risk we face globally. The Royal United Services Institute, the security think tank, points to malign information, often supported, heavily by the way, by state actors, as a direct threat to our security and cohesion.

The World Values Survey revealed less than half of UK respondents now say that most people can be trusted. The latest British Social Attitudes report showed a record 45 per cent of adults say they 'almost never' trust governments of any party to place the needs of the nation above political interests.

At the start of May the BBC carried out research on how people feel about divisions in UK society and the state of public debate. Three-quarters of people now say that UK society feels divided, and six in ten say they feel exhausted by these divisions. Less than half of us say we can share our views without fear.

This erosion of deeper connections, the decline in a sense of 'we' versus 'I', has been a consequence of an online world where social media companies proliferate and, in my mind, was accelerated during Covid.

Not the only way

Here are five urgent, bold choices I believe we can take to directly build trust.

All of them not only support our central task of creating outstanding homegrown content and services but also support the wider challenge of building trust.

These are: the choice for the UK to be a global leader in trusted information; the choice to help support our democracy from the roots up; the choice to deploy cutting-edge technology and AI to help, not harm, our children and their futures; the choice to maximise growth in our economy by investing in every part of the UK; and the choice to ensure everyone benefits from digital transition.

Trust in the BBC

Critically, by focusing on impartiality and transparency, trust in the BBC went up in 2024. Over 80 per cent of UK adults still use us every week and 94 per cent monthly. Amazing numbers in an online age. Three-quarters of UK adults use BBC News weekly, and we're the only UK media brand in the top five most used for young people. We're the world's most trusted global news provider with an audience of 450 million weekly.

We're seeing record growth online driven by rapid innovation, with iPlayer the UK's fastest-growing Video on Demand (VOD) platform in 2024 ahead of all global competitors.

We continue to be the largest investor in UK-made programming. The BBC contributes £5bn to the economy every year – for every £1 of direct economic impact, we generate £2.63 with 50 per cent of our economic impact now outside London, compared to the industry average of 20 per cent.

Noise and the world

We want to help turn the tide by dramatically increasing our news presence on platforms like YouTube and TikTok to ensure we have a stronger position amidst the noise. We are already making progress. We are the biggest news account globally on Instagram, but we want to deploy new technology and skills to create more content that works on these platforms while incentivising links to our services.

We have a plan to meet the need – the appetite – for impartial news across the globe by supercharging the World Service. Imagine the BBC reaching a billion people weekly – over double where we are today. This involves action such as regionalising our content in key English-speaking markets and boosting our offer in the four big languages. With proper government funding, we believe we can drive significant benefits to the UK.

And we need to build Verify across more services globally. Also, we want to empower audiences as they seek answers – combining agentic AI with trusted BBC journalism to create a new gold standard fact-checking tool. Our aim is to work globally with other public service broadcasters to ensure a healthy core of fact-based news.

The BBC and democracy

Second, help to support our democracy from the roots up. Trusted local news is at the heart of the challenge to foster social capital. The BBC helped bolster local news through our Local Democracy Reporting Service (LDRS). As a next step, we want to expand the LDRS from its current focus on local authority reporting to include health authorities, police and crime commissioners, and deep analysis of the work of regional mayors. All available to partners.

But we can be more radical in supporting others. Can we 'open source' all our local video, news, and audio content to enable local media partners to access it too? Can we use the scale and reach of the BBC's platforms to provide more prominent linking to commercial providers? Of course, we'll consult with partners before we confirm plans but we need a plural local news market.

Simultaneously, we want to strengthen the depth of BBC local journalism. Our ambition is to establish specialist 'BBC Insight' teams in all our bases supporting greater investigative reporting, and expanding local BBC Verify and InDepth analysis alongside forensic data journalism.

AI for all of us

Our third choice is to deploy cutting-edge technology and AI to help, not harm, our kids and their futures. We want to transform and grow our education offer. Today Bitesize is the UK's leading revision service, helping millions of children. But AI offers us the chance to do wonderful things in this area.

We're looking at whether we can put the power and reach of BBC Bitesize together with the power of agentic AI creating a personal learning companion for every single child aged 7-16. Evolving for those at different levels of attainment and with different needs. With the BBC's commitment to safety and quality so users can fully trust it.

We want to offer a new BBC family account for every parent of a young child, evolving at key milestones from birth to leaving school, laying the foundations for a lifetime of BBC support.

The UNITED Kingdom

Fourthly, we want to maximise growth in our economy by investing in every part of the UK.

Salford has the potential to be more than a national success – it can be a truly global media and sports hub generating thousands of jobs, and we want to work with others to contribute to that.

We plan to open the doors of our studios for social media creators to be able to generate new work and know that we have their interests at heart. We want to provide every creator with more support, access, and opportunities – from skills training to tools, equipment, and facilities.

Digital for all

Finally, a choice to deliver a digital transition for all.

Over 100 years ago John Reith and the pioneers of radio recognised the power of the new medium, and, wonderfully, amazingly, they harnessed it – in the public interest. They established fundamental principles: everyone should benefit, information should be trustworthy, and programmes should not just amuse people but also enrich their lives.

So five big choices, all directly building trust not only in the BBC but each other.

Entertaining, informing, educating. Bringing us together.

This will all be done in support of our public service mission – never relinquishing editorial oversight. We are looking at new, major partnerships with the world leading big-tech companies, the hyperscalers. As part of this, we are already working on the media supply chain, the processes behind the scenes that gets content from the camera to screen, from microphone to headphone. This will open up huge creative possibilities.

And it will allow us to drive efficiencies and reinvest into world-class content. The UK can lead the market in developing a new wave of smarter platforms, like iPlayer, with improved functionality.

I am interested in the opportunity to create significant value for the public in our ownership of proprietary technology in the media sector.

How to finance it

When it comes to funding we are not asking for the status quo. We want modernisation and reform. But in doing so we must safeguard universality. All the funding models that have been floated in the debate have their merits and drawbacks. But some such as advertising or subscription don't pass the test of building a universal trusted public service.

Beyond that, we keep an open mind. And we continue to actively explore all options that can make our funding model fairer, more modern, and more sustainable.

Will we, us, all of us, watch on as trust dissipates, or will we actively build it? Not just give up and watch it drift but do something. We are not simply victims of the market, I don't buy that, we can lead. The BBC is ready to play its full part—not simply defending tradition, but shaping the future.

But we need help – a shared national vision that builds on the best of us.

With courage, collaboration, investment and imagination, we can create a UK that is more inclusive, more secure, and more successful.

Let us make the choice – together – to leave a legacy of trust.

About the contributor

Tim Davie is BBC Director-General. This is an edited version of a speech delivered by him at the Lowry Theatre, Salford on 14 May 2025.

Note

Tim Davie delivered his vision for the BBC to an invited audience. His carefully crafted speech was nearly 5,000 words long – too long for this book of short chapters. (You can read the full text at: **https://www.bbc.co.uk/mediacentre/speeches/2025/tim-davie-director-general-bbc-catalyst-for-trust/**)

The speech was not widely taken up by the UK national press. It was trumped by Gary Lineker's 'rat' Instagram post that hastened his BBC departure. As is our standard practice with contributions to this and other books we styled and subbed the speech down to 1,603 words. Adhering to the principle of fair dealing we sent the edited version to the Director-General who passed it to his Corporate Affairs team. They thought we should run the speech in full or not at all. We have decided to offer this shortened version.

Chapter 27

A 5,000-word resignation letter

Andrew Beck reads Tim Davie's speech and concludes he's looking for a dignified way out of his job

Every single aspiration expressed in Tim Davie's 14 May 2025 address to BBC staff was eminently laudable, a positive vision for the Corporation as a vital and vibrant, responsive and responsible, twenty-first-century public broadcaster. Only a committed, against all the evidence, shrunken state ideologue or a head-in-the-sand free marketeer could find fault with its ambitions. The real issue with it is that it would take a time machine, an unfeasibly large amount of funding, the repeal of the 1990 Broadcasting Act, and a return to pre-1982 staffing levels to realise it.

Let's look at the five objectives he outlined for the BBC, using costings derived either from the BBC itself or from similar initiatives with other global broadcasters.

Becoming a global leader in trusted information

Davie's goal here is to extend the reach of the World Service from its current 450 million audience to 1 billion, to fully regionalise English content, investing in four world languages (presumably Chinese, English, Hindi, and Spanish; he didn't specify), extending Verify on a global scale, and investing heavily in AI-powered fact-checking tools. The World Service expansion would cost between £250m and £400m, and would require the guaranteed maintenance of government financial support. It would cost between £50m and £100m simply to create a Global Verify and AI tools, and then between £20m and £30m to maintain those services. It would require between £50m and £80m a year to regionalise content.

The common theme, the glue that holds together all of Davie's objectives, is trust. While that is a noble ambition what the BBC has to do is acknowledge how much trust has been lost after the triple whammy of *Gaza: How to Survive a Warzone*, Wallacegate, and Glastopalypse. Those three manifest BBC management failures, and the slowness of corporate response to them, not only attracted the opprobrium of the usual anti-BBC suspects but also many of its friends and supporters. Davie would do well to remember that he is not only BBC CEO but also its editor-in-chief.

Supporting UK democracy

Davie wants to expand the Local Democracy Reporting Service (LDRS), to expand the BBC's Insight offer by creating local teams, and to make content open source for other news organisations. LDRS expansion would cost between £10m and £20m per year. The expansion of the Insight operation would cost between £15m and £30m per year. It would cost between £5m and £10m simply to set up the open sourcing infrastructure and then between £2m and £5m to maintain that operation.

No one could doubt the laudability of this objective but it has to be examined in the context of how hollowed-out is the BBC's local reporting on both TV and radio. Regional news programming runs to barely an hour a day in the week, and is virtually non-existent on the weekend. Where once the BBC boasted a serious network of dedicated regional radio stations providing a full complement of local news and entertainment, now staffing levels have been radically cut, many programmes are shared across sub-regions, and content has lost its tight local focus.

While the BBC proudly states that the LDRS scheme has resulted in the creation of 165 new journalist jobs, those reporters, the LDRs, work for large regional news organisations who are awarded contracts by the BBC. The big three companies — Reach, Newsquest, and National World — account for 143 of those 165 jobs, and LDRs do not report to the BBC but to the contract holder. This leaves the BBC as a commissioning organisation rather than one with directly employed journalists. When Channel 4 started broadcasting in 1982 it operated on an entirely new model for UK TV: it lacked any production facilities of its own, and simply commissioned programmes from a then small independent sector. Channel 4's success, the 1990 Broadcasting Act, and Channel 5's launch all served to profoundly change the UK TV landscape: independent production companies not only provided programmes for the new channels but also for the BBC, part of the Government's attack on what it characterised as monopolies and restrictive practices. From a small start the UK independent TV production sector has blossomed and thrived, and many large transnational TV companies also create programmes for all UK TV channels: there's no squeezing that genie back inside his bottle. Lacking a time machine (*Dr Who* is on hold and its future at the mercy of the Disney organisation) or the capacity to repeal the 1990 legislation, the BBC now finds itself operating more and more as a commissioner. One only has to look at failures to maintain editorial and behavioural standards on *Gaza: How to Survive a Warzone* or *MasterChef* to see the immensity of management challenges for a BBC handling even more commissioned content.

AI and education

This objective is incredibly ambitious: an AI personal learning companion for all 7 to 16 year-olds, and a BBC Family account with lifelong support. The best comparator here is the NHS app in terms of scale and likely cost. The research and development costs of turbocharging BBC Bitesize and making it AI-powered plus the costs of then rolling out this massively enhanced service would be between £100m and £200m. Creating the entire ecosystem necessary to launch and maintain Family Accounts would cost between £20m and £40m.

Maximising growth across the UK

The objective here would build on the long-established commitment to reduce the London-centredness of the BBC operation, as well as reviving the Corporation's commitment to developing the talent of the future, somewhat sidelined in the bottom-line-driven culture of recent years. Salford would become a global media hub. Studios and production facilities would be opened to creators, and those creators would be given the tools and skills training programmes to develop their talent. As with the previous objectives this couldn't be achieved by simply investing in startup programmes and then walking away; it would require significant funding to ensure studios and creators were properly supported (between £30m and £50m per year), as well as establishing and maintaining skill training programmes (costing between £10m and £20m a year).

Digital transition

The final objective flows from, and would support delivery of, the first four objectives: building much smarter platforms on which to offer all of the BBC's massively expanded services, as well as entering into partnerships with hyperscalers, providing the massive computing resources necessary to host and manage all existing and newly created services on the global stage. It would cost between £150m and £250m to develop an iPlayer 2.0 and successive generations of smarter platforms. To enable and maintain this media supply chains would have to be completely transformed. That would cost between £100m and £200m. And creating the BBC's proprietary technology as well as forging partnerships with key delivery organisations would take at least £50m as an initial investment.

Eye-watering figures

The bare minimum funding required to achieve all five objectives is £862m; the maximum is £1.4bn. That level of funding could only be achieved by a handful of strategies. Either a massive increase in the licence fee or by the creation or discovery of a magic funding formula. (Davie has ruled out both advertising and subscription.) Or for the BBC's commercial arms to become astronomically successful and underwrite all their public service commitments.

Or for the government to make a massive investment. None of these are remote possibilities.

Lacking a time machine or the ability to return to pre-1982 or pre-1990 arrangements the BBC will not be able to bring back in-house all programme-making. Where debates about that should have been steered by accountants, they long since lost out to ideologues. Expansion on the scale outlined by Davie is only likely to be achieved by the BBC's becoming a much more efficient and faster-acting commissioning, management, and editorial organisation than it currently is. Expansion of the BBC's commissioning role would inevitably lead to redundancies of directly employed staff. Following intentions outlined in Davie's Salford speech, in July 2025 the organisation announced plans to outsource thousands of jobs in its digital product group, responsible for News Online, Sport, iPlayer, and Sounds. While that could significantly reduce overall operating costs it would reduce the effectiveness of the Cardiff, Glasgow, Newcastle, and Salford hubs. So, operating costs down, local responsiveness down, and managing outsourced contracts up.

Notwithstanding the noble ambitions expressed by Davie in his Salford speech it is difficult to read it as anything other than a long resignation letter. The goals are magnificent. Were they to be achieved the BBC would once again be a world-class news and entertainment organisation able to take on all global competitors. He retains ambitions for the BBC, to see it through Charter review and licence fee negotiations, but he is a realist. Quite possibly by setting impossible targets he has paved the way to make an honourable exit. He might not move on to manage another broadcaster but there are plenty of large organisations looking for their next head honcho. In January 2019 he was offered but turned down the CEO role of the English Premier League. More importantly, because of his previous role heading up the BBC's commercial arm, as well as his openness to innovation, big tech is a more likely career destination. The next time he hears the siren call of silly money he might just accept.

And after? Well, it's difficult to see a future where the BBC's funding hasn't shrunk, where the organisation hasn't contracted in size, and where all that remains of Davie's vision is the text crowding out the space on a headstone in the graveyard of broadcasting ambitions.

Note

We used OpenAI's ChatGPT to explore potential financial scenarios. While this helped shape our thinking, all estimates are illustrative and should not be considered formal forecasts.

Chapter 28

Is Director-General Tim Davie really serious about local news?

Dr Liam McCarthy argues that the BBC needs to embrace its role in local news as a public service response to market failure

Director-General Tim Davie has spoken about his ambition to strengthen local journalism in both the BBC and the wider local news ecologies (Davie, 2025). But ambition is not enough; it needs action, funding and partners to bring it to fruition. To be fair to Davie he is absolutely correct about using the BBC's influence and its local services as a 'catalyst for building trust' and 'social capital' in communities across the UK. However, every DG right back to the *Extending Choice* era of John Birt (BBC, 1992: 30) has talked a good game about local connections but most, with the exception of Greg Dyke, have failed to put new money into local services, with funding shrinking in the two decades since Dyke left in 2004. To meet his ambition Tim Davie needs to re-engineer BBC News across the United Kingdom leading with a Local Digital First Strategy.

The BBC did not kill local news

The BBC must accept that it is part of the local news ecology and not a peripheral player. It needs to stand its ground on behalf of the public who fund it, especially where the marketplace for local news can be seen to be struggling and in places failing. The BBC and its local provision has been under attack from commercial news providers since its inception, but the public who pay for the BBC expect a local service that includes news. Too often the BBC has backed away from investing in services such as local television or providing a more comprehensive online news to placate commercial news providers (BBC Trust, 2008). However, leaving these fields clear has neither helped slow the decline in commercial local news provision or cleared the way for its expansion. A confident BBC should embrace local news as a public service response in a failing market and ensure that innovations such as the Local Democracy Reporting Service and its own local content should be available – with editorial safeguards – to all local outlets.

The local online, radio, and television services of the BBC have been made out to be the main villain in the decimation of local journalism which has seen more than 300 newspaper titles close in the decade to 2019 (DCMS HoC Committee, 2023: 5). But journalism is expensive and the real villain is not the BBC but the concept of accessing content for 'free'. In the digital world paywalls are resented and the alternative of 'free' news comes with online adverts and pop-ups making it almost unreadable on some devices. Deregulation in local radio has seen commercial stations hollowed out to be replaced by national brands such as Heart, Greatest Hits, and Capital – in the latest set of cuts Bauer closed 12 local breakfast shows to replace them with one national programme (*Radio Today*, 2025). Of course listeners will still get local/regional news, but for how long, and will Ofcom bow to pressure and remove that stipulation as well? It is therefore surprising and disappointing that the BBC followed commercial radio by reducing the local content of its own radio stations, further weakening the range of authentic local voices. This has led to the loss of 25 per cent of the weekly audience since 2022, down from 6.3m to 4.78m, as stations have become less locally focused. The loss of experienced staff in radio has also brought some editorial howlers such as the 'systemic failure' of BBC Radio Devon in its lack of coverage of an anti-immigration civil disturbance in Plymouth in August 2024 (*Press Gazette*, 2025). Do these stations still have the staff and skills to produce and broadcast the weekly audience-driven debate programmes that Tim Davie has suggested as part of the fixing of the current democratic deficit? The DG should reconsider the cuts to BBC local radio.

Local radio to local online: a good idea?

The reduction in the BBC's local radio output was a spectacular own goal but it was forced on management to find the money they needed to build up local online news services. This move towards a Digital First policy is part of a new BBC target to ensure its local services in England reach half of all adults, although the radio cuts have not helped. In a digital society this focus online is absolutely correct and early indications are that online connections with licence fee payers are increasing. Ofcom reported that increased online output from the BBC in 2023/24 led to a 40 per cent increase in page views, though it found no significant evidence of these numbers displacing other local sites. According to Ofcom the decline of 20 per cent of page views for commercial news sites predated the BBC expansion (Ofcom, 2025: 8). New BBC online services for Bradford, Doncaster, Peterborough, Wear, and Wolverhampton are serving a public need. The BBC policy of linking to other local news content in each local online story to a wide variety of local news sources from Reach to new providers such as Nub News is valuable online signposting to the market. Nevertheless, the BBC has again come under fire from newspaper groups who see its licence fee services as unfair and now charge the corporation and its short online stories of 'crowding out deeper, local journalism' (*Nottingham Post*, 2025).

The Local Democracy Reporting Service

The BBC's major contribution to the wider news ecologies across the United Kingdom is the Local Democracy Reporting Service (LDRS). Since it was launched in 2018 the LDRS has provided 470,000 individual stories for local news providers and has recently announced its latest set of contracts for the placing of its 165 reporters (BBC, 2025). However, from July 2025 to the end of 2027 more than eight out of ten of the reporters (143) will work for just three publishers – Reach, Newsquest, and National World (Linford, 2025). Where contracts have been awarded in the past to smaller outlets there have been problems, for example Notts TV at Nottingham Trent University won the contract against the local Reach site for Nottinghamshire but has now ceased trading and the contract is back with the *Nottingham Post*. The BBC itself employs a Senior Local Politics Reporter at each local radio station and a dedicated Political Correspondent in each TV region so produces much of its own content but is using LDRS material increasingly on its online sites. Tim Davie wants to expand the remit of the Local Democracy Reporting Service to cover health authorities, and police and crime commissioners, and to provide scrutiny of elected mayors. Perhaps this time it would be better plugged into the existing BBC services which have Home Affairs and Health Correspondents in each region. Similarly, having invested in expensive investigative journalism teams in each region how does Davie think his suggestion of local BBC Verify and data-driven journalism teams might fit in? The LDRS is an important part of the local news mix, but as Rhodri Talfan Davies, the BBC's Director of Nations told the DCMS Committee of the House of Commons: 'it was never the solution to the financial challenges facing the commercial sector. It has helped and it has restored equality and depth to local authority reporting, but it will not turn around the structural challenges facing our commercial partners' (DCMS, 2022). Effectively top-slicing the licence fee to fund the LDRS and any future expansion of its remit is a positive move that should be retained in any new funding formula.

Building a Local Digital First BBC

To strengthen local news the BBC needs to be rebuilt around a news core that is truly devolved with journalists redeployed from what should become smaller London and Manchester newsrooms to the BBC's local bases.

Regional television news programmes on BBC One remain popular within the constraints of a declining overall audience reach for the channel – down by 12 per cent since 2017 (BBC News, 2023). The BBC needs to direct this journalistic and technical firepower for the streaming age creating daily on-demand local video news and sport bulletins as part of its online news offering. This could be delivered this as part a Local Digital First strategy built around the BBC's local radio bases. News happens where journalists are so redeploying the BBC's journalists across the UK is important. They should not be sitting in news factories processing the same limited pool of stories from central news diaries.

Whatever the outcome of the new funding regime for the BBC unless the government proposes to take back funding of the BBC World Service or the cost of free licences for the over-75s the BBC will not be getting any increases to its funding. Therefore a fundamental shift is needed in the architecture of the corporation to release cash for local innovation. The BBC still remains a top-down, London-centric organisation with the power residing within the M25. If Tim Davie is serious about his ambition to address failing local journalism ecologies he needs to rebuild the BBC – around a Local Digital First strategy.

References

BBC (1992) *Extending Choice: the BBC's role in the new broadcasting age*, London: BBC.

BBC (2025) 'New Local Democracy Reporter Scheme contracts announced', https://www.bbc.com/mediacentre/2025/new-local-democracy-reporter-scheme-contracts (Accessed 5 June 2025)

BBC News (2023) 'UK traditional TV viewing sees record decline, Ofcom report says', https://www.bbc.co.uk/news/entertainment-arts-66369532 (Accessed 5 June 2025)

BBC Trust (2008) 'BBC Trust rejects local video proposals', https://www.bbc.co.uk/bbctrust/news/press_releases/2008/local_video_prov (Accessed 5 June 2025)

DCMS HoC Committee (2022), 'Sustainability of Local Journalism', Oral Evidence of Rhodri Talfan Davies, Q205, 25 January 2023, https://committees.parliament.uk/oralevidence/10504/html/ Accessed 30 May 2025.

DCMS HoC Committee (2023) 'Sustainability of Local Journalism', Report, 25 January 2023, https://publications.parliament.uk/pa/cm5803/cmselect/cmcumeds/153/summary.html (Accessed 30 May 2025)

Natalie Fahy (2025) 'BBC 'part of headwinds' threatening local commercial news like Nottinghamshire Live, says Ofcom', *Nottingham Post*, https://www.nottinghampost.com/news/uk-world-news/bbc-part-headwinds-threatening-local-9761274 (Accessed 3 June 2025)

Ofcom (2025) 'Review of Local Media in the UK Part Two'

https://www.ofcom.org.uk/siteassets/resources/documents/tv-radio-and-on-demand/bbc/bbc-annual-report/2024/review-of-local-media-in-the-uk-part-2-report.pdf?v=386116 (Accessed 3 June 2025)

Paul Linford (2025) 'Big three' retain most LDR contracts as four new publishers join scheme, *HoldtheFrontPage*, 8 May 2025, https://www.holdthefrontpage.co.uk/2025/news/more-than-half-of-ldrs-contracts-awarded-to-reach-as-four-new-publishers-join-scheme/ (Accessed 30 May 2025)

Roy Martin (2025) 'Bauer to network breakfast on heritage FM radio stations in England and Wales', *RadioToday*, https://radiotoday.co.uk/2025/03/bauer-to-network-breakfast-on-heritage-fm-radio-stations-in-england-and-wales/ (Accessed 28 May 2025)

Press Gazette (2025) 'BBC local radio station showed 'systemic failure' on night of disorder' https://pressgazette.co.uk/the-wire/newspaper-corrections-media-mistakes-errors-legal/bbc-local-radio-station-showed-systemic-failures-on-night-of-disorder/ (Accessed 31 May 2025).

RAJAR (2025) Quarterly Listening Figures, Q1 2025 and Q1 2022 https://www.rajar.co.uk/listening/quarterly_listening.php (Accessed 28 May 2025)

About the contributor

Dr Liam McCarthy is an Honorary Fellow in the Department of History, Politics, and International Relations at the University of Leicester. He worked for the BBC between 1978 and 2008, was Managing Editor of three BBC local radio stations, and Head of BBC Local Radio Training. His published works include *Finding a New British Asian Sound on BBC Radio* (2023). He is currently writing a book about African American GIs in Britain during WW2.

Chapter 29

Threading the BBC into the lives of the next generation

The BBC is in danger of losing future generations of viewers and listeners. **Dr Martin Moore** examines why

The iPhone alarm trings. Tom, a 22-year old living in a shared house in east London, wakes up and hits snooze. Nine minutes later he stops the alarm and checks Apple news alerts on his home screen. A short while after that, eating breakfast, Tom checks the weather (on the Apple weather app), looks at his Gmail, sees how long it will take him to get to work (via Google maps), and then kills twenty minutes on YouTube. By the time Tom leaves the house he has spent almost all of his time on media, none of it the BBC.

Tom is invented, though there are many people like Tom today in the UK. The average 18-24 year old spends over four and a half hours a day on their phone, supplemented with another hour or so on a computer or tablet (adding up to over six hours in total) (Ofcom, 2024a). Much of this time is spent with the various services of Alphabet/Google (about two hours a day across all devices), TikTok (about an hour across devices), or Meta's Instagram or WhatsApp (no self-respecting 22-year-old uses Facebook). The BBC gains Tom's attention for around three minutes a day (or 104.4 minutes per month to be precise) (Ofcom, 2024b). Less than half of 16-24 year olds, according to Ofcom, even switch on broadcast TV in an average week (Ofcom, 2024c).

Digital natives and the BBC

After the end of the licence fee, whatever the funding model of the BBC, the Corporation faces a fundamental challenge: how to make itself integral to the lives of the digitally native. While any future funding model will mean the continuation of the Corporation, even if this is in a diminished form, the threat to the continued use of its services by the next generation is existential.

Unlike the BBC, Big Tech has woven its hardware and services into the lives of Generation Z. The oldest members of that generation had yet to turn ten when Steve Jobs unveiled the first iPhone in January 2007. Instagram launched as they hit their teens, and the rise of TikTok paralleled their early adulthood. For many of them the BBC is something that was on in the background while they grew up, or where they have fond memories of watching CBeebies (Yonder, 2021).

Only rarely do young people turn consciously to the BBC. The broadcaster has no structural advantage on smart phones as it does on TV and radio. If a teenager is thinking about watching something at home they may consider the iPlayer, but are more likely to turn to a streaming service like Netflix or to YouTube. The BBC is the fifth most-watched streaming service among 16-24s, after YouTube, TikTok, Netflix and Disney+ (Ofcom, 2024e: 18).

This is not to say young people do not believe in the value of the BBC and other Public Service Media. They do, according to recent data. Ofcom's 2024 Review of Public Service Media found that more than two-thirds of 16-24 year-olds are 'quite' or 'very' satisfied with Public Service Broadcasters overall (Ofcom, 2024e). Other research has found that the BBC is still where young people go when a major news event happens, like updates during the pandemic, Russia's invasion of Ukraine, or the Trump trade wars (Craft, 2022). But, when it comes to their daily lives, the BBC is increasingly peripheral.

Why is the BBC so peripheral to the young?

There are many reasons why young people are not consuming much BBC content, and why the BBC is a more marginal part of their lives than previous generations, most of which have nothing to do with the quality of BBC output.

Digital natives navigate media differently than digital immigrants. They do not start their media journey as their parents did, channel flicking between the BBC, ITV, and Channel 4. Or watch programmes at set times. They look for specific programmes, people, or topics, consume them at a time of their choosing, or open their favourite social media streaming service – Reels, Shorts, TikTok – and let the algorithm do the rest. The BBC, which still relies heavily on punctuated linear programming (like the 6 and 10pm news) and has no dedicated shortform video channel, loses out as a result. 'News' can be anything new they learn from their phone. '<u>The</u> news' is different, a product constructed and packaged by legacy media (Craft, 2022). They do not expect to have to consciously seek out either, assuming anything important will find them instead of vice versa (Gil de Zuniga et al, 2017; Toff & Nielsen, 2018). Given the choice of a general news agenda selected by a human editor, and algorithmically selected news that is tailored to them, they tend to prefer the latter (Thurman et al, 2019). And while they may not enjoy being tracked, they assume their media consumption is being recorded and used to inform future algorithmically generated recommendations (Swart et al, 2021). Since they are more likely to consume media alone rather than gathered together in front of a shared screen, they want media they can share and that expresses their identity. Media, in other words, that prioritises their private interest over the public interest. The BBC, which manually curates its news, does not track, and prioritises the public interest, necessarily plays a lesser role in young people's media.

Similarly, the values by which young people assess media content are different. Formality – in terms of appearance and language – does not confer seriousness and credibility, it signals distance and inauthenticity. They are sceptical about aspirations to impartiality (which BBC Director-General Tim Davie has made his leitmotif) and assume all publishers have a bias and an agenda (Eddy, 2022; Channel 4, 2024). When looking for who to follow and who to trust, they seek out individuals rather than institutions – Joe Wicks rather than the BBC.

Yet, most importantly, the BBC is at a disadvantage when it comes to young people's media gatekeepers. The Corporation increasingly depends on big tech platforms to distribute its content to these audiences, tech platforms who adhere to 'radical indifference' when it comes to content distribution (Zuboff, 2022). These US platforms do not care what people consume, as long as it maintains their attention and elicits their engagement. It is not in the platforms' financial interest to privilege legacy media institutions over other content. Even when they do distinguish public service media, they can do so in ways that degrade rather than enhance public trust. Notice how Twitter/X initially labelled the BBC 'government funded media' until the BBC objected (Glynn, 2023). Generative AI will make the situation worse, as the major AI players use public service content as raw material to generate all kinds of customised media. For all these reasons the generational drift away from the BBC is likely to accelerate rather than reverse.

Producing more content and distributing it across more platforms will not solve the problem, it will just cement young people's existing media habits and make the BBC beholden to platform algorithms and commercial metrics. Re-formatting *Question Time* so that it works well on TikTok, for example, will not reconnect young people with the BBC. Equally, while maintaining and enhancing quality standards is essential for the Corporation, this will not be enough to bring back future generations.

The BBC cannot rewire itself into the lives of the next generation unless the structural disadvantages it suffers are reduced, and the BBC is given the freedom – and the resources – to move beyond linear programming.

New services, new roles

On the structural disadvantages, if people prefer to consume media via tech platforms, then these platforms should be obliged to privilege public service media (and British content more generally). This would be a natural and justifiable modernisation of rules regarding due prominence on broadcast TV. Parliament has gone part way towards this with the Media Act 2024. Though this will need to go further, especially as AI leads to cannibalisation and exploitation of public service media content.

The BBC will also need to be given the remit, and the money, to find novel ways to integrate its content and services to young people's lives. This could mean experimenting with new digital services or taking on unfamiliar roles. Ideas suggested for reinventing public service media include a public service search engine (Zuckerman, 2020), public service algorithms (Bennett, 2018), or new digital public spheres (Moore, 2022). The BBC is in the best position to work out how best to serve the next generation – though it can only do this if it has the political freedom and sufficient resources. This will necessarily mean supplementing its funding, probably via a levy on streaming services like Netflix and Disney+, or a tax on the new AI superpowers.

At a time when UK citizens desperately need accurate and verifiable news, content that reflects the UK, media that is publicly accountable, and media organisations who act in the public interest, not those of their shareholders, we cannot afford to let young people's relationship with the BBC fade away.

References

James Bennett (2018) 'Public Service Algorithms', in Des Freedman and Vana Goblet (eds) *A future for public service Television*, London: Goldsmith Press.

Craft (2022) *The Kaleidoscope: Young People's Relationship with News* https://www.wearecraft.agency/the-kaleidoscope

Channel 4 (2025) *Gen Z: Trends, Truth and Trust, January 2025*, https://assets-corporate.channel4.com/_flysystem/s3/2025-01/Gen%20Z%20Trends%20Truth%20and%20Trust_0.pdf

Kirsten Eddy (2022) 'The changing news habits and attitudes of younger audiences', Reuters Institute for the Study of Journalism, 15 June 2022.

Homero Gil de Zúñiga, Brian Weeks, and Alberto Ardèvol-Abreu (2017) 'Effects of the News-Finds-Me Perception in Communication: Social Media Use Implications for News Seeking and Learning About Politics', *Journal of Computer-Mediated Communication*, 22: 3, 105–123.

Paul Glynn (2023) 'Elon Musk: Twitter owner changes BBC account's 'government funded' label', London: BBC, 12 April 2023.

Martin Moore (2022) 'Creating New Electoral Public Spheres', in Martin Moore and Damian Tambini (eds) *Regulating Big Tech*, New York: Oxford University Press.

Ofcom (2024a) *Online Nation Report 2024*, 28 November 2024, London: Ofcom.

Ofcom (2024b) *Communications Market Report 2024: Interactive Data*, London: Ofcom.

Ofcom (2024c) *Gen Z swerves traditional broadcast TV as less than half tune in weekly*, London: Ofcom, 31 July 2024.

Ofcom (2024d) *Ofcom's Annual Report on the BBC*, London: Ofcom, 29 November 2024.

Ofcom (2024e) *Review of Public Service Media (2019-23): Challenges and Opportunities for Public Service Media*, London: Ofcom, 17 December 2024.

Joëlle Swart (2021) 'Experiencing Algorithms: How Young People Understand, Feel About, and Engage With Algorithmic News Selection on Social Media', *Social Media + Society*, 7(2).

Neil Thurman, Judith Moeller, Natali Helberger, and Damian Trilling (2019) 'My friends, editors, algorithms, and I: Examining audience attitudes to news selection', *Digital journalism*, 7(4), 447-469.

Benjamin Toff and Rasmus Kleis Nielsen (2018) '"I Just Google It": Folk Theories of Distributed Discovery', *Journal of Communication*, 68:3, 636–657.

Yonder (2022) 'Exploration of Audience Expectations of the BBC in the current media environment', Research commissioned by Ofcom.

Shoshana Zuboff (2022) 'Surveillance Capitalism or Democracy? The Death Match of Institutional Orders and the Politics of Knowledge in Our Information Civilization', *Organization Theory*, *3*(3).

Ethan Zuckerman (2020) 'The Case for Digital Public Infrastructure', Knight First Amendment Institute at Columbia University, 17 January 2020.

About the contributor

Dr Martin Moore is director of the Centre for the Study of Media, Communication and Power, and a Senior Lecturer in the Department of Political Economy at King's College London. He was previously the founding director of the Media Standards Trust (2006-2015). He is the author of *Democracy Hacked: How Technology is Destabilising Global Politics* (Oneworld Publications 2018) and, with Thomas Colley, *Dictating Reality: the Global Battle to Control the News* Columbia University Press, October 2025).

Chapter 30

A BBC for the YouTube generation

Tara Conlan considers how the BBC might regain a lost Generation Z

The clock is TikToking for traditional broadcasters. The numbers tell the story. Phones have overtaken TV as a more popular form of entertainment, according to the Institute of Practitioners in Advertising.

In June 2025 it was revealed that UK adults are watching three hours and 16 minutes of TV a day, compared with three hours and 21 minutes spent on their mobiles - that's around three times the amount a decade ago. In addition, Ofcom says 92 per cent of people now use video apps such as TikTok or YouTube and TV is no longer the main source of news for UK adults. Some youngsters are also turning to ChatGPT for their news.

With over 80 per cent of UK homes having access to smart TVs, YouTube is emerging as the global king of content the others want to beat. Execs from BBC to Netflix tell me they see YouTube as the main rival. According to ratings company Barb, YouTube viewing picks up around 3pm, when children come home from school. It is expected to become more mainstream as older viewers become accustomed to less formal content on their screens (due to visualised podcasts and the pandemic) and more independent producers pivot towards making family-friendly shows.

Where's the wow factor?

In our creator-driven, social media-saturated world democratisation of the small screen has happened, and mobiles and YouTube are the tech that makes teens go 'wow' in the same way the BBC did for previous generations. Traditional media gatekeepers risk being submerged now the floodgates have opened for direct-to-consumer content.

So, as it gears up for charter renewal, how can the BBC ensure it remains relevant for the YouTube generation of licence fee payers?

It is worth saying: the BBC is still a big beast, with £3.7bn of licence fee revenue to spend, and it is planning to be here beyond the end of its current charter in December 2027. It has just awarded Serco a £40.6m (plus VAT) contract for between five and eight years for its audience and customer services.

But prominence, participation, and trust are three key areas in helping the corporation cut through to Gen Z. However the discoverability playing field, many within the BBC argue, is not particularly level. A substantial amount of traffic comes to streamers via branded remote control buttons. Sources claim these buttons are valued by TV manufacturers at between 30p and £1 each. They are an effective marketing and navigation tool. But they are not always paid for and can be covered by reciprocal arrangements. Apparently Netflix does not pay. It does have a Netflix Recommended TVs page on its website but it did not want to comment about how it gets its name on branded buttons.

Advertising to the rescue?

The BBC does not carry advertising in the UK so, one assumes, cannot enter into such arrangements. Although it gained more prominence onscreen and online through the Media Act 2024, the legislation did not include remote control buttons. Liberal Democrat MP Joshua Reynolds raised the issue in Parliament: on 3 June 2025 he submitted a written question to culture secretary Lisa Nandy asking whether she had "made an assessment of the potential merits of requiring television manufacturers to include a dedicated BBC iPlayer button on remote controls in line with existing buttons for commercial streaming services." He told me: "From the government's response to the question, it seems like they are waiting for Ofcom to direct them. I'm not so sure that's the right thing to do. I don't think Ofcom needs to direct them. They could turn [this] around very easily." But as the relationship between TV manufacturers and the streamers/broadcasters comes under more scrutiny, so too does the future relationship between the public service broadcasters. This needs to be resolved in order to give a concerted push in taking on YouTube.

It is not completely the public service broadcasters' fault they are where they are now. In 2007 the BBC, Channel 4, and ITV's plan to launch the groundbreaking web TV joint venture Project Kangaroo was blocked by the Competition Commission and Netflix et al stole a march. Eighteen years later we are still talking about Kangaroo and hearing more urgent calls for a one-stop streaming shop for the PSBs.

They already partner together on Everyone TV's free streaming service Freely. But I am told that talks have started taking place between the BBC and Channel 4 about bringing some of C4's streaming under the iPlayer umbrella, although a BBC spokesperson said the corporation could not comment "on speculation".

This is about marketing, the bottom line, and that old showiness anxiety: billing. It makes huge sense to be under one name but whose name will be top of the bill, or in this case, on the button? Freely is already on some remote buttons in the UK, but it is free and territory-specific. And it is not on LG or market leader Samsung remotes, which sources claim, is not keen on UK-only buttons.

The 'Best of British' button

So if the PSBs could agree a 'Best of British' (BoB) name they could go under the auspices of globally, that could help them scale against the US streamers. There is Britbox, the streaming service launched by BBC Studios and ITV, offering UK shows in some countries and whose international operations the BBC bought out ITV's stake for £225m in February 2024.

But, many BBC people argue, with the worldwide recognition the corporation has, the 'BoB' name on that button should be iPlayer. A study by Ampere bears this out, showing in February 2025 65 per cent of 18 to 64-year-old internet users accessed Netflix, compared with 59 per cent for BBC iPlayer, 48 per cent for Prime Video, 46 per cent for ITVX, and 34 per cent for Channel 4's streaming service.

Reynolds said: "I think it's well known and understood that the PSBs need to effectively put their eggs in one basket when it comes to what is the streaming platform [...] I think personally, it would be a silly idea to not brand it as iPlayer, because iPlayer is the most recognised brand."

The corporation has thrown millions behind iPlayer's brand and the technology. Its director of product engineering Tanja Lichtensteiger said recently on LinkedIn that the BBC "is on a mission to build the world's first Public Service digital media platform". She was talking about the corporation's technical platform all its digital services (iPlayer, Sounds, News etc) are on, but it signals the Beeb's global intention. As does the fact a company called BBC News Ltd that has been dormant since 2011 recently changed its name to BBC News International Ltd. And Ofcom has recommended that public service content be easy to find on YouTube (Ofcom 2025).

One source says ITV admires iPlayer's capacity and functionality but is not keen on giving up the ITVX branding. Plus on 10 July 2025 it announced it had just done a cross-promotional deal with Disney+.

Can the PBSs get past their legacy and partner? The government's Creative Industries Sector Plan think so, as it is 'considering any potential closer, strategic partnerships or possible consolidation between broadcasters which may benefit their financial sustainability and audiences.' Participation and flexibility are important for youngsters used to taking part in and uploading content on social media. YouTube is Channel 4 forty years ago and the BBC one hundred years ago — now they're both the veteran gatekeepers.

Broadcasters, particularly Channel 4, and streamers have seen where the youngsters are and have successful channels on YouTube: BBC Earth's YouTube has 13.7 million subscribers and Netflix has Still Watching Netflix which 'takes you deeper into the films and shows you love' and has 9.3 million subscribers.

Opening up?

The BBC has pledged to put more of its content on platforms like TikTok and YouTube, particularly news. But could it open up some programming or space on iPlayer for licence fee payers to upload content or participate more in some way? And would its rivals and regulators allow it? In his 14 May 2025 Salford speech Director-General Tim Davie announced that some studio space will be opened up to creators. Yet, in order to compete, there needs to be some element of opening up the output to allow 16-34-year-olds (who are used to the freedoms and interactivity of YouTube, Spotify, Instagram, Substack, Apple Music and Twitch) to participate.

Netflix opened up its content through a 'moments' button on its app that allows viewers to clip parts of shows and share them on social media, thus bringing people back to the platform. The BBC cannot operate on the same playing field as it is more heavily scrutinised and regulated. It can't have just anyone uploading content directly, but perhaps some space or time on BBC Three could be opened up, suitably filtered by AI and moderated by experienced producers.

BBC Three being taken off-air and moved online in February 2016 signalled the de-prioritisation of young audiences and new, rising talent. Traditionally, new comedians like Josh Berry would have been on the channel, but instead they have built followings on Instagram, TikTok and YouTube. BBC Three has come back to some degree, with excellent comedy shorts such as *Danielle Does Life*, starring Danielle Vitalis, and Radio 1 brings youngsters in; but young creatives know they have more freedoms elsewhere.

As Reynolds says: "It's not through public service broadcasters not being open to innovation that places like Netflix and Prime were able to take so much. It's because they were blocked for so long by government and by Ofcom. So, for me, it's a case of [having] a level playing field. I'm 26; for my generation YouTube is TV; there is no difference. I think the quicker the government realise that and allow a bit of that innovation to happen, things will work better for the BBC. Netflix could come up with an idea and implement it on their platform tomorrow if they wanted. Ofcom and the government are just too slow and it stifles innovation." He added the government have focused on AI innovation but if it looked at television "through the same lens of innovation [...] we could be back on top again, globally."

Authentic journalism

A trump card the BBC can play is its impartiality and trust. Would you prefer your children to be roaming round on CBeebies or YouTube? Davie opened his Salford speech saying trust is "the essential ingredient of a secure, cohesive society".

Verified journalism is vital in a world of AI slop and bots. New ventures such as Spread could help the BBC monetise its commercial content as it involves renowned journalists spreading what they're reading, listening to, and watching, while publishers partner with Spread to measure and monetise authenticated, human-only, attention at higher rates with advertisers. Ideal, perhaps, for the BBC's new subscription offering US-based users unlimited access to its news content. Spread co-founder Stu Rogers explained: "We expect the passport to the 'Human Internet' to be media-type agnostic as content creation and user behaviour continues to evolve post-AI. If they aren't already, publishers across the UK, of course [which could] include the BBC, are integrating with Spread to grow reach by prioritising human traffic amidst the onslaught of AI scraping, mirroring the strategies of US publishers such as *The Atlantic*."

Getting the YouTube generation to pay the licence fee in the future is vital. During the review of its charter the BBC is thinking how to phrase the language about the fee, so that even if viewers are only watching streamed video they will still have to pay the licence fee. At the moment, as the TV Licensing website explains, it only covers live TV on streamers.

Reynolds thinks the licence fee "will continue in its current form. Because [...] everyone realizes there's no actual other option. But I worry that we will lose the important things and the important individuals [...] I haven't heard that it's on the radar soon, but I'm concerned in the future, we'll lose the BBC-funded Local Democracy Reporters because they have to focus on core bread and butter. I'm very pro-BBC [...] 43p a day for everything we get is incredible. We were in Japan a few months ago, and one thing the Japanese wanted to talk about [...] more than quite a lot of other things, was the BBC. It is seen still around the world as that gold standard and the best in the world."

Reference

Ofcom (2025) 'Public service content should be findable on YouTube', London: Ofcom, 21 July.

About the contributor

Tara Conlan has written about media for the *Guardian* since 2005 and was previously the *Daily Mail*'s TV editor and columnist. She has also written for the *Observer*, *Evening Standard*, the *Sunday Times*, *The Independent*, *Radio Times*, *Variety*, *The British Journalism Review*, *The Journalist*, *Television*, *The Stage*, and *Broadcast*. As well as contributing to Radio 4's *The Media Show*, the Media Club podcast, Radio 4's *Today* programme, BBC *Ten O'Clock News*, ITV's *News at Ten*, BBC News Channel, and LBC, she is a Royal Television Society juror and an executive committee member of the Broadcasting Press Guild. She has also been a consultant for the newspaper industry's marketing body Newsworks and the TV industry body Screenskills.

Chapter 31

How UK public service broadcasters use YouTube and to what effect

On 21 July 2025 **Ofcom** published *PSBs in the platform era: A YouTube case study Annex 1: Review of Public Service Media.* It contained interesting analysis about PSB news and YouTube

There are various ways people might discover videos on YouTube. Within YouTube, places to discover videos include YouTube's homepage, the Shorts player, Up Next, search, channel pages, and a user's subscriptions page. People might also be referred to videos on YouTube from other services such as Google Search. To understand the relative importance of these sources for discovering videos on YouTube, we used data from Ipsos iris which tracked in-browser activity for around 10,000 UK internet users aged 15+.13 We assume that each YouTube video was discovered on the webpage that the user visited immediately prior to the video. Figure 1 shows the results of this analysis.

Figure 1: Webpages that precede a visit to videos on YouTube

% YouTube video visits from...				
YouTube	Another YouTube video	51.4%	85.6%	100%
	Homepage	15.3%		
	Search	9.5%		
	Channel pages	4.8%		
	Subscriptions page	0.6%		
	Other pages	4.0%		
Not YouTube	Google	4.6%	14.4%	
	Other websites	9.8%		

Source: Ofcom analysis of Ipsos iris clickstream data, 15th January to 15th February 2025. UK 15+ Base of 7,828 panellists. The percentage refers to the proportion of visits to a given type of webpage that preceded a visit to

One-fifth of respondents to Ofcom's News Consumption Survey said that they use YouTube for news. Based on the same survey, we also found that, across all media, PSBs account for 40 per cent of UK audiences' overall share of attention to news.

Given the importance of YouTube and the wider significance of PSBs for news consumption, we wanted to better understand the extent to which PSBs are reaching people with news content on YouTube. To do so, we used the YouTube Data API (Application Proramming Interface) to analyse the presence, popularity, and discoverability of PSB news videos on YouTube. How many videos do PSBs post from their news channels on YouTube? Most PSBs have a primary YouTube channel from which they post news content.

The primary PSB news channels — BBC News, ITV News, Channel 4 News, 5 News, and STV News — have been active on YouTube for well over a decade. As well as posting videos in YouTube's traditional video format, these channels now also regularly post YouTube Shorts. In this analysis we have not included channels from S4C or UTV as neither have dedicated news channels which are active on YouTube. We used the YouTube Data API to count the number of videos posted from the PSBs' primary news channels over time.

Figure 2: Number of YouTube videos posted from primary PSB news channels, quarterly

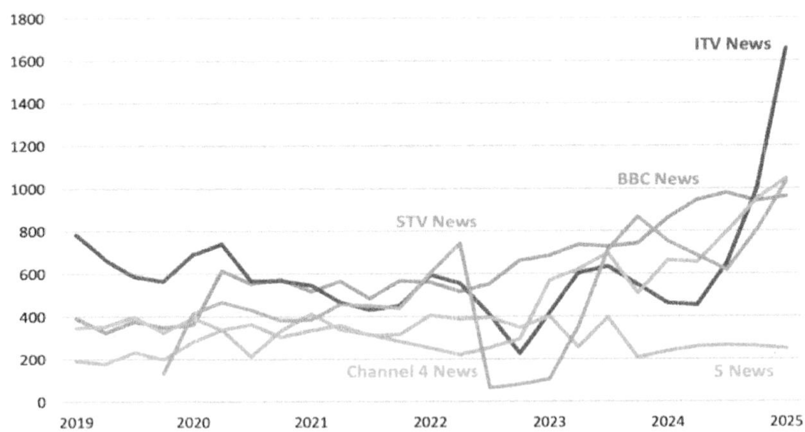

Source: YouTube Data API, Ofcom analysis. This includes regular videos and YouTube shorts.

It shows that the primary PSB news channels all post hundreds of videos every quarter. Over the last few years BBC News, ITV News, Channel 4 News, and STV News have substantially increased the number of videos they post on YouTube. The quarterly number of videos uploaded by ITV News increased by around 66 per cent between the last quarter of 2024 and the first quarter of

2025, rising to over 1,600. This increase was largely driven by a rise in YouTube Shorts uploads.

The next most active primary PSB news channels on YouTube in the first quarter of 2025 were Channel 4 News, STV News, and BBC News, with around 1,000 posts each. Some of the PSBs told us that they were developing new strategies for reaching audiences with news on YouTube so we might expect the increase in activity to continue.

Reach and share of attention

Both metrics are used to understand news consumption, but they capture different aspects of audience behaviour. Reach refers to the percentage of a population that accesses news through a particular platform or service, offering a broad measure of how widely a source is used. In contrast, share of attention goes deeper by measuring the proportion of attention each news source receives relative to others. It is calculated at the individual level and then aggregated, giving more weight to sources used by individuals who consume fewer news outlets. This means that while reach tells us how many people use a source, share of attention tells us how much focus that source commands among its users.

Our analysis focuses on the following YouTube channels: BBC News, ITV News, Channel 4 News, 5 News, and STV News. As well as posting on these YouTube channels, the PSBs sometimes post news content from YouTube channels that aren't dedicated to news (for example, BBC World Service) and the BBC have non-English language news channels (for example, BBC News Hindi).

To get another insight into the PSBs' evolving YouTube strategy for news, we analysed the average duration of videos posted from their primary news channels over time.

Figure 3: Average duration (minutes) of YouTube videos posted from primary PSB news channels, quarterly

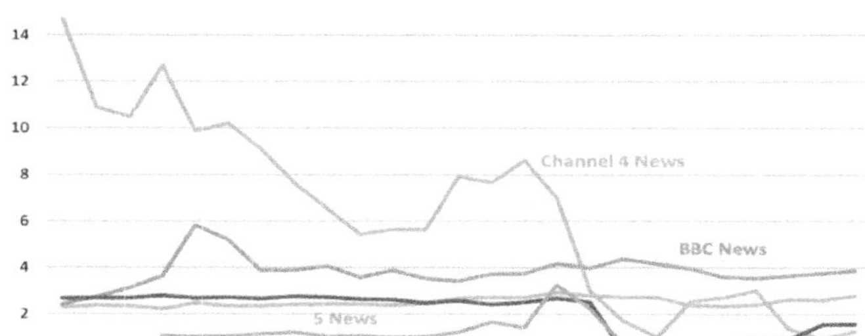

Source: YouTube Data API, Ofcom analysis. We have used the median to measure average duration. This includes regular videos and YouTube shorts.

BBC News posts the longest videos, with an average duration of around four minutes in 2025. In contrast, STV News currently posts the shortest videos, with an average duration of less than one minute. Channel 4 News, ITV News, and STV News all heavily pivoted towards shorter videos in 2023. We have used the median to measure average duration. This includes regular videos and YouTube shorts.

How many people do PSB news videos reach on YouTube?

There are various metrics by which to judge the success of channels on YouTube in engaging with users, including subscriptions, views, watch time, likes, etc. We have chosen to focus on global subscribers and average global views per video because these are simple indicators of engagement based on publicly available data.

Figure 4: Global subscribers and median views per video for popular UK news channels, Q1 2025

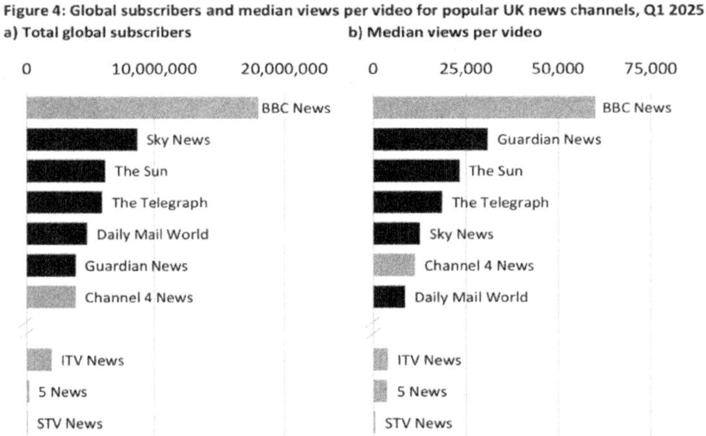

Source: YouTube Data API, Ofcom analysis. As well as primary PSB news channels, Figure 4 includes the five most subscribed non-PSB UK news channels. Median views per video were calculated using view counts as of May 2025 for videos uploaded in the first quarter of the year; subscriber counts are also reported as of May 2025.

Most popular?

As of May 2025, BBC News had 18 million subscribers on YouTube from around the world. In terms of subscribers, this makes BBC News the most popular English-language news channel on YouTube that originates in the UK. Channel 4 News had nearly 4 million global subscribers, which is comparable to some of the most popular commercial UK-based news channels such as Guardian News and Daily Mail World. ITV News had 2 million global subscribers while 5 News and STV News have 184k and 64.5k subscribers, respectively.

Figure 4 includes the five most subscribed non-PSB UK news channels. Median views per video were calculated using view counts as of May 2025 for videos uploaded in the first quarter of the year. Subscriber counts are also reported as of May 2025.

Interestingly, BBC News Hindi has more global subscribers than BBC News but it is not included as the chart only considers English-language channels. There are also English-language channels such as ABC News that have more global subscribers than BBC News, but they do not originate in the UK.

There are other UK-based news channels not included in Figure 4 which have more subscribers than ITV News, 5 News, and STV News. The number of subscribers that a PSB YouTube channel has is correlated with the number of views that its videos receive.

For example, videos from BBC News also receive significantly more views than other UK news channels, with an average of over 60,000 views for videos posted in the first quarter of 2025, as of May 2025. As these are global views, rather than views from the UK, the BBC's popularity in terms of views may be partially explained by its unique global brand. There are many interrelated factors that determine the number of people that a YouTube video reaches. We now analyse one such factor: discoverability.

How discoverable are PSB news videos on YouTube?

Figure 5: Most prominent types of channels in YouTube search results during weeks in 2025

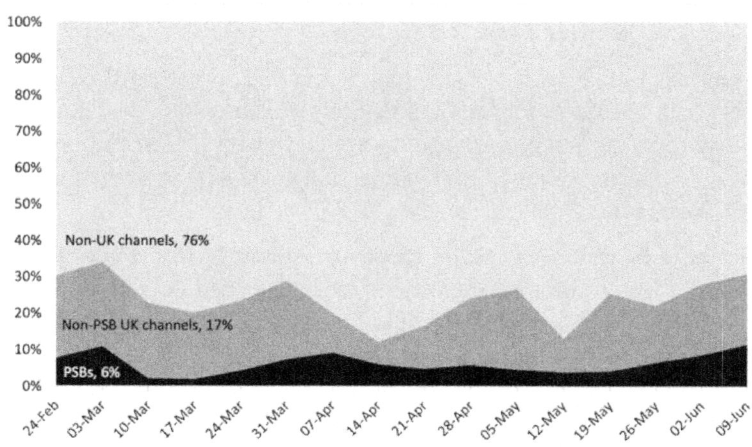

Source: YouTube Data API, Google Trends, Ofcom analysis. The vertical axis refers to the frequency of channels in the top 10 search results during a given week when searching twice daily using a range of popular news related search terms. All dates relate to 2025. PSB content includes all PSB channels, rather than just the primary news channel. Videos from channels that don't label their country of origin are removed from our results, but this doesn't materially affect the conclusions. Percentages may not sum to 100% due to rounding.

Here we focus on search results because the search function is made available via the YouTube Data API, but we are mindful that search is but one of many places on YouTube where videos can be discovered. Many people discover videos via YouTube's Up Next feature and on YouTube's homepage. YouTube also has a dedicated news page and a breaking news shelf on the home page, which were not considered in our previous analysis.

Nevertheless, a significant number of videos are discovered via search, which means that the analysis presented in this section provides some insight into the overall discoverability of PSB news videos on YouTube.

To analyse the discoverability of PSB news videos on YouTube search results, we used the API to search YouTube for news in a regular and systematic way. We ran searches twice a day, at 08:00 and 21:00, between 26 February 2025 and 15 June 2025. To mimic realistic user behaviour we used popular YouTube searches based on data from Google Trends. To reflect general interest in news, we used the top YouTube search terms in the UK from 2024 that were not tied to specific news events. These were: 'news', 'news live', 'news today', 'latest news', and 'politics'. To reflect interest in specific news events we also used a regularly updated set of search terms based on the top and rising news related search terms in the UK on YouTube in the past week. Over the course of the analysis we used 184 unique terms reflecting users searching for specific stories; some examples are: 'starmer trump', 'helicopter crash today news', 'pope francis', 'pakistan india news', and 'uk local elections 2025'. We focused our analysis on the top 10 search results from each query. These search results are ordered by the API based on many factors such as how well the title, tags, description, and video content match the search query. The API also considers location, which we set to the UK.

We note that, unlike when a user searches YouTube from their personal account, the API does not deliver personalised search results based on search and watch history. As such, we would expect the top 10 search results to resemble but not perfectly reflect the videos that users see first when searching for news on YouTube.

The vertical axis refers to the frequency of channels in the top 10 search results during a given week when searching twice daily using a range of popular news related search terms. All dates relate to 2025. PSB content includes all PSB channels, rather than just the primary news channel. Videos from channels that don't label their country of origin are removed from our results but this doesn't materially affect the conclusions.

Our analysis of how users discover videos on YouTube was not specific to news, so the significance of search for news could be higher or lower than for general content. 'Top' refers to the most popular overall search terms, while 'rising' highlights those with the largest recent increases in search frequency.

Our findings are broadly consistent when considering the top 20 videos. They are also consistent when only including the five general news search terms. popular news related search terms, around 6 per cent of the top 10 videos are from PSB channels, a finding which is relatively stable over time. BBC News accounts for the majority of the PSB videos in the top 10 search results. Across the period analysed it accounts for 3.8 per cent of the top 10 search results, making it the second most prominent channel in our analysis. ITV News and Channel 4 News had similar levels of prominence to each other, accounting for 0.7 per cent and 0.6 per cent of the top 10 videos, respectively.

The most prominent channel was Sky News, making up around 4.3 per cent of results. Following Sky News and BBC News, the next five most frequently featured channels in the top 10 search results were Fox News, Jamuna TV, Forbes Breaking News, LiveNOW from Fox, and Firstpost. The next most prominent UK-based channels were The Rest Is Politics, ITV News, and The Sun, making up 1.0 per cent, 0.7 per cent, and 0.7 per cent of the top 10 videos, respectively.

Where do the videos originate?

The vertical axis refers to the frequency of channels in the top 10 search results during a given week when searching twice daily using a range of popular news related search terms. All dates relate to 2025. PSB content includes all PSB channels, rather than just the primary news channel. Videos from channels that don't label their country of origin are removed from our results but this doesn't materially affect the conclusions. Percentages may not add up to 100 per cent due to rounding. Overall, around 23 per cent of videos in the top 10 search results were from YouTube channels that originate in the UK, including the PSBs. Despite our setting our location to the UK and using search terms from the UK, the most common country of origin was the US, whose videos made up 30 per cent of the top 10 results. Videos originating in India were also prominent, accounting for 21 per cent of search results. All other countries accounted for significantly smaller shares of the search results. Although many of the search terms may relate to stories from specific countries, we get very similar results when restricting the analysis to the search terms that did not relate to specific news events (for example, 'latest news'), giving us confidence that the country-of-origin findings are not simply driven by the content of search terms. This analysis has given us a better understanding of the discoverability of PSB news videos in YouTube searched from the UK, but further analysis is needed to understand the discoverability of PSM news content in other places on YouTube (not just search), explore how much prominent news differs by user, and include other online platforms that are commonly used for news (for example, TikTok and Facebook).

Note

This is an edited version of *PSBs in the platform era: A YouTube case study Annex 1: Review of Public Service Media,* which is © Ofcom. For ease of reading the editors have inserted subheadings.

Chapter 32

This is bigger than the internet: Why public service AI is the next great leap

Peter Heneghan argues the BBC should lead the way with a new form of AI

Generative AI isn't just a technological upgrade. It's a once-in-a-lifetime cultural and societal force. The BBC must not follow Silicon Valley. It should lead by forging a new path for public-service AI, rooted in trust, inclusion, and purpose.

In a now-prophetic 1999 interview with David Bowie, Jeremy Paxman playfully dismissed the internet as just another distribution tool. Bowie wasn't having it. With wide eyes and absolute certainty Bowie called the internet an 'alien life form', a force fundamentally reshaping society. "The potential of what the Internet is going to do to society, both good and bad, is unimaginable," Bowie told a clearly baffled Paxman. It turns out Bowie wasn't just right. He was prophetic.

Make no mistake: generative AI isn't *like* the internet. It's bigger. It's embedding faster. And its orders of magnitude are more disruptive. That's why the tech giants are pouring tens of billions into it every year. This isn't the future. It's already here. The question for institutions like the BBC is urgent: will AI be treated as just a quicker way to do old things, or as the structural transformation it really is?

A legacy of innovation, now at risk

For almost a century the BBC has shaped British and global culture. From *Planet Earth* to *The Office*, from the London 2012 Olympics to iPlayer and BBC Sounds, it has defined eras, sparked conversations, and pioneered formats. But the 25 years since Bowie's interview have been difficult. Budget pressures, political interference, and digital disruption have all chipped away at the BBC's relevance and confidence. There is now a real risk that, bogged down by internal matters, the BBC treats generative AI as simply another incremental technological change and misses the opportunity that is staring them in the face.

Since receiving its Royal Charter in 1927 the BBC has consistently evolved alongside technology:

- Wireless and radio gave it a voice.
- Television brought visual presence.

- The early internet broadened its global reach.
- Social media and smartphones facilitated direct interaction.
- Now generative AI, if harnessed correctly, has the potential to completely redefine content creation and audience engagement.

Each technological advancement has reshaped broadcasting. At every stage, the BBC has adapted, often loosening its grip over messaging due to increasing competition and ongoing challenges to its relevance, trust, and authority.

When Winston Churchill delivered his wartime speeches, communication was direct yet one-way, authoritative yet distant. The advent of commercial TV and pirate radio stations, notably Radio Caroline, compelled the BBC to reconsider its approach, responding to public demands for greater cultural diversity and contemporary music. These were significant but incremental shifts. Then came social media and the iPhone and the introduction in 2010 of the front-facing camera that truly marked a turning point.

Passive audiences become active

Today audiences are no longer passive viewers: they actively engage, remix, share, and influence media. Generative tools allow anyone to create sophisticated, multimodal content, text, image, video, sound, and code, cheaply and at speed. For under £100 a month an individual can use ChatGPT to draft compelling scripts, Midjourney to generate stunning visuals, Runway to produce slick films, Lovable to build interactive websites, and HeyGen to deliver it all through lifelike avatars. No crew. No studio. No gatekeepers.

At the 2025 Sundance Festival Gary Hustwit's film *Eno*, a generative documentary about Brian Eno, changed with every screening, an apt reflection of Eno's pioneering work in generative music. Audience interaction influenced how the story evolved in real time. The documentary is never finished. That's the point.

Meanwhile, a Volvo concept car advert, typically a six-figure production, was built entirely with AI in just 24 hours (Hiken, 2024). These aren't novelties. They are signals. Media is changing at its foundations.

The public service response

The BBC cannot out-scale YouTube or out-engineer OpenAI. But that was never its role. The BBC's edge is public purpose and public trust. It should be building something entirely different.

Imagine a large language model trained not just on the BBC's vast radio, television and news archive, but also on its values. Not driven by advertising incentives, but by a mission to explain, educate, and inspire, a model fine-tuned on accuracy, editorial integrity, and inclusion. This is the opportunity: to shape a public-service AI framework grounded in trust, transparency, and accessibility.

The BBC has already made early moves: AI-assisted translation, workflow automation, smart metadata tagging. But these are foundations, not strategy. The next step requires more than pilots. It demands leadership.

A public service AI lab

Rather than bolt-on experiments, the BBC should consider creating a Public-Service AI Lab. Not a tech team in isolation, but a truly interdisciplinary studio bringing together engineers, journalists, designers, producers, and policy thinkers. Its role would be to experiment responsibly with generative formats, AI editorial tools, watermarking, multilingual access, bias detection, and dynamic commissioning models.

It would also create space for innovation outside legacy formats. *EastEnders* and *News at Ten* still attract investment, but they no longer engage audiences raised on Twitch, TikTok, and YouTube. Public service content must shift from broadcasting to participation.

Generative AI can power this shift. Documentaries that evolve based on community feedback. Real-time local news shaped by citizen reporting. Co-created fiction. Contextual explainers that adjust to different comprehension levels. AI can unlock not just productivity, but creativity, accessibility, and inclusion.

British startup Synapse is already developing real-time sign language translation for live video. Combine that with neurodivergent-friendly interfaces and adaptive storytelling formats and you have an entirely new era of accessible media. These are not fringe features. They are essential to what public service means now.

Trust is the BBC edge

But AI is not neutral. The tools being built by the private sector are often designed to capture attention, generate clicks, and flood channels with synthetic content. The BBC must stand apart. In an era of algorithmic noise and deepfakes, trust is the final moat. During the pandemic 94 per cent of the UK turned to the BBC (Advanced Television, 2020). That wasn't a coincidence. It was the product of decades of editorial standards, institutional memory, and public accountability.

If the BBC can bring those same principles to AI — through explainers, workshops, algorithm literacy programmes, and editorial co-pilots that enhance rather than override human judgment — it can once again help the public navigate a world in flux.

But if it doesn't act decisively, others will. And not all of them will care about truth, nuance or public value.

Time to lead

The BBC is no stranger to technological change. But AI is not just another tool. It is a new substrate. A shift from media as broadcast to media as dialogue. From fixed formats to adaptive experiences. From mass audiences to deeply personalised engagement.

If the BBC wants to remain relevant over the next century, it must not just report on this transition. It must shape it. That means treating AI not as an experiment but as infrastructure. Building capability across every content team. Embedding engineers inside editorial units. Partnering with public interest labs. Training teams on prompt design, ethics, and adaptive storytelling. And most importantly, investing in public-service AI as a strategic imperative, not a side project. Public-service AI is not a threat to the BBC's mission. It is the next chapter in fulfilling it.

The alternative? A world of infinite information and diminishing trust, where the BBC is remembered not as a guide through the noise, but as a voice that went quiet just when it mattered most. AI presents a clear choice. It is time for the BBC to lead.

References

Advanced Television (2020) 'Report: 94% of accessing BBC during crisis', Hastings: Creative Media Centre, 20 May.

Asa Hiken (2024) 'Fake Volvo ad made with AI stirs marketers – the creator offers 5 tips for using text-to-video tools', New York: *Ad Age*, 11 July.

Gary Hustwit (2024) *Eno*, Film First/Tigerlily Productions.

About the contributor

Peter Heneghan is the founder of The Future Communicator, an AI and communications consultancy helping organisations navigate disruption and rethink strategy in the age of intelligent tools. He is the former Chief Digital Communicator for the UK government and has held roles at the BBC, Channel 4, and BuzzFeed. A guest lecturer at London Business School on Communications and AI, he advises global brands and institutions, including the United Nations and Diageo. His work sits at the intersection of storytelling, systems design, and generative technology.

Chapter 33

After the BBC licence fee: Rethinking the future of public service media

Deborah Wilson David looks at three alternatives to the licence fee

The days of the BBC's long-standing funding model appear numbered. Shrinking public support, disruptive shifts in media technologies, and a lack of political support, are conspiring to undermine the case for its viability. Lisa Nandy's April 2025 critique (Penna, 2025) only underscored what many already sensed: the licence fee no longer aligns with the realities of twenty-first-century media consumption. As the Government prepares its White Paper outlining the policy direction for the ninth charter in the BBC's history even BBC Director-General Tim Davie acknowledges the need for a fundamental rethink: "We need a model that actively supports the principles of universality, access, impartiality, and social cohesion, while also being fit for the digital age" (Davie, 2025).

The BBC, for all its historic achievements, is now an institution in urgent need of structural reform, creative reinvention, and a critical reckoning with its own complacency. Too often debates about the BBC polarise into simplistic binaries: either tired defences of a golden past or neoliberal assaults from those indifferent or even antagonistic to public service broadcasting.

This is a critical evaluation of three possible options for a post-licence fee BBC. It is also an exploration of how the BBC might adapt to preserve democratic value in a fragmented information environment and by doing so contribute productively to a broader public media ecosystem.

The 'Netflix+' model: A hybrid subscription approach

Among the more realistic funding options, and potentially a more politically palatable alternative, is a hybrid subscription model, reminiscent of commercial streaming platforms. But a direct swap — replacing the licence fee in full with a paywall — would dismantle the BBC's foundational ethos of universal access. Instead, a 'Netflix+' system could offer a publicly-funded core layer of essential public service content, while premium services —flagship drama, exclusive sports, original documentaries — would be placed behind a paywall.

In theory this protects public access whilst allowing the BBC to compete commercially. But in practice there are risks. The BBC has historically favoured high-profile, high-cost productions: period dramas, celebrity formats and other prestige projects, often to the detriment of local, regional, educational, and minority content. A two-tier system may only worsen this imbalance, concentrating investment in areas with higher commercial appeal.

Furthermore, the BBC's existing digital platforms, such as iPlayer, lag behind rivals in functionality, curation, and user experience. Tim Davie has warned that without urgent reform, the BBC risks becoming 'just another app' in a crowded digital world. In a subscription model, that danger becomes existential.

If the BBC is to compete against premium content providers, it must first tackle its digital shortcomings and cultural risk-aversion. BBC executives have claimed to be 'modernising', yet the organisation often appears mired in bureaucratic inertia. Without genuine transformation, the 'plus' side of this model may be nothing more than a poor imitation of Netflix, undermining both public trust and market viability.

Most crucially, subscription fragments audiences. The BBC's legitimacy has long rested on universality — a shared cultural space accessible to all (so long as they pay their licence fee), but a tiered model risks deepening divides between those able to pay and those reliant on limited, state-funded content. If premium tiers are the space where elite content is to be found, the BBC risks becoming an agent of digital inequality rather than its remedy.

The Citizenship Dividend: A universal basic media income

A more radical alternative draws inspiration from the concept of Universal Basic Income (UBI). The Citizenship Dividend model would give every adult media credit to spend on any accredited PSB provider they choose, be it the BBC or other accredited public service providers. This would decentralise funding and transform audiences from passive recipients into active commissioners, reallocating public money through user choice.

This model would challenge the BBC's long-standing monopolistic hold on public funding and the appeal is clear: it would force the BBC to earn public trust and loyalty, rather than rely on brand nostalgia. Critics from independent producers to regional content creators have long argued that the BBC fails to represent the full diversity of UK voices. With this model, smaller, independent outlets, especially those reflecting regional or underrepresented perspectives, could flourish.

Of course, accreditation would be a fraught process. Who decides which providers qualify as public service? Could populist or politically extreme platforms exploit the system? These are valid concerns. But they do not negate the value of shifting agency to the audience. As Davie has noted, the BBC must 'actively champion British values of fairness, freedom, tolerance, and dialogue'— not merely assume its entitlement to represent them.

This model also introduces a much-needed cultural shift. The BBC is not in the habit of framing its public service obligations as a privilege — and one that is funded by the public. A Citizenship Dividend could flip this perspective with the audience as the major stakeholder rather than a grateful beneficiary.

With multiple players competing for public funds, the incentive to experiment, diversify and connect with underserved communities would increase. The BBC has appeared to struggle here, hampered by bureaucratic governance and cultural conservatism. The kind of media landscape this model would offer could be more agile, more responsive, and ultimately more democratic.

The infrastructure model: BBC as digital public utility

A third, and arguably the most transformative, option reimagines the BBC not primarily as a broadcaster, but as civic infrastructure. Like a public transport system or the NHS, the BBC could be positioned as a backbone for digital citizenship — providing the tools, platforms, and cultural infrastructure needed for a healthy digital democracy.

In this model the BBC shifts from content creation to enabling others, for example hosting local news APIs, supporting open-source education tools, and convening digital forums for debate. Tim Davie has spoken of the BBC's role in 'social cohesion'. As civic life migrates online, that cohesion may depend less on shared programming and more on shared infrastructure.

Yet the institutional shift required is immense. Despite years of digital first rhetoric, the BBC remains slow in delivery. Critics inside and out speak of risk aversion, siloed leadership, and missed opportunities, innovation projects being buried under layers of compliance and executive sign-off.

To be a true digital utility the BBC would need to embrace open standards, decentralised partnerships, and user-led design. Its current broadcasting legacy is as much a burden as a strength in this respect. It would need a new form of accountability: to communities and to those who are shaping the future of digital public life.

The Public Interest News Foundation report on local news ecosystems underlines this need (Heawood and Padania, 2025). It found over 4 million people in the UK now live in news deserts — communities without a single dedicated local news outlet. The current BBC-funded Local Democracy Reporter (LDR) scheme is criticised as 'a sticking plaster', channelling funds to corporate publishers while failing to regenerate independent local journalism.

An infrastructure model would also help resolve the tension between content and connectivity. As broadband access becomes a prerequisite for civic life, the BBC could be tasked with supporting digital literacy, ensuring accessible interfaces for disabled users, and investing in regional data infrastructure.

A reimagined BBC could act as a platform and aggregator, not a sole provider — supporting a plural local media environment rather than dominating it. As the report recommends, public funding should be redirected toward accountable, community-based outlets, allowing the BBC to play a coordinating, not colonising, role.

Synthesis and strategy: Moving from legacy to leadership

These models — subscription hybrid, user-directed voucher, civic infrastructure — are not mutually exclusive. A credible future for the BBC may lie in combining all three. But the precondition is reform. None of these alternatives will succeed if the BBC remains organisationally rigid, culturally complacent, and insulated from genuine accountability.

The core challenge is not funding alone. It is institutional legitimacy. The BBC faces an erosion of trust — not just among right-wing ideologues or market fundamentalists, but among younger audiences, marginalised communities, and creative sectors who see it as increasingly out of touch. Its internal culture often prioritises continuity over experimentation, and executive leadership remains disproportionately drawn from narrow professional backgrounds.

Meanwhile the erosion of local journalism, the rise of disinformation, and the declining trust among younger audiences all point to a need for systemic renewal. The future of public service media will not be saved by sentimentality. It requires structural innovation, plural voices, and civic imagination.

To chart a credible post-licence fee future, the BBC must be honest about its failures. It must admit that its universality has often been symbolic rather than substantive; that its regional outreach has too often been performative; that its governance lacks the diversity and independence it claims to champion.

Davie's speech candidly acknowledges: "We must build a BBC that is open, honest about our failings, and fast-moving in an environment that is changing at pace." This is not just rhetoric — it's a warning. The BBC's greatest challenge is not funding, but relevance. It must earn its place in the future not through legacy or nostalgia, but through service, openness, and transformation. If it succeeds, it can become the backbone of a new democratic media landscape. If it fails, others must be empowered to take its place.

References

Tim Davie (2025) 'The BBC – A catalyst for building trust', Lowry Theatre, Salford, 14 May.

Jonathan Heawood and Sameer Padania (2025) *Media wealth building: The report of the Local News Plan Project*, Public Interest News Foundation: London.

Dominic Penna (2025) 'BBC licence fee is 'unenforceable' and targets women, claims Culture Secretary', *The Daily Telegraph*, 25 April.

About the contributor

Deborah Wilson David is Head of the Department of Journalism and Media at Nottingham Trent University. She has combined broadcasting and education for thirty years. Her research interests are broadcasting history, particularly the early days of the BBC, the BBC's reporting of World War II, and BBC local radio. She sits on the Board of the US-based Broadcast Education Association, representing the Association's International membership, and served for six years as the Vice President of the European Journalism Training Association.

Chapter 34

The evisceration of PBS in the United States

David Cay Johnston examines the Trump plan to destroy US public broadcasting, offering lessons for the UK

Awful as the BBC licence fee debacle is, imagine for a moment a British Prime Minister who ran for office denouncing the BBC as an abomination, accusing it of spreading anti-British propaganda and of favouring one political party, and then moving to eviscerate government funding with a goal of turning off its transmitters.

That's exactly what's happening in America. 'Ending Taxpayer Subsidization of Biased Media,' was the White House headline on Trump's 1 May 2025 executive order ending all federal funding for America's two public broadcasting organisations effective 1 July (The White House, 2025). PBS stands for Public Broadcasting System, founded in 1969, while NPR is the new shortened name of what began in 1970 as National Public Radio. More than 350 local nonprofit television stations carry PBS programming while NPR is a network of more than a thousand nonprofit radio stations.

The executive order asserted that public broadcasting never 'presents a fair, accurate, or unbiased portrayal of current events to taxpaying citizens'. Trump directed a funding agency, the Corporation for Public Broadcasting, 'to cease federal funding for NPR and PBS' for violating a law that says it may not 'contribute to or otherwise support any political party' (Cornell Law School). He also removed some Corporation board members, a move the agency says was illegal. Trump's Executive Order asserts that 'which viewpoints NPR and PBS promote does not matter. What does matter is that neither entity presents a fair, accurate, or unbiased portrayal of current events to taxpaying citizens'.

Never mind that there's no evidence to support these assertions. Trump, as I've documented for decades, creates his own reality. As president what he says is, in his view, The Truth, while reporting he dislikes is 'fake news'. A key part of Trump's view on this is that journalists should not be allowed to report anything unless he approves. So far, he has not been able to fully impose this dictatorial view, but his order to terminate PBS and NPR funding is a major step in that direction, along with baseless lawsuits against two commercial broadcast companies, ABC and CBS.

The Associated Press, which Trump tried to ban from the White House for refusing to call the Gulf of Mexico the Gulf of America, described this executive order as 'the latest move by Trump and his administration to utilize federal powers to control or hamstring institutions whose actions or viewpoints he disagrees with. Since taking office, Trump has ousted leaders, placed staff on administrative leave and cut off hundreds of millions of dollars in funding to artists, libraries, museums, theaters and others' (Associated Press, 2025). Trump also ordered an investigation into what he says is rampant discrimination at PBS and NPR. His administration says that white men are the primary if not only victims of discriminatory practices that favour unqualified minorities and women.

And it's not just the domestic PBS nonprofit television and NPR nonprofit radio networks that Trump seeks to destroy. Trump & Co. also claim, preposterously, that the Voice of America (VOA), the US government's propaganda arm since 1942, spreads 'anti-American' ideas with 'leftist bias'. Elon Musk and other Trump appointees fired most of the VOA staff, seeking to replace these civil servants with people from One America News Network, a faux news outlet known for its reliably adoring coverage of Trump.

Why public broadcasting?

With nonprofit broadcasting in the public interest endangered on both sides of the Atlantic, will the signals weaken and then stop? Or can an enduring benefit arise that will keep these treasures on air and online?

Nearly half of America's 3,143 counties have only one news outlet and 203 more have none (Northwestern University, 2025). In vast swathes of rural America public broadcasting is the sole source of local news as weekly and daily newspapers have shut down and commercial broadcasters stick to more populated areas. Without NPR stations many people in the dozen Midwest and Plains states known as Tornado Ally would have no warning when deadly vortexes bear down on them with the power to flatten whole neighbourhoods.

Despite the life-saving benefits of NPR, the American right has sought an end to taxpayer subsidy from the get-go. Like dandelions in spring, anti-tax Republicans annually introduce legislation to end public service radio which the American far-right denounces as an abomination. Just as reliably all the legislation does is tamp down the volume of money going to support public broadcasting.

Public broadcasting has long been under attack by organisations that market right-wing ideology, notably the Heritage Foundation. Trump is busy implementing a plan developed by Heritage folk, known as Project 2025, that would transform the United States into an autocracy with Trump as the *de facto* dictator. One Heritage Foundation fellow wrote that 'NPR and PBS used to justify their unjustifiable taxpayer funding by telling people that poor children would be harmed if their educational programming was cut. Then, in 2015,

Sesame Street got a private deal with HBO, and a stream of educational content came online.'

In 2016 Big Bird did indeed fly the PBS coup, along with the rest of *Sesame Street*, for HBO, a premium priced cable channel. However, tykes whose parents can't afford HBO can still watch Elmo, Grouch, Prairie Dawn, and their pals in skits sponsored by 'advertisers' like the letter W. They just see episodes nine months after they are first aired on HBO, a delay of no significance.

PBS Kids airs about 30 programmes, each tailored by education experts to help children develop their reading, maths, critical thinking, and relationship skills (PBS, 2020). Developing rigorous intellectual skills in children undermines authoritarian power so PBS Kids must go.

The cost of PBS programming

In recent years PBS's funding arm, the Corporation for Public Broadcasting, has received about $500m per year from Congress. That's roughly $1.50 per American, a proverbial drop in the bucket. Defence spending totals about $3,000 per person, a spending ratio of roughly 2,000:1. Trump wants more military spending.

In America campaigns run by the community leaders who typically serve on the boards of nonprofit PBS and NPR stations, by farming and other groups who have an economic and safety interest in getting reliable news that in many rural areas is available only from public broadcasters, religious social justice groups, and various charitable endowments, are fighting back. Public broadcasters are also suing the Trump administration arguing it has engaged in numerous illegal actions.

Total control

This resistance won't faze Trump. He believes that any news organisation is biased unless it advocates for him. The goal is control, complete control. Trump is still consolidating his power, but his direction and intent, which I've warned about since 2011, are clear. Praising those he seeks to destroy is, at times, central to these plans.

During a televised meeting of his cabinet in 2019, Trump said, "I'll have to start watching PBS much more", referring to a news report he had not watched, but that he said he was told was accurate. Chuckling could be heard in the background. He said *PBS News Hour* 'covered it very accurately. And I actually put a quote out last night about what they said, I thought that was very accurate' (Barajas, 2019).

That's Trump employing a core tactic: muddy clear waters and create doubt about where he stands. He may issue strident calls for violence, as he did on 6

January 2021, but then he'll toss in a line advocating for peace to spread uncertainty, to fashion a rhetorical loophole for his benefit.

So why the attacks on PBS, NPR, and on the US government's propaganda ministry with its dedicated services in English, Arabic, Russian, and other languages? Why claim that *PBS News Hour* is overly expensive when it costs just $27m a year, or about 8-cents per person?

Imposing a dictatorship requires limiting independent and serious news coverage. The goal is ending journalism, replacing it with Orwellian official declarations, as we have seen in every dictatorial society, most notably in recent years in Hungary under the Viktor Orbán regime. Vladimir Putin has effectively ended journalism in Russia as evidenced by *The New York Times* Moscow bureau operating out of Istanbul.

Saving American public broadcasting may well hinge on gaining support among Republicans, including those in rural areas with only public broadcast news reports. Almost 70 per cent of Democrats support federal funding for PBS, three-and-a-half times the Republican level of support (Lipka and Matsa, 2025).

From Beijing's perspective, Trump has given China a valuable gift by strangling VOA, along with ending most American humanitarian aid. For decades VOA broadcasts into China let people hear accurate news of the rest of the world, good and bad, including about corrupt American presidents (Yuan, 2025).

Public broadcasting in the UK and the US has proven a valuable investment in creating and sustaining thoughtful options in a world of cheap and increasingly crass commercial broadcast options. Tossing away these national treasures would be worse than a tragedy. It would be a sign that people don't care enough about a government that serves the people to fight for it and that's just the mindset that wannabe dictators want to foster.

References

Associated Press (2025) 'Trump signs executive order directing federal funding cuts to PBS and NPR', 2 May.

Joshua Barajas (2019) 'WATCH: Trump says he'll 'have to start watching PBS much more'', *PBS News*, 3 January.

Cornell Law School Legal Information Institute (n/d) '47 U.S. Code § 396 - Corporation for Public Broadcasting', available at: https://www.law.cornell.edu/uscode/text/47/396

Michael Lipka and Katerina Eva Matsa (2025) 'Americans more likely to support tan oppose continuing federal funding for NPR and PBS', Pew Research Center, Washington DC, 26 March.

PBS (2020) 'PBS Kids – Everything', available at: **https://pbskids.org/everything/**

The White House (2025) 'Ending subsidization of biased media', Washington DC, 1 May.

Li Yuan (2025) 'Trump Could Hand China a 'Strategic Victory' by Silencing Voice of America', *New York Times*, New York, 28 March.

About the contributor

David Cay Johnston, a Pulitzer Prize-winning investigative reporter and four-time bestselling author, is a professor of practice at Rochester Institute of Technology.

Chapter 35

The BBC: Time to change or fade away

Janine Chandler writes a love letter – of sorts – to the Corporation

The BBC is in trouble. Not today, maybe not tomorrow, but very soon that trouble will become existential. The world around it has shifted — and it's still clinging to a map that no longer matches the terrain. So this is a love letter, of sorts, but a tough one. This is because the BBC matters. But if it doesn't change, it soon won't matter.

Change is not optional anymore

The money's tight. The licence fee is frozen. Inflation doing its thing. Meanwhile Netflix, Amazon, and Apple throw billions at content like it's pocket change. They're global. The BBC is national. You can't win an arms race when all you're holding is a butter knife.

And politics? Let's not even start. Every new government sees the BBC as a branding opportunity. The left thinks it's sold out. The right thinks it's gone woke. It's impossible to win. And that constant bashing eats away at public trust, which used to be the BBC's superpower.

Audiences have changed too. Radically. Grandma still watches *Strictly* at 7.30 on a Saturday. Her grandson doesn't know what day of the week it is — he's busy bingeing on TikTok or tuning into a YouTuber halfway across the world. They're both audiences. But they live on different planets.

And then there's culture. Not 'what's on *The Culture Show*'—but actual culture. We don't want one big national conversation anymore. We want our own. We're in the era of niches, not nations. Personalised playlists, not prime-time schedules. The BBC still tries to be everything to everyone. That used to be its magic, now it's part of the problem.

Tech? A blessing and a curse. iPlayer was ahead of its time. But it hasn't kept the lead. The BBC should feel like a tech company with a soul. Instead, it often feels like a TV company with a panic button. It's not just about apps. It's about ways of thinking—agility, experimentation, responsiveness. Tech isn't a department. It's a mindset.

Even the climate is pushing change. Green credentials matter. Audiences notice. Staff care. You can't claim to lead the national conversation while your own carbon footprint's stuck in the 1990s. How stories get made matters now, not just what they say.

All of this stacks up to one thing: adapt or become background noise.

Why doesn't the BBC just change?

Because it's hard. Really hard. Because the things that made the BBC brilliant now make it brittle.

Success is sticky. The BBC has done extraordinary things. Set global standards. Changed lives. But that success becomes a comfort blanket: "This worked before. Let's just tweak it." That's not change. That's rearranging the furniture while the house burns.

And audiences are pulling in opposite directions. Older viewers want what they've always had. Younger ones want something completely different. Serving both means hard decisions — about where to invest, what to cut, who to let down. That's a nightmare for a brand that's supposed to belong to everyone.

Inside the organisation, change hits walls: good people, stuck in old systems; committees; layers; chains of sign-off. Innovation dies in meeting rooms where no one wants to be first — or wrong. People care deeply, but that care often shows up as resistance: "Not my programme. Not my network. Not my team." It's human. But it holds everything back.

And talent? The BBC has amazing storytellers, but it's not where the tech talent flocks. They want to move fast, break things, and build again. The BBC moves slowly, avoids risk, and worries about headlines. You can't build the future if you're scared of tomorrow's front page.

And let's not forget competition. The BBC isn't just up against ITV or Channel 4 anymore. It's up against MrBeast, Spotify, Fortnite, Substack. Places that don't just compete for eyeballs, but for time, attention, and trust. Places that speak in the native tongue of the next generation. The BBC often sounds like it's still clearing its throat.

And through it all, politics looms. Every move the BBC makes becomes a debate. Every debate becomes a delay. Every delay becomes another reason not to try something bold. Playing it safe starts to feel like survival. But safe is the riskiest move of all right now.

So what's the play?

Be bold. Be focused. Be fast.

The BBC can't be everything. But it can still be *essential.* It can be the platform we trust, the place for truth in a time of noise, the space where public service meets twenty-first-century storytelling. It has to move from broadcast to conversation, from monologue to many voices, from trying to hold the centre, to connecting the edges. It needs to stop obsessing over protecting what it was, and start building what it could be. That's a shift in mindset—not just strategy.

The good news? The talent is there. The love for the mission is still strong. And the BBC has changed before—sometimes under pressure, sometimes by choice.

This time, the pressure is on. The choice is ours.

Chapter 36

How are UK public service broadcasters doing? The Ofcom verdict

The media regulator **Ofcom** takes the temperature of UK Public Service Broadcasters (PSBs) every five years. Here's their not entirely positive July 2025 diagnosis

The UK media landscape is undergoing rapid transformation. Traditional broadcasters are in a fierce battle for audience attention, while global tech giants flood the market with an ever-growing range of content.

Services like Netflix and YouTube offer hyper-personalised experiences that are hugely popular with viewers and advertisers. In this environment, the PSBs are finding it much harder to fund the production and distribution of high-quality UK content to all audiences.

Public service media (PSM) has a long and proud tradition in the UK. The PSBs – the BBC, ITV, STV, Channel 4, Channel 5 and S4C – are the key providers of PSM. They are universally available and highly valued for trusted and accurate news and informative and entertaining UK stories that reflect the diversity of the whole of the UK. This critical content supports participation in democratic society through holding governments and institutions to account and keeping audiences informed about local, national, and international events. The PSBs also provide sporting and cultural programming that brings the country together and promotes a sense of shared values. Audiences enjoy PSM content on other broadcast services, subscription video on-demand (SVoD) services, and video sharing platforms (VSPs).

We have set out six recommendations for action, focused on:

- prominence and discoverability for PSM content on YouTube and potentially other third-party platforms;
- stable and adequate funding to sustain a broad range of PSM content;
- urgent clarity on the future of TV distribution;
- ambitious partnerships amongst the PSBs;
- investment in media literacy to support audiences; and
- streamlined regulation that strips away any outdated unnecessary restrictions, protects audiences from harm wherever they are and to encourage growth and innovation.

Overview

Services like Netflix and YouTube offer hyper-personalised experiences that are hugely popular with viewers and advertisers. Algorithms, tailored recommendations, and instant accessibility are reshaping how a growing number of audiences discover and consume media. Emerging technologies, such as generative artificial intelligence (GenAI), are revolutionising how content is created, distributed, and consumed. These seismic shifts are well underway. **This review calls for urgent action, both now and in the coming years to strengthen and maintain public service media (PSM) content which provides trusted and accurate news, tells UK stories, and represents the diversity of the nations and regions of the UK.** It is critical that the PSBs provide content across multiple platforms ensuring audiences can easily find it.

Regulation alone will not address all of the challenges facing PSM: public service broadcasters must innovate and make content that engages audiences. An important part of UK culture is under threat. The PSBs remain the key providers of PSM. With the BBC at their heart, the PSBs benefit from a blend of public and commercial funding. Together they offer distinctive services and a broad range of content which reaches all UK audiences. Their competitive dynamic has driven high-quality programming. The PSBs are universally available and have requirements to deliver trusted news, including local news, and an unmatched breadth of high-quality UK programmes that meet the needs and interests of UK audiences. They also provide sporting and cultural programming that brings the country together and promotes a sense of shared values. Without PSBs there would be significantly less UK content and there is a risk that society becomes ever more fragmented and polarised.

UK creatives lead the world

The UK creative sector is globally admired. The UK has one of the most successful creative sectors in the world – it is worth £124bn (over 5 per cent of the UK economy), with film, TV, music, and radio contributing £22bn. The PSBs are the cornerstone of the UK's production sector, supporting production across the nations and regions and contributing to skills development.

Without the PSBs we would not have the highly skilled, creative workforce that has become a global leader in the production of television, film, and digital media, and which attracts significant investment into the UK. Global streamers and other UK broadcasters also contribute to the rich variety of PSM that audiences enjoy. A range of broadcasters deliver accurate and duly impartial news and, along with global streamers, commission high-quality UK drama and entertainment. However, unlike PSBs, they often sit behind a paywall, and they are not required to be universally available, commission UK content, or invest in the production sector across the whole of the UK.

Radio and VSPs

Commercial and community radio also provides news and programming, including local news, that allows audiences to keep in touch with their local communities. In addition, there has been significant growth in viewing on video sharing platforms (VSPs) such as YouTube, increasingly being watched on the TV now that more than seven in ten households have connected TVs. They have a fast-growing body of user-generated and professionally produced content that covers a wide range of interest areas and is popular with young viewers and increasingly with older ones as well. **PSM content is fighting to be seen and heard. Viewers now spend less than half of their in-home viewing on linear TV and this is declining. As people move online they are watching programmes on a much larger range of services.** Broadcasters' video on-demand players only account for 9 per cent of all viewing, significantly less than subscription streaming services (15 per cent), and video sharing platforms (19 per cent).

The PSBs are responding by putting content on third party services, such as YouTube. Their strategies are evolving as they learn what works, but our research shows that PSB content only forms a small proportion of what UK audiences watch on YouTube and they are competing with every other content creator in the world.

The PSBs will therefore need to work much harder to create content that audiences want to watch on these platforms that determine what content is promoted to users. This makes it harder for audiences to find PSB content, which undermines its universality, and may mean they are exposed to fewer genres or viewpoints. This trend is even more stark for children and young people – for example – 15 year old children spend significantly more time watching YouTube than PSB services combined. **If children do not turn to PSB content as they get older, the future of PSM is at risk.**

News

Seven in ten adults now get their news from online services, with around half of adults accessing news on social media platforms. This delivers benefits in terms of the breadth of news available, but also means algorithms have a significant role in determining what audiences see and that high-quality, reliable news, including from the PSBs, may not be easy to find. Our analysis has found that users who consume news on social media are less likely to correctly identify important factual information, have less trust in institutions and are more polarised in their views. There is also a greater chance of encountering misinformation and disinformation. It is not surprising that people have significantly less trust in news on social media than broadcast news services which are required to provide duly accurate and impartial news.

Less money available

In this increasingly dynamic environment, the PSBs are finding it much harder to fund the production and distribution of high-quality UK content to all audiences. **PSB revenues from the TV licence fee and linear TV advertising have declined by more than a quarter in real terms since 2016,**

with growth in broadcast video on demand (BVoD) revenues failing to compensate. Costs are also rising – PSBs have to provide content across linear and online services and they are increasingly investing in more expensive high-end content to attract viewers to their services. This has put significant pressure on broadcasters' commissioning budgets and ability to continue providing both a breadth of content and some genres that attract less advertising revenue such as news and children's programming.

The vital reforms in the Media Act will help support PSBs, including by making their on-demand players prominent on connected TVs. However, given the increasing levels of content audiences are watching and listening to on different services, it is unlikely to be enough on its own to secure the future provision of PSM content.

Third-party platforms, including VSPs like YouTube, are now an increasingly important part of the UK media sector and play a key role in delivering content to UK audiences.

Recommendations for action

There is no silver bullet that will address the challenges that the sector is facing. We recommend that action focuses on six key outcomes. These will require change from everyone involved – the PSBs themselves, social media and VSPs, Government and Ofcom.

The six key outcomes are:

1. **Prominence and discoverability for PSM content on the third-party platforms that audiences increasingly turn to.** To deliver on this the PSBs need to keep adapting to audience preferences by constantly challenging themselves to test and iterate new ways of distributing and creating content for diverse audience groups. It is critical that the PSBs and YouTube work together to ensure that PSB content is prominent on its service, and on fair commercial terms. The Government should consider whether this needs to be underpinned by legislation. More widely, the Government may wish to explore prominence for news on social media and other platforms, even though implementation would be complex and would need to reflect the different ways that platforms promote content to users. In the meantime, the PSBs need to work with other VSPs and social media platforms to ensure their content is available and easily discovered by users.
2. **Stable and adequate funding to sustain a broad range of PSM content, including trusted and accurate news, and programmes that showcase the diversity of the whole of the UK and bring the country together.** Stakeholders have called for a range of measures to support funding for PSM content like levies and changes to tax credits to fund specific PSM genres. It is for the Government to consider these, and to lead work on the future funding of the BBC through its Charter Review. If there is to be new funding we recommend that it should prioritise genres that are socially

valuable but commercially less viable and attract lower advertising revenues, such as news, local news, and children's programming. Ofcom's regulation will continue to support the provision of content that reflects the diversity of the UK – particularly in the nations and regions – including through targeted and proportionate quotas.

3. **Urgent clarity on how TV will be distributed in the future.** The PSBs are required to be universally available. As viewers increasingly move online, they have to broadcast over Digital Terrestrial Television (DTT) while also investing in distribution across multiple platforms.
4. **More ambitious partnerships amongst the PSBs.** Modern media organisations need technology to reach audiences and compete with global platforms who they depend on in some cases to reach viewers. Scale is critical for the PSBs' and domestic broadcasters' ability to connect with all audiences in a fast-moving sector.
5. **Investment in media literacy is vital for everyone's ability to use digital services and to understand and critically engage with news and content**. Media literacy is defined as the ability to use, understand, and create media and communications across multiple formats and services. With the emergence of new technologies (including new forms of AI) the media landscape is only going to get more complex and personalised. Broadcasters are in a unique place to support audiences to critically engage with news content from a range of sources, distinguish fact from fiction, provide transparency about how they establish facts, and raise awareness about conspiracy theories and prevalent fraud schemes.

   The BBC plays a further role, supporting media literacy through its children's education initiatives. It is also considering how it can further support young people's digital literacy skills so they can better assess trusted information and recognise disinformation.
6. **Streamlined regulation which strips away any outdated unnecessary restrictions**. The majority of the current legislative and regulatory framework was designed for a linear world. It needs a fundamental review to determine what is required to support audiences as they shift their viewing and listening online and to encourage growth and innovation.

Ofcom is already implementing the Media Act which provides critical support for the PSBs, in particular through giving them greater flexibility to meet their obligations across their linear and online services and making their on-demand players prominent on connected TVs. We are also working with Government on its BBC Charter review which will play a central role in supporting the future of PSM.

If no action is taken, the very existence of the PSBs – who are the main providers of PSM – will be threatened. Time is running out to save this pillar of UK culture and way of life.

Note

This is an edited version of *Transmission Critical: The future of Public Service Media* published on 21 July 2025, and which is © Ofcom. For ease of reading the editors have inserted subheadings and have emboldened certain sentences to highlight important points in the report.

AFTERWORD

Does Tim Davie need to get a Willie to save the BBC licence fee?

John Mair offers the current Director-General some advice

Let's deal with the Willie point first. Margaret Thatcher had Willie Whitelaw as her flak-catcher, and that relationship worked. Most recent Director-Generals have had a flak-catcher, a public number two who spotted trouble before it happened. Davie seems to have eschewed that. Maybe it shows in the series of BBC crises. Tim has two years to save the BBC at least in its current form. Let me be his adviser, flak-catcher. The level and type of licence fee is key.

Here's my ten-point plan.

1. Be much more open. Bring the viewing public in on decisions. It's one-way traffic now. Remember your Procter & Gamble and Pepsi training as a marketer before you joined the BBC. A huge audience survey was undertaken in 2025. Whether that was flawed or not in design and execution what did it really tell the Corporation? The survey was asking the wrong questions to the wrong people, that is, current BBC users, and was clearly designed to provide evidence for more licence fee. If you ask people they will want more of what they have. But it won't really get any new insights. If you really want to bring the audience with you and co-create a future do it properly. Engage BBC users and non-users properly through a BBC Futures Roadshow or BBC assemblies. You need to allow time for people to learn, reflect, and engage with experts and evidence before together creating a future.

2. Reveal the cost of various services now and in the future. People simply do not know. Should they? If they knew what went into programming — the budget, the people behind the scenes, the process, the time — they might be shocked or they might be sympathetic. All they know now is the megabucks earned by presenters and BBC executives. This fits with the 'inform, educate' part of the Reithian mantra. This could take the form of podcasts or programme series.

3. Decide on priorities. What is vital and what is not to the BBC and the licence payers? Has the brand stretched too much to offer too many services? Does the BBC have fingers in too many pies?

Does universality mean populating every new platform? Podcasts: Should programmes be made for iPlayer or Sounds alone? What is broadcasting?

What can the BBC close without offending too many people? The World Service? The Proms? BBC Orchestras? The digital radio and TV stations: Radio 6 Music, Radio 4 Extra, the Asian Network, BBC Three? There will be a small amount of noise if you cut any of them but you can ride it out.

Remember the importance of grassroots and local radio. Revamp them that so they appeal to the younger and lost demographics. Think of some of the newer commercial radio stations and how well some of them are doing.

4. Programmes, programmes, programmes are the secret of the BBC but so too are the people who make them.

5. Get the staff much more onside for they can be the best sales staff for the Corporation. Encourage them to be vulgar yet subtle. Ownership is key. Get them fighting for their BBC and their future. BBC staff need to be change-fit. You need to radically change and therefore staff need to think and act differently otherwise they will burn out. Current research shows that only 12 per cent of transformational projects work. The main reason for that is staff are not ready for change; they lack change fitness.

6. Offer alternatives to the current straight licence fee. Listen to the critics and critiques. Do not rule out hybrid forms. For a start the BBC is the national TV and radio archive. Take advantage of that. The media world has moved on rapidly in the last twenty years. Use that. People now accept subscription for media content. Work out how to make subscription attractive in addition to the licence fee.

7. The armadillo defence, simply putting up a barrier, against the many attacks does not work. Some attacks may bounce off but sooner or later one or two get through. They certainly enter public consciousness. The anti-BBC right-wing hyenas have a field day in your absence. On GBNews and TalkTV I regularly defend the BBC against half-stories and ill-informed presenters and I have little hard evidence with which to rebut those stories. It would be much better if you did it. Get all the senior management team out there defending and attacking. They are paid well to do it.

8. Be bolder in your journalism as it is the foundation of all the Corporation does. Don't let the BBC be boxed into the corner of a minefield called Gaza. Put on a one-day public conference of all the UK and big international broadcasters to talk Reporting Gaza. The exclusion of reporters from the war zone is an international scandal.

9. Survival in reduced mode should not be an option. Be bold with the culture secretary, whoever holds the government post or the responsibility, as 2028 approaches. They are 'here today, gone tomorrow'. The BBC will survive them.
10. Remember you are the BBC but don't rest on your laurels. Each and every day is a new one to reconnect with audiences old and new. They love the BBC. They just have to be reminded why.

Printed in Dunstable, United Kingdom

66484394R00127